iPads in Higher Education

iPads in Higher Education:

Proceedings of the 1st International Conference on the Use of iPads in Higher Education (ihe2014)

Edited by

Nicos Souleles and Claire Pillar

Cambridge Scholars Publishing

iPads in Higher Education:
Proceedings of the 1st International Conference on the Use of iPads in Higher Education (ihe2014)

Edited by Nicos Souleles and Claire Pillar

This book first published 2015

Cambridge Scholars Publishing

Lady Stephenson Library, Newcastle upon Tyne, NE6 2PA, UK

British Library Cataloguing in Publication Data
A catalogue record for this book is available from the British Library

ISBN (10): 1-4438-7626-7
ISBN (13): 978-1-4438-7626-1

TABLE OF CONTENTS

PREFACE

This edited volume of papers presented at 'ihe2014' (1st international conference on the use of iPads in Higher Education) aims to contribute empirical research in an area where there is an obvious need for further academic study. Although the iPad computer tablet is increasingly adopted across many universities worldwide, there remains a noticeable gap in the literature on the instructional potential of this tablet in different academic disciplines. In addition, what is called for is a critical examination from the perspective of different research methods, to unpack the potential contribution as well as limitations of the iPad for teaching and learning. In this respect, the mission of this volume is to address these challenges and – to use a well-known idiom – get the ball rolling.

Subsequently, this volume of conference proceedings is of interest to a wide range of people, including academics from different disciplines who are implementing mobile learning and learning with iPads, instructional designers and instructional technologists who provide support for such implementations, researchers who want to be informed on the different applications of this tablet in the sector, as well as academics in general who wish to explore the potential of the iPad for teaching and learning.

These proceedings cover the following academic disciplines: Urban Planning and Management, Urban Studies, Education, Environmental Management, Biology, Medical Education, Master of Business Administration, Teacher Training and Education, Physics, Languages, Field Work, Conference and Meetings Management, Hospitality, Art and Design, Computing and Mathematics and Physiotherapy and Occupational Therapy. In addition, the articles make use of a wide variety of research methods, such as: Surveys, Questionnaires, Focus Groups, Long-Term Studies, Qualitative methods, Pilot Projects, Multimodal Approaches, Observations, Use of Technology Implementation Models, Action Research, Ethnography, Field Studies, Document Collection and Analysis, Content Analysis, Case Studies, and Mixed Methods. What these articles share in common is a critical reflection on the instructional potential of iPads for teaching and learning.

Lastly, the editors acknowledge the significant contributions of Dr. Fernando Loizides, Dr. Salomi Papadima, and the doctoral students Stephania Savva, Antigoni Parmaxi and Dimitra Perdiou. We also wish to thank the reviewers of the conference papers: Dr. Andri Ioannou (Cyprus University of Technology), Dr. Jane Costello (University of Newfoundland), Dr. Fernando Loizides (Cyprus University of Technology), Dr. Marguerite Koole (Athabasca University), Prof. Tony Shannon (Karl Von Busse Institute of Design) and Dr. Nathaniel Ostashewski (Curtin University).

On behalf of the ihe steering committee

Dr. Nicos Souleles
Claire Pillar

www.ipadsinhe.org

USING IPADS AS A DYNAMIC LEARNING TOOL TO DEVELOP SKILLS IN GRAPHIC COMMUNICATION AND ENHANCE SPATIAL AWARENESS

ELISABETE CIDRE[1]

Abstract

This paper will present interim reflections on an ongoing pilot educational project being undertaken with the 2013-2014 new undergraduate cohort of Planning students in the three existing programmes at the Bartlett School of Planning (BSP) in University College London (UCL): Urban Planning, Design and Management (UPDM), Planning and Real Estate (PRE) and Urban Studies (US). The main purpose of this project is to enhance the University-level agenda for key transferable skill development (academic, self-management, inter-personal, but most importantly, communication) via active production of design (e)artefacts of paramount value for employability in the Built Environment – the iportfolio. It also aims to contribute to wider pedagogical and theoretical debates on the nature and value of the use of technology in Built Environment higher education. The project is developed in two stages, over the academic year. During terms 1 and 2 (October-December and January-March), the project will pilot the use of iPads as a dynamic learning tool in graphic communication, and will explore the potential of technology-enabled features and utilities to improve student engagement and foster individual learning. In terms 2 and 3 (April - June), the project will pilot the use of iBooks as a dynamic learning resource in phenomenological pedagogy, with the aim of building on the capacity for our graduates to become reflective practitioners. It will do so by promoting the co-development of iportfolios as design (e)artefacts that enable and reinforce the values of self-regulated and flexible learning and ongoing personal/career development.

---

[1] University College London, United Kingdom. Email: e.cidre@ucl.ac.uk

1. Rationale of the Project

The use of technology is definitely changing the ways we teach, learn and practise in the creative built environment disciplines. This calls for the use of e-resources, features, utilities and tools to be embedded within experiential and iterative learning methods, as no doubt the use of technology will appeal to a contemporary and young cohort, one which has e-mastery embedded in the way it communicates, learns and socialises. Undergraduate Year 1 Planning students often have no prior design or studio experience, and are for the first time being asked to develop a language of design that enables them to communicate design ideas. This is an iterative learning process, highly based on exploratory approaches rooted on constructivist and experiential theories of learning (Dewey, 1938; Savery & Duffy, 1996). These contend that enhanced understanding is achieved through engagement with others, i.e. "social interactions as pedagogy" (Shaffer, 2007), discovery and personal experience.

This project aims to bring a fresh look at the use of technology in experiential learning methods by using the iPad as a dynamic learning tool and the iBook as a dynamic learning resource. Within the Faculty of the Built Environment (where BSP sits), it will be an innovative mechanism for staff and students to explore within the creative learning environment. The use of technology will appeal to students to articulate their learning experiences and creativity, whereby they will be encouraged and nurtured to produce their own iBooks to showcase their own (design) work. By doing so they will be iteratively developing their e-portfolio as a design artefact. The project is being embedded in the curriculum over Terms 1 and 2 alongside the modules where communication ability and spatial awareness are developed - Graphic Skills (Term 1) and Urban Design Skills (Term 2).

In the weekly module "Urban Lab I: Graphic Skills" (October-December) students learn different methods and techniques of graphically presenting urban analysis and archival research. In this module students work in groups and in pairs, combining the "traditional" use of sketching, figure-ground study, technical drawing, mapping and layout techniques, and, for the first time, using the digital possibilities (apps) enabled by the iPad (i.e. Adobe Ideas, Adobe Photoshop, etc.). Students were given sketchbooks and iPads and encouraged to use the iPad as a dynamic and interactive learning tool to help them develop their skills in graphic communication and enhance their spatial awareness, two key objectives for the development of conceptual built environment knowledge and literacy. Using iPads is also allowing the students to develop their group projects in a more dynamic (e)community, as by using the Adobe Creative Cloud suite of resources, they can create and develop content simultaneously, as well as share, access and publish it whether in the class or offsite, automatically syncing different users in different locations.

Interim evaluation of the project will be conducted via a survey questionnaire and focus groups, where students will reflect on their elearning experience over the taught 10 weeks. The cohort of 61 students will complete a survey in the last taught session of term 1 (to ensure a high response rate), where a combination of "multiple-choice" and "attitude battery" questions will be used. The "attitude battery" format is useful to measure strength of opinion from respondents (i.e. how useful was the use of the iPad in this module), where a scale of five (5) points is provided (ranging from bad to excellent, daily use to do not use, etc.). Five points are chosen as this is considered the optimum number for an attitude battery questionnaire, with respondents losing the ability to differentiate with more points (McLafferty, 2003). Open-ended sub-questions will also be used (why/why not?) to allow a broader scope of data, and more meaningful responses to be collated, which will help devise the themes for discussion in the focus groups.

The focus groups will run at the beginning of term 2, in an informal and sociable setting, while on a field trip abroad to a European city. The focus groups will consider how the project can be explored further during Term 2 when the iPads will be used for their group and individual work in the bi-weekly module "Introducing Urban Design: Urban Design Skills" (January-March), in conjunction with e-resources created in partnership with the 2012-13 cohort: the Urban Design Images group resources, available via the MyPortfolio and Moodle VLEs (Virtual Learning Environments).

The Urban Design Images group displays still images that provide a reference image library of six spatial categories (experiential and behavioural qualities, hard vs. soft materials, leftover space, street furniture, townscape, urban fabric). Each category has its own folder and these are compiled in a page, the Images Archive. In addition, the webpage Urban Design in the Web provides a synopsis and links of urban design-related web projects and resources. New features are currently being developed by the tutors (funded by UCL ELDG, between June-December 2013) to add to the experiential and behavioural qualities category, identified by the students as "challenging and contentious and more open to subjective interpretation". By exploring these qualities in more depth while developing their projects, we aim to develop an iBook of Experiential and Behavioral Qualities of Space, in a collaborative partnership of staff and students, throughout term 2. This interactive textbook (of text, evolving illustrations, image and sound narratives [filmed using iPads], quizzes) aims to enhance the understanding of not only spatial but also phenomenological awareness, "shorten[ing] the road to self-experience" (Findeli, 1990).

The iBook is seen here as a useful Open Educational Resource (OER) "openly available for use by educators and students, without an accompanying need to pay royalties or licence fees" (Butcher, 2011). The iBooks' content and all of the interactive features can be easily accessible in any Apple device as the iBook app can be downloaded for free from the app Store. A lite version can also be created for access in Android devices as a PDF file. The use of mobile devices (iPads) in the learning of graphic communication and urban design skills and development of an enhanced spatial awareness will ultimately seek to encourage undergraduate students to take an active role in the iterative production of (their) design (e)artefacts by producing their own e-portfolio(s) as an iBook. As such, students will be invited to an extra-curricular workshop on "how to do your own iBook". By using and developing their own iBook(s) students will be building their own employability skills through flexible online learning.

References

Butcher, N. (2011). *A basic guide to open educational resources (OER).* Vancouver: Commonwealth of Learning & UNESCO.

Dewey, J. (1938). *Experience and education.* New York: Macmillan.

Findeli, A. (1990). Moholy - Nagy's design pedagogy in Chicago (1937-46). *Design Issues,* *7*(1), 4-19.

McLafferty, S. (2003). Conducting questionnaire surveys. In G. Valentine (Ed.), *Key methods in geography*. London: Sage.

Shaffer, D. W. (2007). Learning in design. In R. A. Lesh, J. J. Kaput, & E. Hamilton (Eds.), *Foundations for the future in mathematics education* (pp. 99-126). Mahweh, NJ: Lawrence Erlbaum Associates.

Savery, J., & Duffy, T. (1996). Problem based learning: an instructional model and its constructivist framework. In B. G. Wilson (Ed.) *Constructivist learning environments* (Chapter 11). NJ: Educational Technology.

iPADAGOGY: iPADS AS DRIVERS OF TRANSFORMING PRACTICE IN TEACHING EDUCATION

PAUL HOPKINS[1] AND KEVIN BURDEN[2]

Abstract

The tablet computer (iPad) offers a range of affordances to the teacher and learner in higher education, including mobility, social interactivity and customisation (Kearney, Schuck, Burden & Aubusson, 2012), and the standards (standard 3) for trainee teachers in England require that teachers "successfully identify and exploit opportunities to develop learners' skills, in communication, reading and writing" (DfE, 2013). This project is exploring the broader professional learning of teachers, occurring within the university and on vocational placement and in the students' homes. Using a mainly qualitative approach of student logs and questionnaires and interviews with both tutors and students, it is looking at how the presence of such technologies in the hands of an entire course cohort affects the nature of learning and teaching, including the move towards an inquiry-based rather than a delivery model. The data will be analysed using an inductive thematic coding method. In addition, the project seeks to explore the wider institutional impact of mobile technologies for learning and teaching purposes, including the pedagogical and logistical consideration across and beyond the institution.

1. Introduction and Literature Review

With the growth in ubiquitous ICT and the emerging use of mobile technologies in and outside of the classroom it is becoming increasingly important to prepare trainee teachers to use and harness flexible technologies, such as mobile and tablet devices, both for their professional

[1] University of Hull, United Kingdom. Email: p.hopkins@hull.ac.uk
[2] University of Hull, United Kingdom. Email: k.j.burden@hull.ac.uk

and personal learning (Aubusson, Schuck & Burden, 2009). The use of mobile technologies in teachers' own professional learning offers the potential for teachers to access current educational information (e.g. video clips, articles, lecture and presentation notes), and transfer valuable learning and teaching resources between their various bases, which include the university itself, their school placements and their homes (Wishart, 2009; Aubusson et al., 2009). In addition, it offers opportunities for students to collaborate with other students (and teachers) and to analyse and reflect on their own practice and learning. Many of these are generic employability skills which are valued across many different cognate areas of the university and are therefore of interest to many different stakeholders beyond the Faculty of Education where this project is rooted.

In a rapidly changing world, teacher professional learning needs to provide opportunities for critical reflection and access to changing knowledge bases; mobile technologies offer a potentially powerful means to enhance teachers' professional learning through:

- The discussion of pedagogical issues within a community of colleagues and with other trainees, both within and beyond the institution;
- Ready access to online information and resources;
- Shared reflection on digitally captured classroom experiences.

Although some authors have identified mobile learning as a possible way of alleviating some of the problems associated with the itinerant nature of teacher training (Aubusson et al., 2009; Wishart, 2009), Wishart, McFarlane and Ramsden (2005) also discovered that trainee teachers appreciated the portability that mobile devices afforded for transferring resources, and especially the just-in-time access to the Internet made available through the device. Trainees and teachers in this study found the mobile device particularly useful for management activities such as record keeping and note taking. This project sought to build on this research, using a more enhanced mobile device (the iPad), to extend our understanding of the ways in which the latest technologies might enhance current provision in Initial Teacher Education (ITE), supporting new forms of pedagogy and learning, especially that of inquiry-based learning (Justice, Warry, Cuneo, Inglis, Miller, Rice & Miller, 2001), both within the institution and during the periods of time when students are working outside thc university on teaching placements. This is integrated with a new approach to learning using an inquiry-based learning model, which is facilitated by the 1-1 affordance of the mobile device.

In spite of the potential benefits that mobile technologies might bring to Inquiry-Based Learning (IBL), there remains a rather limited body of research on teacher learning with mobile technologies. Much of the current research investigates the integration of ICT into school curricula (Bain, 2004; Staples, Pugach & Himes, 2005). Whilst there have been some small-scale projects, which have explored the use of mobile technologies in ITE (Wishart, 2009), these have not tracked trainee teachers through their school placements nor have they investigated the impact of access to such technology after the students leave the institution when they find employment as teachers.

Also, research on mobile technologies in education has tended to focus primarily on use by pupils, and on the ways that teachers can support that usage, whilst very little research has been conducted on how teachers and trainee teachers themselves might learn with these new technologies, or indeed with any digital technologies (Naismith et al., 2004; Fisher, Higgins & Loveless, 2006). Further, as third generation mobile technologies, which offer increased connectivity, are a relatively new phenomenon, there has been little opportunity to assess the impact of these next generation technologies for professional learning. Fisher et al. (2006) argue that if different approaches to learning and teaching, and different relationships between students and teachers are to occur, it is essential to understand teachers' learning and the role that digital technologies might play in this. This project sought to build on the review by Fisher et al. (2006) of teacher learning with digital technologies by considering what mobility, with its characteristics of being personal and portable, might contribute to the experience of trainee and early career teachers, and what benefits this might ultimately bring to institutions involved in the process such as the university provider and the recipient schools.

2. Post-PC Technologies for Professional Learning

In recent years there has been a discernable shift in education away from fixed personal computers towards more pervasive devices (sometimes referred to as "Post-PC Technologies") such as mobile phones and tablet computers, which are highly personal, rather than corporate, technologies. Although mobile phones have been around for almost a decade it is only in recent years that they have become virtually universal, with UNESCO estimating there are around six billion subscriptions across the world (UNESCO, 2012). Their use as tools for learning, however, especially in formal contexts such as schools and universities, remains contentious and largely unexplored, both for practitioners and policy makers alike, who face the dilemma of reconciling the potential gains of these devices with the much publicised dangers and concerns, real or perceived, when used in the classroom or lecture theatre. More recently students are beginning to purchase and bring to the campus their own mobile computers, including laptops, notebooks and tablet technologies. There remains, however, an urgent need to clarify how such portable technologies can be used most effectively for teaching and with what impact:

> While the field is expanding, crucial issues underpinning practices and their sustainability remain to be addressed such as the role of teachers and the type of professional development required to prepare them for teaching their students to learn with these devices… (Ng, 2013, p. 2)

In the Faculty of Education at the University of Hull there is a more pressing need to understand the phenomenon of mobile learning better (m-Learning), since many of our students embarking on professional programmes such as teaching are likely to encounter situations in their work placements (post primary schools) where these technologies are being used by teachers and students alike. This is likely to be common across many other professional contexts and disciplines, especially where students experience a prolonged period of teaching or study in a work-based environment, such as healthcare, medicine, dentistry and some aspects of logistics. Hence the need to support students in their use of these emerging technologies, from both a personal and professional perspective, is common to a wide range of cognate areas and disciplines across the university sector and particularly the University of Hull.

The university therefore funded a two-year project embedded in the Faculty of Education to support the development of trainee secondary teachers when using personalised tablet computers. The faculty purchased 150 second-generation iPads (iPad 2s), which were allocated to all students starting in September 2013. The devices were supplied with a core set of applications. These were decided in consultation with the tutors and drawing on the project leaders' experience from other projects in the UK, and their use and impact will be monitored and evaluated by staff from within the Faculty over the course of the academic year of study for the cohort (2013-2014) and then repeated for the following cohort (2014-2015). The devices will be collected back from students at the end of their programme in June 2014, and will be reallocated to the second cohort of students the September of that year. It is anticipated that many of the lessons gathered and learned in the first year of the programme will be incorporated into a more expansive provision starting in year two. The first year can, in some ways, be considered an extensive pilot programme.

Based on previous evaluations and research undertaken by members of the Faculty of Education, it is anticipated this two-year project will generate significant insights into a range of issues associated with the move towards more personalised, individual technologies, such as the iPad, helping to inform our institutional understanding and awareness of how best to support and exploit this trend in terms of learning, teaching and the underlying logistical and infrastructure requirements to make it a reality.

3. Research Design, Aims of the Research

In order to gather, interpret and disseminate this data, staff associated with the project, supported by other colleagues and colleagues across the university, are conducting a two-year evaluation of this project, which will focus on a range of different impacts, including:

- The impact on lecturers and their teaching approaches/styles when all students have access to ubiquitous, connected technology like the iPad, particuarly in the delivery of a professional studies curriculum rooted in an inquiry-based learning methodology;
- The technical and logistical infrastructure required to support students in their use of mobile technologies, both on and beyond the university campus (this includes the impact of wide-scale usage of tablet devices on the Wi-Fi infrastructure);
- The impact on students as learners in terms of organisation, metacognition and competence in using technology to support their learning and understanding;
- The extent to which the use of a personalised connected device can assist students and tutors in tackling some of the problems associated with work placement, such as the provision of ongoing support and advice; the sense of isolation experienced by individual students; the dissemination of resources and ideas for students remote from the university.

Hence these potential impacts will form the broad canvas for a two-year evaluation of this project.

4. Research Questions

This study provides a large-scale, in-depth investigation of how the use of a mobile computing device (i.e. the iPad) facilitates a more effective ITE experience for trainees. The overarching research question addressed by this project is therefore: How does the use of mobile technologies support, enhance and extend the professional learning and practice of trainee teachers and their lecturers/mentors?

4.1 Sub-Questions

1. What aspects of trainees' own professional learning do mobile devices best support? Does this vary according to the subject specialism of the trainee?
2. What is the impact upon lecturers and their teaching approaches when all students have access to an Internet-enabled device, like the iPad?
3. In what ways does the use of mobile technologies support students and their tutors/mentors during teaching placement when students are remote from the university context?
4. What are the logistical issues required to support ubiquitous mobile pedagogies (e.g. technical support; infrastructure issues)?

5. Methodology

The research design aimed to provide a robust and in-depth source of longitudinal data to track the progress of the initiative across two academic years (2013-2015). The research design adopts a mixed methods approach, which includes an interpretative study to explore the views, attitudes and practices of trainee and early career teachers from a personal perspective, along with a qualitative approach to identify changing patterns of use over the academic year. The research seeks to explore and investigate new phenomena in terms of how trainee and early-qualified teachers use, modify and evaluate the use of mobile technologies for their professional learning. In keeping with the research questions outlined above this suggests the adoption of methodologies and research instruments, which are sympathetic to the exploratory nature of the research itself. Rossman (1988) identifies a number of salient features, which underpin the research design we will be using, these being:

- The link between qualitative research approaches and natural settings: our research will be located in relatively natural settings, populated with actual users (teachers and students) undertaking authentic activities and tasks. In addition, the research team will be highly involved in the actual experiences of participants, which also characterises "naturalistic" and interpretative research.

- Qualitative research is emergent rather than tightly pre-figured: this is a crucial consideration for the type of activity we are likely to be engaged in, which will change during the course of the project. This may affect the research questions, as different themes or patterns begin to emerge from the data, which we initially collect. Even the data collection methods are likely to change from those we have outlined below, since this is a novel area of experiences, and it is likely we will discover alternative instruments and approaches as the phenomenon itself becomes clearer.

Qualitative research is fundamentally interpretative: we are exploring a largely new and hitherto unexplored phenomenon, and an interpretative research paradigm is therefore entirely appropriate as it is essentially inductive, rather than deductive, describing the setting, before starting to analyse the data for emerging themes and categories which inform the final interpretation.

The sample includes the entire cohort of trainee teachers who will be training for post-secondary education; in 2013-2014 this amounts to approximately 135 students. These include six subject areas: English, Mathematics, Science (Biology, Chemistry, Physics and Physics with Maths), Modern Foreign Languages (French, German and Spanish) and Geography and History. In order to maintain the ethical integrity of the project, all of the trainee teachers on this course have been invited to participate in the research, and have been offered the opportunity to withdraw if they so wish. At the time of writing (October 2013) none have opted to withdraw from the project, though one student did decline to take part, citing their worries about losing / damaging the device.

In terms of data generation, there are a number of research instruments, which will be used to generate data during the project. These are:

- Online baseline and exit surveys of students to identify changing levels of skill sets and attitudes towards the use of technology;
- Semi-structured interviews of students and lecturing staff conducted by researchers at the end of phase II (November 2013) and phase IV (February 2014);
- Blogs and self generated artifacts produced by students during the course of the year (these will be collected through a Dropbox folder set up for each subject group);
- Regular student reports on their usage;
- Tracking of the applications loaded onto the devices;
- Periodic surveys;
- Video case studies of particular usage.

6. Inquiry-Based Learning

A core function of the iPad is to facilitate a move from a lecture /seminar based model of learning to an IBL model. With students having access to the devices we can be confident that they have access to the materials, which are uploaded onto a website, before the IBL session. Building on the work of Justice et al. (2001), we have developed a suitable model for teacher education students (Hopkins, 2013). An ongoing concern has been how we prepare teacher education students with suitable insights into the theoretical underpinnings of education whilst also allowing them to concretise this into the practice in their school based parts of their training. The use of the devices and the IBL or flipped learning model will allow this. Initial feedback after the first weeks has been very positive from both the students and the tutors delivering this new model as opposed to the lecture and seminar model, which was followed in previous years. There is no doubt in our minds that the iPads have made this methodology possible in a way that would have been almost impossible without the devices – as access to technology both prior to and during the IBL sessions is essential to effective implementation.

7. Initial Data

The initial baseline survey data explored the existing technology base of the students, the ways in which they had experienced technology in learning and teaching and the idea that these were "digital natives". Not surprisingly, access to technology was high, with especially high ownership of laptops and almost all students having access to mobile devices of some sort. The relatively low ownership of game players might also be surprising.

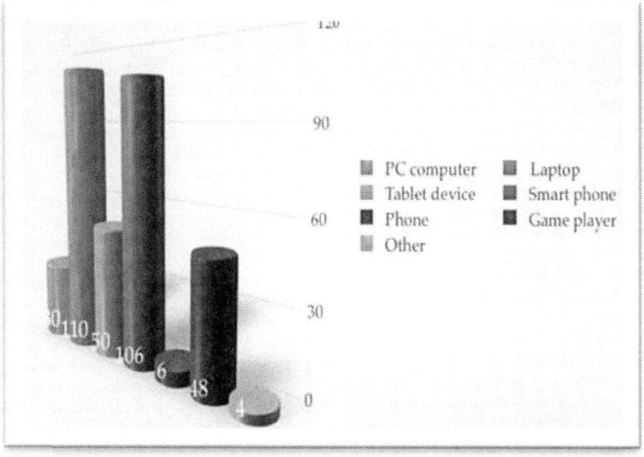

Figure 1. Technology ownership – students September 2013, n=115

When asked how they currently used technology for learning the figures followed similar patterns for the desktop and laptop, but were different for mobile devices. Learning was mostly seen as writing assignments, accessing web sources and using communication such as email.

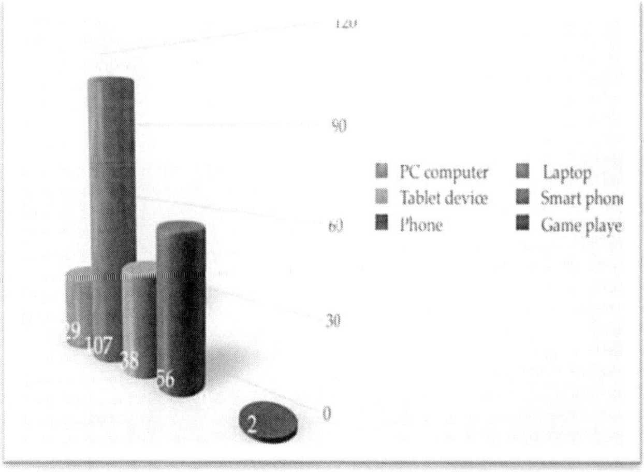

Figure 2. Technology used for learning – students September 2013, n=115

The students were also asked how often, in their undergraduate teaching, they had experienced technology used in the teaching to which they had been exposed.

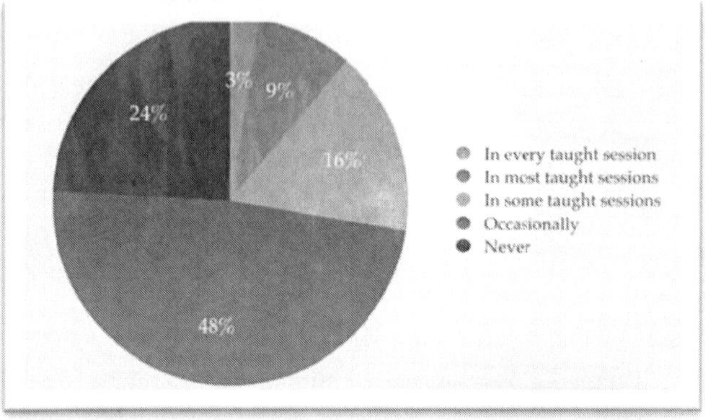

Figure 3. Technology used for teaching – students September 2013, n=115

The experiences of the students were that technology had been used to some degree in about three-quarters of their teaching, but when asked the type of technology this was overwhelmingly uni-directional technology, was mostly projection or presentation technologies, and with very few exceptions was synchronous with the teaching event. Very few of the students have experienced any remote or asynchronous teaching as part of their undergraduate degree.

Initially, the students were asked to keep a Wiki of their own use of the iPads. However, this was found to be technically challenging for many of the students, and so we reverted to the use of emailed reports sent to the researchers. At the time of writing this paper only the first three weeks of this data is available. This amounts to about 200 emails of data, the scope of which ranges from 400-500 word reports showing an analytical and reflective account of usage to a short descriptive comment of use or non-use. Initial analysis can group the comments into four areas:

a) The iPad as a resource access device

Given the nature of the inquiry-based learning and the provision of materials for the students to access before the IBL sessions this was one of the most prevalent reported uses of the device. The use of the device has allowed for the distribution of multimedia resources for students to access including e-books and other e-resources via the library services.

Comments from students include:

> "…iPad mainly for... FiPS (professional studies) reading, subject method reading and research within subject method sessions…"
> "…Looking at Prezis, to do pre-reading without having to print it out/ carry documents around…"
> "…Keynote power points during method sessions, research during university based days…"
> "…Especially finding it handy for reading downloaded journals…"
> "…I have used iBooks and Pages more than any other apps, these have helped with reading and writing."
> "Being able to save various documents in iBooks has proven very useful, and it has certainly saved on paper…"
> "…I do love is the podcasts, I have downloaded many to do with history and listen to them on my way into university or school."

b) Taking notes, organising work and making resources

As well as accessing resources the students have been using the devices in sessions to take notes and to organise their learning, including the use of applications such as Dropbox and Calendar as well as list makers and checklists. Whilst many students are still also using traditional resources such as pen and paper more and more are using the devices to take notes (using a word processor application) to map ideas (using post-it or mind mapping applications) or using the camera to capture shots from groups work or the notes from the tutor's screen.

Comments from students include:

> "…Taking notes, creating mind-maps…"
> "It has helped my learning in that the resources are to hand without having to print them all out, making organisation much easier…"
> "…Used it to make presentations using Keynote and to make notes using pages…"
> "…Note taking and pre-reading for class…"
> "…To take pictures of the posters we made in FiPS, and to fill in the journal…"
> "…I use the iPad to take pictures for inspiration for future planning and resources…"
> "I find the iPad very handy to show documents quickly to other people and share information…"
> "The iPad as been useful when reading articles in class being able to highlight and annotate things on it…"
> "My favourite app so far though is "Paper". I have been using this app to draw pictures that I will then be able to use as my own resources in PowerPoint or active inspire…"

> "I have also taken photos of some of the work that we have produced in method sessions…"

c) Reflective practice

We are beginning to see the students thinking about how the devices can be used for reflective practice. This allows them to capture data about their practice, and then easily share this with their mentor either in the university or in their partnership placement practice school. This kind of practice is transformational (McCormick & Scrimshaw, 2001) in terms of what they could previously do with the technology.

> "I have had the opportunity to record short starter activities and teaching tasks which have allowed me to critically evaluate the way I teach…" (History student teacher)
> "I recorded my micro-teaching lesson today with my iPad so it will be helpful to have a look at it with my mentor in school and try to raise some aspects that I can improve…" (Languages student teacher)

d) Classroom usage

The students are starting to go into their partnership schools and classrooms, and there are some opportunities for them to be able to use the devices in the classroom. Students are also investigating with mentors how these might be able to be used more widely in the school.

> "I used the device to record students where there were not enough Dictaphones…" (Geography student)
> "Useful apps for the classroom I have downloaded are a name generator and a timer…" (English student)
> "The ability to draw on top of documents using Sketch is a great alternative for when a Smart board is not available…" (English student)

What is interesting here is again the opportunity for transformational practice that the affordances of the technology allow (Aubussion et al., 2009), those of mobility and customszation especially with the incredible cheapness of the software, often free and rarely above £1.00.

e) Some initial issues

The introduction of the devices has not been without problems. Two of the devices (from a total of 150) had some technical issues that resulted in the devices having to be brought back to the centre for repair, and to this end we do have a stock of "replacement" devices, which can be used for this purpose. In addition, the mindset of using the device and the practical learning in using it, especially for those who have come from a non-Apple background, caused a number of issues. Comments from the students include:

> "I have been having some problems to manage all the information, personally I think that we have access to (so) many information what can make it confusing…" (Languages student)
> "I have also found that it is easy for me to forget to do things on it, such as the journal as I am not seeing it in my bag everyday like I would have it was in paper format…" (Languages student)
> "I can't use my iPad at my placement school, I don't have the Wi-Fi password yet…" (English student)
> "I have noticed that it is difficult to keep track of work as it is available in a range of places, and it is quite easy to skip past something when it isn't completed…" (Languages student)
> "I won't be able to use it in school because they have a no iPad policy…" (Languages student)
> "While my placement school has no problem with my use of the iPad within my teaching, they equally prefer working "on paper" for administrative purposes. This will therefore require me to copy up their handwritten observation notes onto the digital file…" (English student)

We have also experienced some technical issues with the provisions of Apple TVs in the teaching classrooms and the distribution of applications for specific groups, rather than the whole cohort.

8. Conclusion and Implications

At the time of writing, the project in still in progress and so the data is still in its initial stages (see above). We expect that by March 2014 we will have rich data from the university-based experiences of the students over the first 12 weeks of the course and their time on placement from November 2013. We will be able to further analyse data from the baseline surveys using descriptive statistics and deductive coding to create a broad overview of patterns of use before the deployment of the technologies. We hope that the conference committee sees that this is an exciting and innovative project – we believe it is the biggest of its kind in teacher education in England at this time, and already the unanalysed data is showing an excitement about the use of the devices in both the student and the tutor population of the Faculty of Education allowing innovative learning to take place.

The implications for both our own institution and wider arethat it offers a serious challenge to the lecture as a key teaching strategy and a move to a more inquiry-based and personalised learning style that has the potential to allow multi-model and multi-synchronous teaching and learning. Whilst this has been postulated widely for many years, we believe that the tablet technologies offer a practice as well as a pedagogic solution.

References

Aubusson, P., Schuck, S., & Burden, K. (2009). Mobile learning for teacher professional learning: Benefits, obstacles and issues. *Research in Learning Technology, 17*(3), 233-247.

Department for Education (2012). *Teachers' standards*. London: Department for Education.

Fisher, T., Higgins, C., & Loveless, A. (2006). Teacher learning with digital technologies: A review of research and projects. *Report 14. Futurelab Series*. Bristol: Futurelab.

Justice, C., Warry, W., Cuneo, C., Inglis, S., Miller, S., Rice, J., & Miller, S. (2001). A grammar for inquiry: Linking goals and methods in a collaboratively taught social sciences inquiry course. In *Society for Teaching and Learning in Higher Education* (Ed.), The Alan Blizzard award paper: The award winning papers. Windsor, Ontario, Canada: McGraw-Hill Ryerson.

Kearney, M., Schuck, S., Burden, K., & Aubusson, P. (2012). Viewing mobile learning from a pedagogical perspective. *Research in Learning Technology, 20*(1), 14406.

Hopkins (2013). A development of the Justice et al inquiry based learning model for the teaching education students. Retrieved October 31, 2013, from http://www.mmiweb.org.uk/hull/site/ibl/ibl.html

McCormick, R., & Scrimshaw, P. (2001). Information and communications technology, knowledge and pedagogy. *Education, Communication & Information, 1*(1), 37-57.

Naismith, L., Lonsdale, P., Vavoula, G., & Sharples, M. (2004). Literature review in mobile technologies and learning. *Report 11. Futurelab Series*. Bristol: Futurelab.

Ng, W. (2013). Conceptualising m-learning literacy. *International Journal of Mobile and Blended Learning, 5*(1), 1-20.

Rossman, G. B. (1998). *Learning in the field: An introduction to qualitative research*. Thousand Oaks, Calif: Sage Publications.

UNESCO (2012). *Turning on mobile learning: global themes*. UNESCO: Paris.

Wishart, J., McFarlane A., & Ramsden, A. (2005). Using personal digital assistants (PDAs) with Internet access to support initial teacher training in the UK. *Proceedings of the mLearn 2005: 4th World Conference on Mobile Learning.*

Wishart, J. (2009). Use of mobile technology for teacher training. In M. Ally (Ed.) *Mobile learning: Transforming the delivery of education and training* (pp. 265–278). Edmonton, Canada: AU Press.

iPADS AS COLLABORATIVE TOOLS TO ENHANCE BIOLOGICAL IDENTIFICATION SKILLS IN THE LAB AND FIELD

SARAH L. TAYLOR[1] AND TRISH PROCTER[2]

Abstract

According to the Chartered Institute of Ecology and Environmental Management, today's biology graduates lack the key species identification skills required by prospective employees. This mismatch between students' skills and employers' requirements has serious implications for employability after graduation. Interactive species identification apps on mobile learning devices, such as iPads, have the potential to encourage active engagement with the process of identification and provide a means for students to (re)connect with nature. A pilot study funded by a Keele University teaching innovation grant and School of Life Sciences teaching equipment grant investigated the potential of iPad educational apps to boost species identification skills. Working in pairs, twelve final year undergraduate students were given one hour to locate eight target trees on the Keele campus using the Here&Near app and then utilise four tree species ID apps (FSC trees, ForestXplorer, LeafsnapHD and Isoperla's TreeID) to identify the tree species. The students completed pre- and post-activity evaluation questionnaires and produced a post-activity reflective audio commentary using Fotobabble. The pre-study questionnaire revealed that 92% of students thought tree ID apps would aid identification skills, while only 50% of students agreed that iPads would facilitate collaboration. The post-study evaluation revealed that not all tree apps were equally useful in learning, along with a transformation of student opinion regarding the collaborative aspect of the activity. The second phase of the study is to embed a modified version of the tree tour into a first year undergraduate practical, and evaluate how this affects the ability

[1] Keele University, United Kingdom. Email: s.l.taylor@keele.ac.uk

[2] Keele University, United Kingdom. Email: p.procter@keele.ac.uk

to correctly identify trees on the lab exam. The preliminary results from this study indicate that a group-orientated collaborative problem-solving approach encouraged communication and development of skills based on all their senses (visual, verbal, etc.).

1. Introduction

Species identification and taxonomy are key skills required by prospective employers that are often perceived by students and staff as outdated and boring. A study by Nimis et al. (2006, as cited in Nimis, Riccamboni & Martell, 2012) found that lengthy paper-based classical keys are difficult for the layperson to use, and are not appropriate for educational projects or citizen science. Students become quickly disengaged with species identification, feeling overwhelmed by the options and preferring to flick through books and look at the photographs/diagrams rather than go through the formal process of identification using descriptive and illustrative keys. Such a surface learning approach to identification means that students cannot identify similar species in different habitats as they do not know the traits that define a given plant family, etc. Academic institutions have also stepped away from traditional taxonomic courses. For example, in 2012 Birmingham University decided to abandon the Biological Recording programme despite it being the only such Masters course on offer in the UK that provided habitat and species identification skills for ecological consultants (BBC News, 2011). A report by the Institute of Ecology and Environmental Management (IEEM, 2011) revealed there has been a national decline in species identification skills at a time when it has never been more important to protect the nation's biodiversity and sustainability of ecosystems.

Identification is a critical skill for a biologist that is an active, experiential and exploratory learning activity (KeytoNature, 2010). Students must experience the target organism using all of their senses: smell it, touch it, listen to the way it sounds when you crumple it in their fingers and look at it from multiple angles (tasting is not recommended as it may be poisonous!), etc. Therefore, species identification brings together a unique set of skills that involve visual learning, visual thinking and visual communication (Stanley, 1996). Identification is not about the final answer, but about the process used to achieve the final answer, and as such should not be done as a solitary activity. The problem here is that verbal communication is something that is often lacking between students. I have personally witnessed students sitting side-by-side in a tutorial messaging each other via Facebook, rather than engaging in oral communication. The prolific integration of technology into our lives (spell-checker, predictive texting, Satnavs, etc.) means we are losing the ability to use all of our senses, to think on our feet, and question what we see, hear, feel, etc. Multi-sense learning involving the brain and our body is critical not only to science, but also develops a broader set of skills needed to cope with day-to-day life tasks.

Species identification provides the perfect forum for a constructivist approach to knowledge creation by building on prior experiences of species, and requires the observer to ask questions, such as "how is this different to the last plant?" Much of the prior knowledge used in the constructivist model of identification is gained subliminally through childhood adventures - making mud pies and capturing "creepy crawlies" in backyards and local woods with friends. But for a whole generation of today's children, the pleasures of a free-range childhood are missing (Louv, 2005). Monbiot (2012) considers the removal of children from the natural world to be a second environmental crisis. It is therefore down to universities to educate adults in the ways of nature and to provide these childhood experiences. Mobile learning devices offer the opportunity to engage today's students in the process of species identification in ways previously out of reach in a field setting, and can be used as a means of bridging the communication gap to help students work collaboratively.

The Field Studies Council has rolled out iPhone and iPad apps of their highly acclaimed laminated species identification keys (FSC, 2012). Interactive key apps for mobile devices are useful in education, in the promotion of nature-aware tourism and in projects of citizen science (Nimis, Riccamboni & Martell, 2012).

This study investigates the potential of a collaborative iPad-based problem-solving activity to enhance tree identification skills. The specific objectives are: (i) develop a guided tree tour using the Here&Near app, (ii) critique the suitability of four tree species apps (FSC trees, ForestXplorer, Leafsnap HD and British tree ID), and (iii) evaluate the impact of the activity on student learning. This paper will focus on the preliminary findings of the pilot study (phase 1), which was completed in November 2013, and the implications this has for the test study rollout in February 2014.

2. Study Design

The project comprised a pilot study in semester 1 and a test study in semester 2. Twelve final year undergraduate students were selected on a first come first served basis to participate in a pilot study workshop in semester 1. To encourage engagement, students received a £10 Amazon voucher and a certificate of participation on completion of the feedback components. The pilot study group received the class materials developed for a first-year ecology module, along with a short session on how to use the iPad. Student pairs were given one hour to go out and identify eight tree species growing on the Keele campus. Trees were located using a tree tour in the free Here&Near app (Dvoychenko, 2012), and students were required to make a note of how easy trees were to locate. For each tree species, students were required to try out four tree apps. Three of the apps were free: FSC trees by Field Studies Council (2012), ForestXplorer by Forestry Commission (2013), and LeafsnapHD by Columbia University, University of Maryland and Smithsonian Institution (2011). The fourth app, TreeID by Isoperla (2012), was purchased at a cost of £2.49.

Evaluation was in the form of pre- and post-activity questionnaires and a reflective audio diary using the free Fotobabble (2012) app. Students were numbered 1 to 12 so that pre and post evaluation could be tracked while ensuring student anonymity. Students were required to rate the apps using a four-tiered scoring system (1, poor; 2, mediocre; 3, good; and 4, excellent), and statements such as "Tree apps will improve species identification skills" using a five-tier rating system (strongly disagree, disagree, neutral, agree, strongly agree). The results from the pilot study will be fed into the test study in semester 2 of 40 first-year undergraduate students. Lab exam scores for questions relating to tree identification will be compared to previous cohorts to see if the iPad activity has enhanced learning. Students and teaching staff will also be required to evaluate the activity on the end-of-module teaching evaluation questionnaire.

3. Preliminary Findings

The pre-study questionnaire revealed that 92% of students thought tree ID apps would "aid identification skills", supporting findings by Nimis, Riccamboni and Martell (2012). The British TreeID app received the highest rating with an average score of 3.4, and students felt the cost of £2.49 for the TreeID app was reasonable. The LeafsnapHD app had the lowest rating of 2.2 out of a possible four, as students found the image analysis frustrating and did not aid learning. The consensus was that no one app alone could cope with the range of targeted trees species.

The pre-study assessment of the capability of "iPads to facilitate collaboration" highlighted a degree of variability in student opinion, with only 50% of students agreeing that iPads would facilitate collaboration. This is surprising considering multimedia have quickly become the means of modern communication (Gliksman, 2013, p. 14). Comparison to the post-study assessment revealed that one-third of respondents had increased their ranking and no students disagreed with the statement (Figure 1). This was also highlighted in the reflective diaries and open comments on the evaluation sheet, which included "it [collaboration] showed me that there is disagreement in certain plant identifications". The students liked the fact that they could use abstract screenshots in Fotobabble and got quite inventive with the special effects (Figure 2). The collaborative approach made students feel "safe to fail", and the fun aspect of the task helped to keep the students engaged.

The iPad has a 5-megapixel camera, which can be used to collect photos/videos of the specimens and the habitat in which they are growing and of students carrying out the fieldwork. Such multimedia can help affirm identification back in the laboratory and promotes the ethos of "take only pictures leave only footprints".

This is particularly important when dealing with protected habitats, such as Sites of Special Scientific Interest (SSSIs), as collection of specimens is prohibited. There is hope for the future. The IEEM (2011) report has put species identification on the main agenda, and the abandoned Biological Recording course was rescued by Manchester Metropolitan University (MMU, 2012). Species identification is an excellent way for our students to (re)connect with nature, while gaining key employability skills.

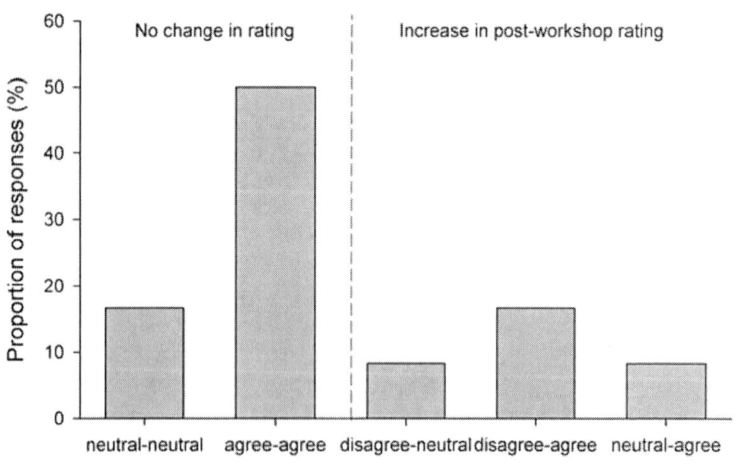

Figure 1. Pre- and post-workshop evaluation of the statement iPads facilitate collaboration

Figure 2. Fotobabble screenshot used in one of the audio reflections

4. Conclusion

The preliminary results from this study indicate that a group-orientated collaborative problem-solving approach encouraged communication and development of skills based on all their senses (visual, verbal, etc.). The tree tour was hampered by the patchy nature of the outdoor Wi-Fi signal, which reduced GPS accuracy and prevented access to the ForestXplorer app. In future targeted trees will be restricted to the Wi-Fi hotspots and only the two highest rated tree species apps (ForestXplorer and TreeID) utilised. The second phase of the study is to embed a modified version of the tree tour into a first-year undergraduate practical in February 2014 and to evaluate how this influences the ability to correctly identify trees on the lab exam.

Acknowledgements

This study was funded by a School of Life Sciences teaching equipment grant and a Keele University teaching innovation grant. Many thanks to the following final year undergraduate students who gave up their spare time to participate in the pilot study workshop: Amy Collier, Davy Falkner, Holly Farrington, Abi Gazzard, Kristen Hirsh-Pearson, Katie Marsh, Kenroy Millwood, Alex Melson, Max Reboul, Ben Salt, Richard Sant, and Nathan Wisniewski. Finally, thanks to Craig Armstrong and

Yassir Rashid in Computing Services for their technical assistance in the mysterious workings of Apple Configurator.

References

BBC News (2011). University to cut "unique" course. Retrieved December 30, 2014, from http://goo.gl/BoHP7C

Columbia University, University of Maryland, & Smithsonian Institution (2011). Leafsnap: an electronic field guide. Retrieved December 2, 2013 from http://leafsnap.com/

Dvoychenko, S. (2012). Here&Near, notes by location and GPS tools. Retrieved December 30, 2014, from http://goo.gl/whKKQf

Fotobabble (2012). Fotobabble. Retrieved January 5, 2015, from http://www.fotobabble.com/s/mobile

IEEM (2011). Ecological skills: Shaping the profession in the 21st Century. Retrieved December 30, 2014, from http://goo.gl/I8awC4

FSC (2012). Field Studies Council iPhone apps are here... Retrieved April 17, 2013, from http://www.field-studies-council.org/publications/iphone-apps.aspx

Forestry Commission (n.d.). Get the forest in your pocket with our free app. Retrieved December 2, 2013, from http://www.forestry.gov.uk/mobileapp

Gliksman, S. (2013). *iPad in education for dummies*. New Jersey: John Wiley & Sons, Inc.

Isoperla (2012). Tree identification. Retrieved December 2, 2013, from http://isoperla.co.uk /TreeIdiPhone.html

KeytoNature (2010). Handbook - pedagogical approach? Retrieved April 16, 2013, from http://goo.gl/T2pDRA

Louv, R. (2005). *Last child in the woods: Saving our children from nature-deficit disorder*. London: Atlantic Books.

Manchester Metropolitan University (MMU) (2013). UK's last wildlife recording course saved - MMU to offer unique Biological Recording awards. Retrieved December 4, 2013, from http://www.mmu.ac.uk/news/news-items/1628/

Monbiot, G. (2012, November 19). If children lose contact with nature they won't fight for it. *The Guardian* Retrieved April 17, 2013, from http://goo.gl/WAbc1

Nimis, P.L., Riccamboni, R., & Martell, S. (2012). Identification keys on mobile devices: The Dryades experience. *Plant Biosystems, 146*(4), 783–788.

Stanley, E.D. (1996). Taking a second look: Investigating biology with visual datasets. *Bioscene: Journal of College Biology Teaching, 22*(3), 13-17.

USING THE KEYNOTE APP AS A RESEARCH TOOL: A CASE STUDY IN MEDICAL EDUCATION

VERONICA MITCHELL[1]

Abstract

Research in medical education has traditionally drawn on scientific evidence using quantitative methodologies. However, qualitative methods now bring new insights into the humanistic elements of healthcare. In the Health Sciences, traditional methods of data collection can now be transformed by the affordances of new technologies. The iPad enables alternative types of engagement with research participants. For instance movable images can provide deeper insights into individual experiences. The Keynote application (app) offers such an opportunity. In a recent Master's research project in Higher Education Studies, the iPad was used as a valuable tool to draw on students' critical reflection in terms of their Obstetrics practical curricular task. Using a simple image on the Keynote app of the iPad, this project involved undergraduate medical students, who shifted the images to indicate their assessment of their personal and professional growth. By talking to their actions as they adjusted the size and position of symbolic circles, the iPad acted as a vehicle facilitating deeper reflection and revealing rich insights. Both the novelty of using the tablet and the added sensory input contributed to motivating the student engagement. As products of individual student insights these images were interpreted to indicate shifts in students' knowledge, empathy and reflection from their fourth year Obstetrics experience to their insights two years later in their final year. The findings from this project demonstrate how the iPad fosters personal meaning-making, thereby enhancing the quality and efficacy of our educational practices.

---

[1] University of Cape Town, South Africa. Email: veronica.mitchell@uct.ac.za

1. Introduction

Advances in technology are revolutionising education at all levels of teaching, learning and research. Teachers are under pressure to become "pedagogical engineers" as they need to choose "the most relevant instructional approaches and technologies" (Hung, 2001, p. 286). Similarly educational researchers can adopt new opportunities arising from emerging technologies. The iPad offers numerous affordances that can supplement traditional forms of inquiry.

This paper describes my Higher Education Studies Master's research project (Mitchell, 2012) at the University of Cape Town (UCT), in which I explored undergraduate medical students' engagement with their practical Obstetrics curriculum. The iPad was used as an effective tool to add depth to students' reflective insights.

What follows in this paper is a theoretical outline providing a background to the project, then a description of the research process and findings with a focus on the use of the iPad as a facilitating tool. The topic of the study was the curriculum that forms the cornerstone of formal education, yet there is a paucity of research around it, particularly from the viewpoint of students' experiences.

As students engage in the designed curriculum, numerous forces drive, shape and modify it to shift towards an enacted curriculum. Barnett (2000, p. 260) explains curricula as:

> ...being lived by rather than being determined... [with an] elusive quality about them. Their actual dimensions and elements are tacit. They take on certain patterns and relationships but those patterns and relationships will be hidden from all concerned, except as they are experienced by the students.

By understanding the curriculum through the lens of students' actual experiences, valuable insights can be gained towards fostering improved educational practices.

While qualitative research data in the Health Sciences are frequently collected through interviews, focus groups and participant observations, the iPad offers a modality that can attract students' attention and encourage them to interrogate their experiences to a deeper, authentic level through an appealing user interface.

My qualitative research project aimed to examine how individual students in the Health Sciences Faculty (HSF) at UCT negotiated the curriculum-in-action in their Obstetrics practical rotation. Students were asked to reflect on their experiences with anticipation for their final year re-entry into the learning block.

Although the Department of Obstetrics and Gynaecology instructs fourth year students to submit individual reflective commentaries at the end of their disciplinary rotation, these descriptions of students' personal and professional growth tend to offer only a glimpse of their observations and experiences in the Obstetrics practices in local clinics. These commentaries also provide a feedback mechanism offering the potential for useful insights that are not frequently surfaced in course evaluations.

While developing students' reflective capacity has become an integral part of medical training, it remains a challenging task for both educators and students (Hatton & Smith, 2006). Using the iPad supports recommendations that new approaches are needed to motivate and engage the new generation of medical students (Sandars & Homer, 2008). The Keynote application (app) was an integral component of my research project.

2. Research Project

Recognition of my own preference for visual learning and teaching, reinforced by students' appreciative feedback in using visual tools, inspired me to use the Keynote app, adopting a multimodal approach in my research project. Beyond text and interviews, I used a visual framework that disaggregated the curriculum into three circular components representing Knowing, Acting and Being based on Barnett and Coates' (2005) triple-fold schema. Below I will explain the conceptual theory underpinning the chosen methodology where the iPad added an innovative and beneficial dimension. A description of the Keynote images used and the variations achieved in the research will be followed by a brief explanation of the findings. Specific quotes from the students offer further meaning to this conceptual exploration of the curriculum.

The triad of circles (Figure 1) provides a conceptual tool "to distinguish curriculum components and relationships" (Barnett, Parry & Coate, 2001, p. 437). Firstly, the circle representing the Knowing domain encapsulates the structure of the curriculum, the topics that are included in the knowledge field as well as the requisite techniques. Barnett (2009, p. 432) refers to knowing as "an individual's personal hold on the world", while knowledge is viewed as "a collectively attested set of understandings in the world". Due partly to the social construction of knowledge, the knowing domain is "never static… always in a state of flux", as agency, ownership and the will to act contribute to the purposeful act of knowing (Barnett & Coate, 2005, p. 59).

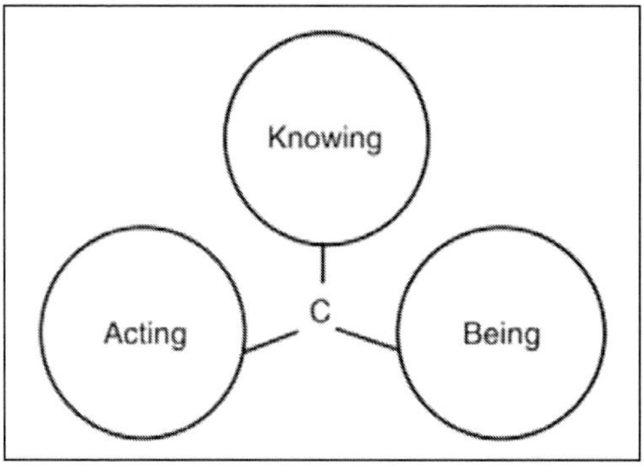

Figure 1. General schema (Barnett & Coates, 2005)

Secondly, referring to the Acting domain, Barnett and Coate (2005, p. 62) explain that by "acting out the practices of a discipline, the student has to become the author of her own actions". Although "part of the currency of curricula" (Barnett, Parry & Coate, 2001, p. 442) is to develop skills and behaviours, multiple interpretations emerge as different students determine their own actions in their curricular journey as they learn by doing to achieve the Faculty's graduate competencies. Viewing the curriculum as a project of acting with its challenges, Barnett and Coate (2005, p. 135) question how students "act in the world, to engage effectively with others".

Thirdly, the Being component views the curriculum in terms of the students as individuals who are Being and Becoming. When students work through the curriculum they interpret their learning from their individual standpoints. This ontological component of the curriculum integrates the personal involvement of the student. An open mind willing to explore alternative dimensions, an authenticity where connections can be made and reliance of personal judgment all contribute to students engaging in a curriculum through the dimension of their own being. Barnett and Coate (2005, p. 64) suggest "the language of being… attempts to do justice to the inner lives of students" thereby shifting the objectivity of students as receptors of the curriculum towards critical subjects with a voice and a will determined by their own life-worlds.

According to Barnett, Parry and Coate (2001) there are three aspects to theorising curricula through this framework. Firstly, the weighting is variable as the importance and prioritizing of each component is viewed from different perspectives. Secondly, the degree of intersection of the domains can demonstrate the extent of overlap or integration that is evident - a particularly relevant aspect for this study. Thirdly the patterns of change of the curricula tend to be driven by "epistemological differences in the knowledge fields" (2001, p. 439). Barnett and Coate (2005, p. 106) suggest that the:

> …domains of knowing, acting and being are indicating processes that should, to a certain extent, be developed together and be working together… A certain level of integration is required between the dimensions of knowing, acting and being in order for the students to embark on a fuller level of engagement with curricula involving themselves, their knowledge and the activities they are required to undertake.

3. Using the iPad

The iPad added an extra dimension to the research participants' reflective process as described below. After talking about their Obstetrics experiences guided by semi-structured questions, students were invited to use the Keynote app on the iPad. Because this app is familiar to me as a tool for PowerPoint presentations in class, it was easily accessible with the extra affordance of sharing with others. For the research participants the iPad proved to be a new tool offering a novelty attraction. They were keen to participate and enthusiastic about the process. Each student became familiar with the iPad and the app as they moved and resized the circles, showing appreciation for the tacit kinaesthetic appeal of the tablet's user interface.

I was able to draw on a similar but different visual framework used in their first year curriculum, in which students assessed their professional development in terms of reflection, empathy and knowledge, thereby facilitating and scaffolding the process. Students were encouraged to familiarize themselves with the triple-fold schema then to work with it as a conceptual representation of the curriculum.

For each student I prepared a PowerPoint slide on the iPad containing three coloured circles symbolizing Knowing, Acting and Being (Figure 2). The circles were symmetrical with a stable composition; a setup described by image reading experts Kress and Van Leeuwen (2006, p. 80) as being "equal distance from each other, given the same size and the same orientation towards the horizontal and vertical axes".

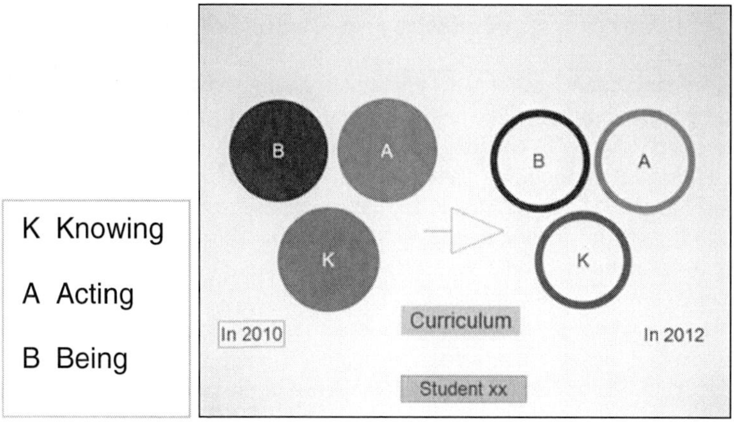

Figure 2. Slide used for interview

The image on the left guided students' review of their past experiences in Year 4, an event familiar to the them, while the right hand image was the anticipated symbol of what is to come in Year 6. Each of the three domains had a different colour carried through between the two components that were labelled 2010 and 2011/2012 depending on when our interview took place. The curriculum was represented as a text label to remind students of the context. An arrow indicated the move to a higher level of study. Each student's abbreviated name on the slide was personalised to encourage their ownership of the image, although names were later replaced with a pseudonym. Students were asked to actively position and adjust the size of the circles in the triads, and to share their thoughts aloud as they considered their past learning experiences in 2010, then to anticipate the future using the same representative circles.

When the students shifted the circles in terms of size and the degree of overlap, they were encouraged to consider the relationships of the curricular components. Because both the past and the present images were correlated, students were able to observe any changes that were evident in their perceptions of their experiences. The images on the Keynote app were emailed to the researcher and printed, enabling them to be interpreted in terms of the sizing of each of the three circle elements and the positioning of the triads.

4. Findings and Discussion

All participants seemed to appreciate an opportunity to use the iPad and become familiar with how it worked. It acted as a facilitating tool to the conversation – an enabling third party.

The novel methodology and kinaesthetic appeal was valued, appearing to bridge the intergenerational gap between researcher and students. The Keynote app is an uncomplicated app to use. It provided a beneficial visual component to the research project enabling me to draw deeper insights into students' representations of their experiences through the triple-fold schema. As students made sense of their experiences through the visual images, their active participation seemed to encourage their reflective process. There was a palpable sense of pleasure and satisfaction as each student completed their task. One student suggested that "it was fun".

Jewitt and Oyama (2001, p. 152) suggest that interpreting experience through circular frames may represent a microscopic view of the personal and affective aspects of a study. By using a design component, students' personal meaning-making moves beyond conversation mode into a visual element in which they can choose and shift their interpretation. It may be viewed as a narrative interpretation in which the students as research participants are the actors. Yet they also take on the role of producers of a completed product that portrays their meaning. For the purpose of this paper and to demonstrate my findings I will focus on the data drawn from the interpretation of the circle images supported by the significant comments from students Joan, Sipho and Thabo.

The composition of the graphics in terms of position and arrangements of the circles indicated valuable information when modified by the students. What students said to explain their judgments as they sized and moved the constituent parts of the triads indicated the multiple factors influencing their experiences. Their comments and their actions reflected their thoughts and feelings about their personal engagement with the curriculum.

Taking a macro view of the images on the Keynote slides, student Sipho's circles (Figure 3) were closest to the configuration of the framework learnt in Year 1 and to the given triad, keeping to the familiar. He indicated a wish to conform and little initiative to break away from the expected. However he recognized that observing abuse of power in the workplace conflicted with his perceptions of healthcare.

In terms of circle overlap, which is used as a symbolic expression of integration in the images, the relationships of the three domains varied. For instance Thabo (Figure 4) suggested: "In fourth year from what I understand, the Knowledge and the Being were big, and then Acting was less, but they are all interrelated". He added that "Acting was with Knowing, I mean they are all a part of each other". Joan (Figure 5) expressed pleasure connecting her Knowing to her Acting by using her skills and gaining competence. She explained: "I really enjoyed delivering, using my hands and doing practical things". Sipho overlapped the Knowing and the Acting as he praised the teaching he received in the block pointing out: "The nurses there they taught us, because we didn't know, we had no idea like what should be prepared, what does it mean to be delivering a baby… all the practical components of it, but they actually took us step by step".

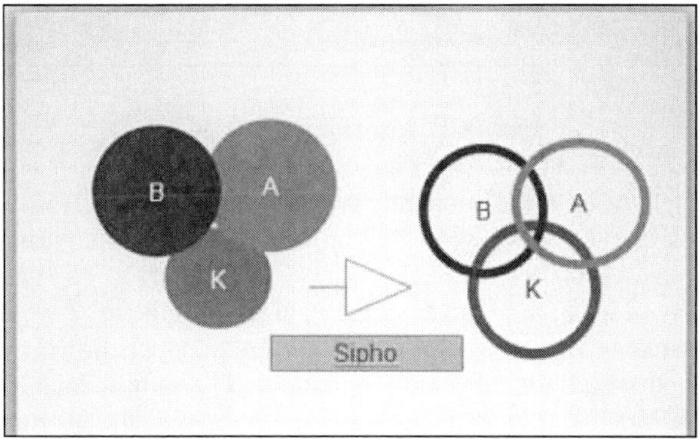

Figure 3. Interview with Sipho

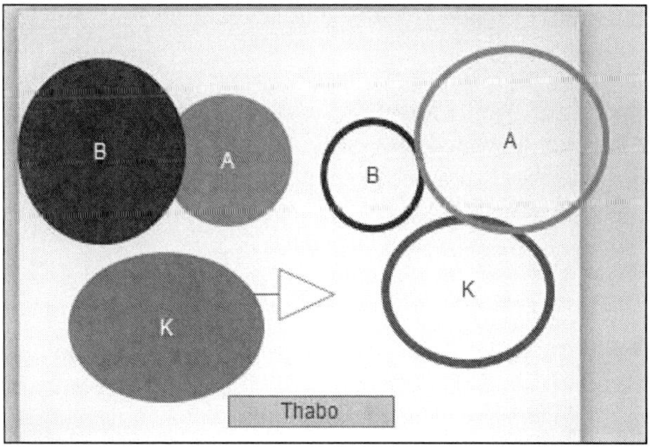

Figure 4. Interview with Thabo

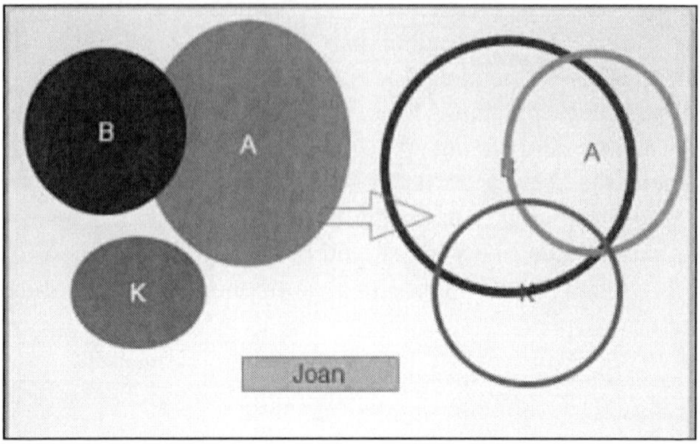

Figure 5. Interview with Joan

Varying shifts were evident as students worked on the triads demonstrating their developmental progress through the years. Student Sipho's images showed a small change from Year 4 to Year 6 with increased overlap. Sipho interprets his goal as a graduate "I would like all the three circles to become more solid and to be much firmer and… they will all come together, they are all integrated" – while Joan shifted her circles significantly in both images in recognition of the centrality of her Being once in final year. As Joan moved the circles together representing her future work she suggested: "…by the end of six years you have kind of learnt to hold yourself together a lot more, you've got a better understanding of yourself, I think and there is more insight". Thabo's initial separation of the Knowing component is later linked although he then subordinates his Being to a position on the periphery. Thabo enlarged the circles moving them away from each other to the extent that Acting even goes beyond the boundaries of the frame.

As indicated, the iPad app contributed towards deeper insights into the students' individual learning experiences. However there were challenges.

5. Limitations

In terms of the tablet technology, none of the students involved in this study owned an iPad. They were excited to use it, however they needed a few minutes to become acquainted with the touch screen and visual concepts. The Keynote app did not pose any extra challenges.

There is recognition that the conceptual images may be too complex. Jewitt and Oyama (2001, p. 151) suggest that the authenticity of the images is difficult to discern as we are probing "beyond the surface" to explore "some deeper hidden truth".

Findings in one instance indicated a variation between what the student said and the representation of the image; the student's circles were evenly distributed and sized yet his narrative indicated a range of importance.

6. Conclusion

The iPad expands our research options. In this research project with fourth year undergraduate medical students, technology enhanced the quality of their reflective processes to critically engage and explore their curricular experiences.

The Keynote app offered affordances that improved the researcher-participant relationship and communication, facilitated students to reflect in a more meaningful manner and enabled a more flexible, more creative approach to be used. Students welcomed the technology and valued the acquisition of new skills. They appreciated the production of images that reflected their authentic thoughts and feelings.

Acknowledgements

I wish to thank Hilary Watters (Falmouth University, United Kingdom) for engaging in a conversation with me in which she reflected on her practice as an artist to identify the kinaesthetic appeal of the iPad user interface. Also, my husband Dave who recognized the empowering affordance of the iPad for my visual impairment, and purchased an early model during a brief visit to Boston, United States.

References

Barnett, R. (2000). Supercomplexity and the curriculum. *Studies in Higher Education, 25*(3), 255 265.

Barnett. R., Parry, G., & Coate, K. (2001). Conceptualising curriculum change. *Teaching in Higher Education, 6*(4), 435-449.

Barnett. R., & Coate, K. (2005). *Engaging the higher curriculum in higher education*. SRHE & Open University Press. London.

Hatton, N., & Smith, D. (1995). Reflection in teacher education: Towards definition and implementation. *Teaching and Teacher Education, 11*(1), 33-49.

Kress, G., & van Leeuwen, T. (2006). *Reading images: The grammar of visual design.* 2nd Ed. Routledge: London.

Mitchell, V. (2012). *The curriculum in medical education: A case study in Obstetrics* (Unpublished MA dissertation). University of Cape Town, South Africa.

Sandars, J., & Homer, M. (2008). Reflective learning and the net generation. *Medical Teacher, 30*, 877-879.

EMBEDDING THE IPAD AS A LEARNING AND TEACHING TOOL: A CASE STUDY OF STAFF AND STUDENT PERSPECTIVES IN A MANAGEMENT SCHOOL

MARY MORRISON[1], JEAN LEAH[2], FIONA HARVEY[3] AND CAROL MASTERS[4]

Abstract

This paper considers the use of iPads in the University of Southampton Management School. The iPad is an extremely popular mobile technology device and has broad educational application, as demonstrated by the research and case studies at primary and secondary school level. Rather less has been documented about the iPad at Higher Education (HE) level, but even at the University of Southampton, where there is no formal support for using them, they are increasing in popularity. The Management School invested in tablets to experiment with mobile assessment in 2012, and this gave some insights into the potential and limitations of tablet use in higher education. However, when staff and students on the MBA programme were provided with an iPad at the beginning of the 2013-14 academic year, this presented an ideal opportunity to consider this in more detail and examine the perceptions and practice of the two user groups. A questionnaire was designed and made available to all MBA staff and students at the beginning of the semester, which collected some

[1] University of Southampton, Management School, United Kingdom. Email: msm@soton.ac.uk

[2] University of Southampton, Management School, United Kingdom. Email: J.H.Leah@soton.ac.uk

[3] University of Southampton, Management School, United Kingdom. Email: Fiona.Harvey@soton.ac.uk

[4] University of Southampton, Management School, United Kingdom. Email: c.masters@soton.ac.uk

quantitative data, but also invited open comment on a number of issues. Semi-structured interviews with a small sub-group of participants gave further detail. The results of this initial research are presented here, and indicate that while the overall reaction is positive – acknowledging the benefits of "new" technology or different ways of teaching and learning – there are also barriers to uptake or use. For instance, students used the iPads quite extensively in the first week, and indicated that they had underestimated the potential of the iPad as a learning tool (even if familiar with their use in a business or personal setting). Staff also explicitly stated that they saw considerable potential in iPad use in their teaching and were happy to trial new technology. There was a clear preference for more support in their use, even from experienced technology users. The intention is to revisit the group at the end of the first semester to consider progress and changes in practice.

1. Introduction

The iPad is a potentially powerful tool for organisation, communication, research and learning. However the extent to which it is used or is welcomed, may be driven by personal preference, technical expertise and practicalities such as Wi-Fi coverage and technical compatibilities.

At the beginning of the 2013-14 academic year, the University of Southampton Management School supplied each MBA student with an iPad to be used as a central research and learning tool. The School has the benefit of experience with iPads and tablets both within the School and elsewhere in the institution. This study evaluates (from both the staff and student perspective) the use of iPads and a range of apps, and to what extent their use relies on technical expertise. It is anticipated that this will inform future practice both in the School and beyond.

2. Context

It is helpful to consider the context of this study at the institutional and School level, and to consider recent experiences with iPads.

2.1 Institutional Context

The University is a large, well-established HE institution, part of the Russell group of research-intensive UK Universities, based in the South of England. In common with many UK universities, the University has seen significant growth in student numbers. Figures for the University as a whole have shown an increase in annual student enrolment (including postgraduate research (PGR), postgraduate taught (PGT) and undergraduate (UG) from under 21,000 in 2008-9, to 22,365 in 2012-13. Latest figures for 2013-14 suggest over 23,800. This has intensified the need to maximise use of teaching and learning spaces, extend the teaching day, such as teaching during lunchtime, beginning the teaching day at 8am and teaching on some courses until 9pm, and has stretched hard-pressed administrative systems. At the same time effective learning opportunities for all students, many of whom are from overseas, must be sustained.

The University is organised into eight Faculties offering over 250 programmes ranging from Fine Art to Mechanical Engineering. The common approach to teaching and learning remains predominantly one of a traditional face-to-face experience where the standard large lecture is often followed by a smaller seminar or class each week. This approach prevails at UG, but at PGT level there is more variety. There is an expectation that all lecturers use the Virtual Learning Environment (VLE) for their modules, in this case Backboard. However, there is no requirement for the VLE to be more than a repository or information-accessing platform.

At the same time, the growth in mobile technologies has meant that a significant number of staff and students use the new technologies with growing confidence, but not all naturally adapt their use to an educational context, nor is the mobile technology specifically supported by the central IT department. It is difficult to say how many staff or students have or use an iPad, particularly as many own them personally but use them for work or study. Unofficial figures from the University Information Technology (IT) department, dating back to 2010, suggest that around 800 iPads or iPad minis were ordered through them in the three years, but only around 80 other tablets were ordered in the same period. Although this only represents University-supplied tablets, it would still suggest a strong preference for the iPad over other tablets, and continued purchase of them despite the lack of formal IT support.

In 2011-12 the University reinforced the need to support staff in the use of technologies in the educational context, and launched the Centre for Innovation in Technologies and Education (CITE). CITE aims "to provide faculties with a dynamic, responsive and collaborative partner to enable them to fulfil their ambitions for enhancing the student experience through effective, sustainable and quality assured applications of learning technology" (CITE, n.d.).

The key staff in CITE soon established formal and informal support groups to share ideas and developments in the use of mobile technology that could be applied and was appropriate to teaching and learning at University level. One specific support group was the "iPad coffee club" established by CITE staff member Fiona Harvey. The coffee club invites anyone interested in the use of iPads or android devices to share apps and ideas as to how to apply them.

2.2 School Context

The University of Southampton Management School has grown considerably in recent years. In 2013 over 850 postgraduate taught students joined the School, along with 280 new undergraduates. This marks a considerable increase from earlier years. In 2008-9 there were fewer than 1200 students in total in the School while in 2013-14 this increased to over 1600. The PGR population has remained fairly steady, while the key growth has been in taught students – with both PGT and UG populations showing substantial growth.

These increasing numbers provide added impetus to identify good practice and introduce appropriate change (including technological) to enhance the student learning experience. This might be to speed up or simplify a process (generally more of a challenge when dealing with larger student numbers), or it might be to introduce a new way of working that offers additional opportunities for the staff and students.

This paper will consider the use of the iPad in an example of both kinds. Firstly, it will consider the use of the iPad (and Android tablets) in assessing a large cohort of students, in an effort to simplify the process and provide improved and speedier feedback to students. Secondly, it will consider the provision of iPads to an entire cohort and the main teaching staff, as a means of providing core texts and as a tool for learning and teaching.

3. iPad and Assessment in the Management School

The quality of feedback to students is a recurring theme in HE in the UK. The School agreed a modest budget for the purchase of an iPad and an Android tablet to experiment with using them to improve feedback. The staff involved were the two Education and Experience Fellows, plus an adjunct lecturer taken on to teach this module only.

Fairly large groups of the School PGT cohort are required to take skills modules. One of these is Presentation Skills, where the group (over 135 in 2013) were given an introductory lecture and then set a task. This was to give a short presentation to a small group, which includes two staff assessors. Pre-2012 the assessment feedback was in written form using a paper template. Students received a hard copy of the handwritten notes summarising the markers' views, and the final agreed mark. This had to be collected from the School Office, and the handwriting was not always easy to read. The process was therefore not completely satisfactory.

Given the University strategic goal of rolling out an online assessment package, it was decided to combine testing this with a trial of tablets. Tablets were thought to be preferable to using laptops as they were smaller and did not form a barrier or major distraction to the speaker, and also generally faster to access and use. Initially the intention was to find a way to write onto the tablet with the notes being converted into text to go into an assessment template. However, this was fairly rapidly revised given the relatively limited performance of handwriting conversion apps (such as Myscript memo). Although it was possible to get a fairly reliable transfer of script to printed text, it was not easily possible to combine this with the feedback form or package, thereby requiring cutting and pasting and being a fairly slow process. Additional problems were presented by sketchy Wi-Fi coverage and a lack of support from IT specialists. This meant relying on knowledgeable and interested colleagues, or research, trial and error.

The new esubmission and marking system (called eAssignments) was being rolled out, and it seemed an ideal opportunity to combine a trial of both hardware and software. eAssignments (given enough bandwidth) could be accessed via the iPad and other tablet, and although the package had not been optimised for tablets of any kind, it had reasonable functionality. This still required considerable up front work, to check through the system and to input the learning outcomes and relevant level descriptors. The system allows a mark to be chosen against a criterion, and automatically allocates a corresponding comment. Additional free-text boxes enable one assessor to enter draft typed comments as they allocate marks, while the other still makes a handwritten record. Comments and marks are combined and moderated after the session. Once the date of mark release is set, students are emailed that their mark is available. They can log on to see it and read the feedback sheet, which they can also print if they wish.

This means that the feedback is more legible and the process much faster. Students did not have to queue to pick up a paper version from the Faculty Office, and administrative staff did not have to spend time handing back coversheets to individuals. However, the set-up was very time-intensive for the staff actually doing the assessment. Tablets and eAssignments were used for the first time in autumn 2012 and were felt to be sufficiently beneficial to use them again the following year. The set-up time was considerably reduced in the second year of use (Autumn 2013) and the assessors found the process easier.

Experimenting with iPad and tablet usage suggested that personal preferences and/or confidence in using new technologies were important, as were the institutional infrastructure and tablet compatibility with existing systems. Familiarity with iPads or other tablets was an obvious advantage, as this means a greater awareness of the potential and functionality of the device. It also revealed some problems of using the system on a tablet, as certain functions did not work or they behaved unpredictably. For instance, even when whole numbers were selected the system still sometimes allocates a fraction. This and other problems had to be fed back to the staff developing and servicing eAssignments. Wi-Fi coverage was critical, and as a result of this pilot the coverage was improved in the School, so all floors had reasonable coverage. The Wi-Fi service in the MBA suite of rooms was also upgraded, which made the use of mobile devices more feasible.

4. Research Design and Rationale

Making iPads available to the MBA staff and students provided an opportunity to study how staff and students engaged with them. The MBA team intended the iPad to be an important tool in the learning and teaching process - effectively being part of a blended learning approach. This study will consider whether that happened and how, and to what extent it was dependent on prior knowledge or support.

The term blended learning is disputed. Driscoll (n.d., p.1) noted this and identified four broad definitions, the second of which is "to combine various pedagogical approaches (e.g., constructivism, behaviorism, cognitivism) to produce an optimal learning outcome with or without instructional technology". This paper adapts the above definition to recognise that the iPad is a personal learning tool, rather than an instructional tool. The definition used therefore is "the appropriate use of theories, methods and technologies to optimise learning". This should offer the best experience for both staff and students, rather than a strict adherence to one approach, and should enable the adoption of varied methods and appropriate technologies to facilitate student learning and accommodate different learning preferences.

The provision of iPads in this case is one example of what that blended learning might look like – where students who have many face-to-face sessions also have an iPad, which they are encouraged to use to access their core text books, and which they can use, or be required to use by their lecturers, in many other ways. Similarly, the lecturers can also use it for research, class activities and the online assessment of assignments, amongst other things.

There is limited research on the use of iPads in UK HE. However, evidence from a recent Naace report (n.d.) suggests the iPad has considerable value as an educational tool. This report was based on a case study in a UK secondary school, but suggests the conclusions are widely applicable in other educational contexts. We intend to explore some of these themes, such as reduction of workload, facilitation of collaborative work, appropriate use of apps and so on (ibid. p.4).

5. Research Design

The MBA cohort is relatively small, and follows a dedicated pathway of study, without crossover with other programmes. This facilitated a case study approach, which is recognised as an appropriate framework for gathering qualitative data. This approach is one that seeks to understand individual views as well as understand their reality of a specific happening or "direct experience" (Cohen, Manion, & Morrison, 2011). In the context of this study the "direct experience" is the introduction of an iPad at the inception of the programme of study. This approach also recognises that their understandings are subjective, but may be viewed as valid in the sense of being true. The richness of this data would be captured via semi-structured surveys and one-to-one interviews

6. Context of the Case Study

The MBA team provided an iPad to all students joining the MBA and staff with substantial teaching responsibility. The student intake to the programme is international, and they are only accepted with a minimum of three years' work experience.

The iPad was to be a central tool for students and staff so, for instance, the core texts were made available as e-books. Staff and students were given a guide to using the iPad – which was based on one produced by the Academic Development Centre at the University of Kingston. The original gave some user tips, and a list of apps. The guide produced for the MBA updated and expanded this guide, giving institutional information and links, and providing an updated and expanded app list. A £25 iTunes voucher was supplied with each tablet so that key apps could be purchased at no additional cost, and quite a number of the essential apps were free. The e-books could be downloaded and read via the Bluefire app, (recommended by the book supplier Kortext) or they could be accessed online via the Kortext company site.

7. Methodology

The study of the MBA staff and students set out to establish the baseline of staff and student prior knowledge and expectations at the beginning of the semester, and how this changed with time. This was undertaken via a questionnaire made available online via the University in-house survey package (Appendix). All 25 full-time MBA students were emailed in week one with a request to take part in the survey, with the cooperation of the programme team, and twelve (12) students completed it. Seventeen (17) MBA teaching staff were emailed a similar request, and eight of those completed the survey.

Respondents from each group were approached for a more detailed discussion about the questions in the survey and to explore their perceptions in more detail. All staff and students will be invited to participate in a second wave of research at the beginning of semester two, which is about halfway through the MBA programme.

8. Results

The quantitative results of the questionnaire are presented in bar charts showing values as a percentage of either group. Where comments are presented these will not necessarily map onto the number of respondents, as some made multiple comments. All issues raised have been acknowledged in some way, and comments have been grouped under representative headings.

Prior use of tablets was fairly high, over 66% in both groups (Figure 1). In comparison with students, there was a greater proportion of staff that had already used an iPad, and a slightly higher proportion of students who had not used a tablet of any kind.

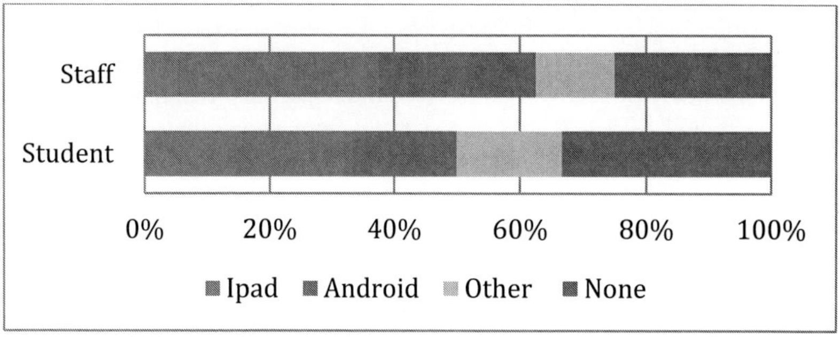

Figure 1: Prior use of iPad and tablets (as percentage of respondents in groups)

Participants were then asked about their experiences of using tablets so far, and some offered additional comments. Not all participants answered the questions where there was free text response, but eight students and three staff commented.

Comments	Students	Staff
Portability – using on the move	3	2
Paperless working	2	
Presentations	2	
Communication tool	3	1

Table 1. Experience with iPads

If participants did not own a tablet they were invited to comment as to why. Two staff members and four students offered comments that fell into the categories in thc table below.

Comments	Students	Staff
Superfluous (e.g. already owning smartphone)	2	2
Reluctance to register with Apple or Google	0	2
Preferred laptop with full keyboard	1	
No identified need for a tablet	1	

Table 2. Reasons for not trying a tablet before

When asked for their initial reaction to the provision of iPads on the MBA, all staff and students made comments that could be categorised as in Table 3 below. Comments were predominantly positive, many referring to its potential as a teaching and learning tool and a new and different technology. This indicates that both students and staff would seem to favour the use of iPads as part of a blended learning approach.

When it came to considering what apps might be used for, both groups rated "making notes" as the most likely use of the tablet, with communication second (see Figure 2). Students seemed to suggest that the iPad would be of least interest to them as an organisational tool, whereas staff indicated that group work was the category least likely to apply. A small number of participants noted other uses. One staff member suggested that the iPad would be most useful for presentations. Four students made additional observations about its use, such as an alarm clock and calculator, or a tool for entertainment – watching videos. Two other students suggested that reading e-books or accessing materials on the VLE would be most useful. The responses generally seem to suggest that again both groups acknowledge the potential of the iPad in blending learning in a variety of ways.

Comments	Students	Staff
Considered to be a good/different teaching and learning tool	6	2
Positive about new/different technology	2	7
Considered this to be a sign that students are valued	2	1
Concerned about barriers and lack of system integration	1	1
Portable, light, better than books		2
Concerns about reading on iPad		1
Useful outside MBA too		1
Better than iPhone and paper		1

Table 3. Comments on provision of iPad

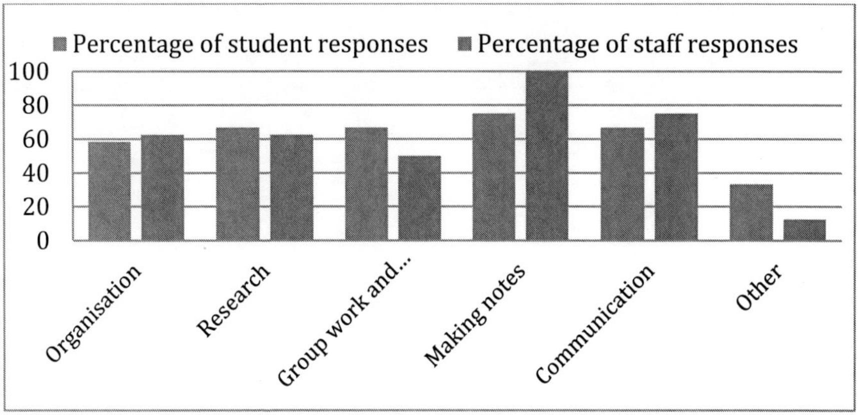

Figure 2. Expected use of Apps

Half of the staff that responded to the survey had read the guide, while 9/12 students read it. Students were particularly happy with the information supplied on apps and that would seem to be reflected in the figures for downloads (see Figure 3 below). Staff downloaded far fewer apps – but of course a major difference is that many staff had not at the point of survey started teaching on the MBA, and informally some commented that there was therefore no reason to use the iPad as yet.

Comments	Students	Staff
Useful	8	3
Can use iPad already	3	1
Do not need it yet (e.g. not teaching on MBA until later)		1
Never (or prefer not to) read user guides	1	2
No time		1
Good to learn about Apps	5	

Table 4. Comments on the guide provided

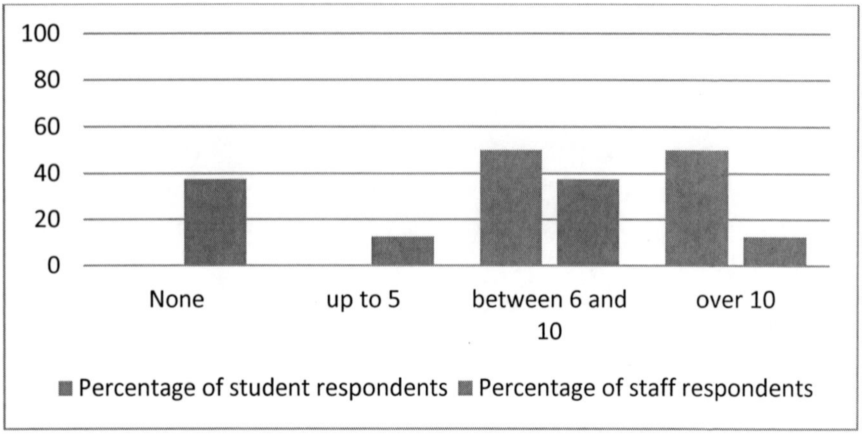

Figure 3. Number of apps downloaded in the first week

The figures for hours of use in the first week are consistent with responses for downloads, showing that 50% of staff respondents did not use their iPad at all. The students were required to download the core texts so their hours of use should be higher.

Figure 5 shows how apps have been used so far. The highest proportion of respondents' use of apps in either group is for communication – with over 60% of staff indicating that they had used the iPad for this. The highest figure for students was for research. Both these, i.e. using email or doing web-based research, represent the simplest activities possible on an iPad, and appropriate early in the semester.

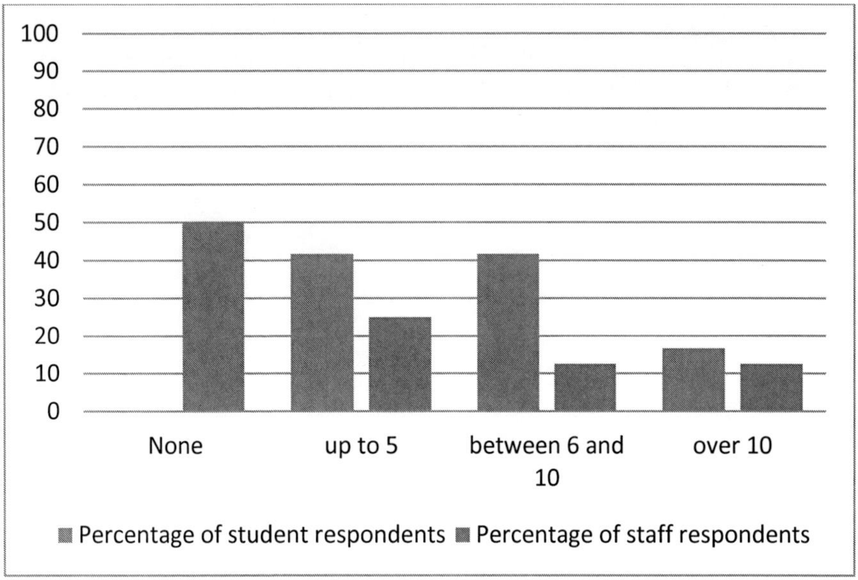

Figure 4. Hours used in the first week

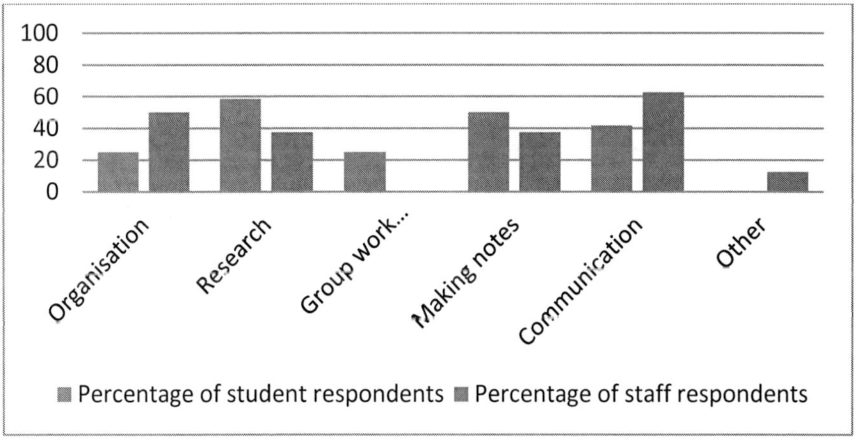

Figure 5. The use of apps so far

All participants were given the opportunity to make general observations or other comments about using the iPad, and these are summarised in the table below. There is a clear grouping of comments that again referred to the potential value of the iPad and its ease of use, while some did refer to barriers or problems experienced.

Comments	Students	Staff
Very useful/ potentially useful	2	2
Easy to use	4	4
Familiar with iPad		1
Not yet started/ had no time		2
Wi-Fi not always reliable/ available	3	3
Cannot use data sticks		1
Would like keyboard/ find iPad typing awkward	3	
Software (apps) crucial if to be of use in HE		1
Heavier than it looks	1	

Table 5. General comments

9. Interviews

In addition to the online survey a sub-group of staff and students agreed to undertake interviews. These were semi-structured, and were designed to gain a more defined or detailed understanding of the points and perspectives gleaned from the questionnaires. The significant or key points raised will be used to inform practice within the School and will be the basis for developing this research.

Staff were chosen to be interviewed on the basis that they had actually started teaching the MBA by the time of interviews, while students were self-selected, responding to a request for volunteers. The purpose of the interviews was to go over the same questions raised in the survey, but ask clarification and explore their comments in more detail.

9.1 Staff Interviews

The two staff interviewed (three had been approached but it did not prove possible to find the opportunity to interview the third) made comments which raised some common themes, despite one of the interviewees being fairly familiar with technology, while the other described himself as "technologically illiterate". The major area of concern was how to use the iPad appropriately as a pedagogic tool.

Both staff saw the supply of iPads as providing opportunities to work and teach in different and new ways, possibly doing some things that could only be done with an iPad. However, both also mentioned the need to have time to become familiarised with the technology and also to have time to "mentally adjust". One commented that to prepare materials and learning opportunities properly would require considerable investment of time. The importance of support and the correct environment to do this was mentioned by both, for instance mentioning that staff needed to be given opportunities to use technology effectively.

One of the staff felt that the iPad provision was significant and a recognition of the special status of the MBA and its students. He also felt that trialling iPads in a relatively small group like this was a good idea.

There were concerns raised by both interviewees. One stated that it was important not to use the iPad simply because it was there – i.e. the technology should facilitate and enhance the learning process where appropriate, but it should not dictate it. He also commented that he still gave paper copies of key articles to students and that the students seemed to treat hard copies with more importance than e-copies. The other staff member, while recognising its potential, was unsure that it was right to adopt the iPad as a learning tool. He had additional concerns that students for whom English was a second language would struggle with the speed of exchange afforded by the iPad.

9.2 Student Interviews

The intention was to interview three students, and three interviews were arranged. However, one student had to cancel at short notice as they were invited to a visa interview, so only two interviews were completed.

The student comments also showed considerable overlap, but were more concerned with actual usage of the iPad and apps on a practical rather than theoretical level. Both students interviewed seemed to say that they had an iPhone and laptop and didn't think an iPad would add anything, but they both found it really useful. One described the iPad as the most "useful useless device" because she could not see why she needed it but now used it all the time. Both said that they had underestimated the potential of the iPad. One expanded on this – it is bigger than the iPhone so better for reading, but much more portable and faster to access than a laptop. The apps that facilitated access to timetables and the library were mentioned as real timesavers, but there were still apparent issues with functionality. There might be workarounds for these (such as how to transfer the individual student timetable from the "My Southampton" app to the calendar – but this was not obvious and could be the sort of "implicit knowledge" that might be shared at a face-to-face session.

Both students interviewed were quite familiar with Apple products. One was familiar with some of the apps in the world of work, but had not considered their potential as a study tool. She commented that it required more thinking "outside of the box" to transfer practice from professional practice to study.

Despite their familiarity with Apple technology, both students clearly expressed the view that more support for iPad usage would have helped. This was firstly in the context of recognising the potential and getting started. One thought that those students who were less technologically "savvy" seemed to not be using their iPads very much, and thought that they (and all) students might have benefited from a more structured and detailed introduction. The written guide was good, but a session on "how to" might have been better. There are lots of issues with compatibility between apps, and students could perhaps have benefited from advice on how to work around them – unless it is thought that learning from experience is preferable.

10. Conclusion

It was felt that the use of iPads in assessment in the presentation skills module was beneficial to both staff and students, offering legible and timely feedback. It is too early to draw firm conclusions on the use of iPads within the MBA programme. Initial indications are that the reaction to the introduction of iPads has been mostly positive – seeing the iPad as having great potential as a learning and teaching tool. It is presumed that usage as a learning and teaching resource will increase as staff and students become more familiar with their iPads and the range of apps available. Therefore the intention is to survey and interview again after the end of the semester (i.e. January 2014) to consider what changes there may have been in usage or practice. The original survey will be re-run, with additional interviews to supply more detail, so the work is still very much in progress.

11. Post Conference Addendum

A second phase of research was planned for the end of the first semester, to see how usage or perceptions had changed in that time. The survey was re-run with slightly amended questions, which reflected the fact that a semester had passed, and another round of face-to-face semi-structured interviews was undertaken.

11.1 Phase Two Survey

The survey was commenced in week two of semester two. This was timed to allow students to complete their semester one examinations and return from a European field trip. The response rates were disappointing with only five out of 25 students responding and three out of 17 staff. This was thought to be for a variety of reasons, some to do with individual commitments and others technical. Being in the middle of the academic year, both groups were busier, and it was also some time since the issue of the iPads. This meant it was more difficult to elicit responses so the sample size is small. However the written responses from the survey reinforced points made within the interviews.

11.2 Phase Two Interviews

The interviewees included the two students and two staff from the first phase, plus an additional one from each group. As before, the survey questions were used as the basis for semi-structured interviews, with the opportunity to explore responses given in more depth.

There were various common themes which emerged in all interviews and which were common to both groups.

The responses indicated a good degree of consistency with the phase one interviews. All were requesting more guidance – although what format that could take is less clear. One notable change was that the student in phase one, who was surprised at how much she was using the iPad, greatly reduced her use over the term. She said she preferred to use a laptop, although still valued the iPad as a back-up tool.

Staff responses	Student responses
Limited use in class (due to lack of time to prepare, lack of familiarity). Increasing informal usage (communications, easy access to video and images, texts, use of Facetime with students for meetings). Noted student usage of iPads (e.g. with an employer visitor, or as additional tool/ screen). Would like more guidance.	Culture and familiarity with technology important. Varied approach, one used iPad as key work and library space, others as additional or only backup tool, (preferred laptop even for reading). Various ideas about how to embed further (advice on apps (e.g. a dedicated collaborative space), or accounting for learning differences). More advice or guidance could help (suggested this for staff too). Direct requests from staff would prompt use Should make it clear that iPad techniques/ apps and skills can be developed and transferred to work.

Table 6. Phase two interviews

Interestingly there seemed to be some lack of agreement as to the meanings of particular terms that for the authors were self-explanatory. When asked if the iPads had been the basis for group work, the respondents said no. However, one student then gave an example of how they had used Google docs to work together on a document, so there was a difference in the understanding of what group work actually meant.

Barriers	Facilitators
Keyboard (lack of real keyboard reduces use). Insufficient guidance/ advice. Lack of Wi-Fi (e.g. none in halls of residence). Problems of compatibility with University systems. Lack of support from the University IT department. Inaccuracy of touch screen – a good stylus would be helpful.	Portability Speed of access Ebooks

Table 7. Barriers and facilitators

Various technical issues were cited as barriers – the lack of a standard keyboard and a lack of compatibility with University systems being two. It is also a major issue that the halls of residence do not have Wi-Fi so students must be on campus to make use of the University Wi-Fi. The main facilitators remained speed and convenience, and the fact that many of the key texts were available via the iPad.

11.3 Phase Two Conclusions

The provision of iPads to this small MBA cohort provided a good opportunity to carry out this study, although the survey response rate, particularly in the second phase, was disappointing. If this were to be repeated it would be worth considering different strategies to increase engagement. This might be asking students to complete it during a session, perhaps using Nearpod. Since staff requested more guidance, it could be that a workshop with a demonstration of how to use the Nearpod app could have been the ideal opportunity to complete the phase one questionnaire. However, the reality is that achieving engagement with surveys is not easy when participants have competing priorities, so the second phase would still have been a problem. The interview approach worked very well, with both staff and students happy to devote time and thought, and this produced rich data.

At the outset, it was noted that the MBA programme team intended iPads to be a valuable tool for both students and staff. The general reaction to the supply of iPads is positive from both groups – being seen as a way to add value to the programme, suggesting innovation and progression. Even the student who became less enthusiastic over the term still thought the supply of iPads a good idea. Another said, "It really improves the MBA", and added that as the MBA "is based more on debate, the iPad definitely facilitates that".

Although they were supplied to teaching staff the MBA team did not make particular demands about iPad use, beyond enabling access to ebooks and making recommendations for apps. But the reluctant adopters showed a marked change in attitude to the use of their iPads between the beginning and end of the study, becoming more interested in finding ways to use them. All staff interviewed said that they wanted to explore opportunities, and needed more support and advice about the potential as a teaching and learning tool. Given the initial reluctance expressed by these staff members, it seems as if this "light touch" approach may have worked to the advantage of the MBA team.

Comments from students and staff about the potential of the iPad (e.g. diversity of applications, speed of use, suggestions for additional apps) indicate that it remains a powerful tool for blended learning as defined in this study. However, it seems that confident usage within the programme (by student or staff) depends either on clear guidance on a particular application, or on a level of familiarity which can only really be achieved if individuals are using the iPad for a broad range of activities and learning informally. The diversity of approach reinforces the idea of the iPad as a personal, customisable working and learning tool rather than being seen as simply a piece of equipment to be used for a particular application. Students can be encouraged to see the iPad as a tool for study and work, and staff encouraged to see it as a tool for research, administration and teaching.

This study contributes to the understanding of the potential of the iPad in HE, and supports the Naace report (n.d.) view that it has considerable value in education. The data collected will certainly help develop the use of the iPad in future years, and should support the programme team to develop further ideas for offering guidance and enhancing the student experience within the Southampton University MBA and elsewhere in the School and institution.

Note

Mary Morrison and Jean Leah are Education and Student Experience Fellows in the University of Southampton Management School. Fiona Harvey is Education Development Manager in the Centre for Innovation in

Technologies and Education (CITE), and Carol Masters is Senior Teaching Fellow in Accounting and Finance and Senior Tutor in the Management School. This paper was possible with the support and cooperation of the MBA team, including MBA Director Dr Edgar Meyer and MBA Programme Development Manager Mr Christian Letteriello. The authors would like to extend thanks to them and to all the other staff and students for their input and support.

References

Cohen, L., Manion, L., & Morrison, K. (2011). *Research methods in education* (7th ed.). New York: Routledge.

CITE. (n.d.). About CITE. Retrieved December 29, 2014, from https://www.cite.soton.ac.uk/about-cite

Driscoll, M. (n.d.). Blended learning: Let's get beyond the hype. Retrieved December 5, 2013, from http://goo.gl /6mJzu9

Naace (n.d.). The iPad as a tool for education. Retrieved December 29, 2014, from http://goo.gl/tqycx

APPENDIX

iPad and tablet survey
Questions for staff and students with minor amendments (Early in term, then in April - adapted slightly where logical)

1. You have been given an iPad for the MBA programme. Have you used a tablet before? (Y/N)
   a) If yes, was it an iPad or other OS such as Android? (Please specify)
   b) If yes, how long have you had your other tablet? (less than 6 months, 6-12 months, 12-24 months, more than 24 months)
   c) If yes what is your experience of iPad/ tablet use elsewhere (at work or home) and what could we learn/ gain from this? (Text box)
   d) If no, was there a particular reason that you didn't have a tablet? (Please specify)

The MBA iPad
2. What did you think about being given an iPad? (text box)

3. Do you expect it to be a tool for
   a) Organisation
   b) Research
   c) Teaching and learning
   d) Making notes and recording data and information (audio, video or other)
   e) Communication
   f) Other (Please specify)

4. You received a user guide. Have you read it? (Y/N)

5. Did the user guide help you use the iPad? (Y/N) (Please explain)

6. How many hours have you used it in your first week of prep or delivery ("first week of study" for students)?

7. How many apps have you downloaded?

8. How many apps have you used? (Can you list them?)

9. How would you categorise those apps:
   a. Organisation
   b. Research
   c. Teaching and learning
   d. Making notes and recording data and information (audio, video or other)
   e. Communication
   f. Other (Please specify)

10. Do you have any general comments about how easy or difficult it is to use the iPad? (This could include Wi-Fi access and reliability, technical issues or personal preferences).

GIVE THEM A FISHING ROD... THE USE OF IPADS BY EDUCATION STUDENTS

LIAT EYAL[1]

Abstract

This study attempts to present the variety of possible uses for mobile technologies, and iPads in particular, in the learning process. The objective is to evaluate a unique implementation model that was tried out at a teacher training college. The methodology is based on a qualitative research paradigm. The findings show that students use the iPads in various contexts: (a) for ongoing personal use, (b) for planning lessons, (c) for active integration in the classroom, and (d) for creating and developing content and games. These findings are presented in a chart that shows the different uses as levels in a hierarchical taxonomy.

1. Background

The growing use of mobile technologies presents new challenges in the field of teacher training and classroom instruction. Professional literature shows that mobile learning has yet to be defined unequivocally. One of the accepted definitions is: "…any type of learning that takes place in learning environments and spaces that take account of the mobility of technology, mobility of learners, and mobility of learning" (El-Hussein & Cronje, 2010, p. 20). Other researchers address the different uses of mobile technology, such as support for the learners and their participation in creative, cooperative, critical, and communicative learning activities (Cobcroft, Towers & Smith, 2006).

Traxler suggests that mobile learning is intended to provide support for authentic and personal learning processes, and is situation-dependent, and that in the future mobile learning will enable a wide range of learning

[1] Levinsky College of Education, Israel. Email: eyaliat@gmail.com

methods (Traxler, 2007; 2010). Rossing, Miller, Cecil, and Stamper define mobile learning as the most effective use of digital and wireless technology in empowering the learning process (Rossing, Miller, Cecil & Stamper, 2012).

Mobile technology offers several advantages in the educational context: access to learning anywhere, anytime, without the need for extra resources, learning that has an environmental impact like encouraging situated learning or collaborative learning (Naismith, Lonsdale, Vavoula & Sharples, 2004), informal learning that enables constructivist teaching, which enables teachers to function as facilitators (Mouza, 2008), and developing of interpersonal and social ties (Melhuish & Falloon, 2010). Additionally, mobile devices support the development of visual and textual literacy (Kelly & Schrape, 2010; Valentino, 2010). However, as with any technology, the use of mobile technology in learning is not without its limitations: the relatively small screen size, Internet connectivity (Alexander, 2004), the need to frequently recharge the battery (Georgiev, Georgieva & Smrikarov, 2004), and obstacles related to socio-economic factors. Nonetheless, in my opinion, the more pointed questions related to the use of mobile device centre around its educational and pedagogical contribution to learning, and the relationship between educational processes and the technological environment.

2. Literature Review

2.1 iPads Use in Education

There are those who maintain that learning in itself does not change, it is only the mode of learning that changes. In this respect, iPads are a means for advancing empowerment processes. Mobile learning integrates different components, including the learner and the teacher-facilitator. Technology enables educators to design and develop interactive learning activities (Monahan, McArdle & Bertolotto, 2008; Price & Rogers, 2004).

Teachers can enhance the learning process through the development of applications designed to support learners, and which serve as a kind of coach or support to help the learner through the process, with their presence gradually reduced as they become less necessary (Chen, Chang & Wang, 2008; Chen, Kao & Sheu, 2003). You can create a simulated environment for the learner, and allow him to practise under conditions that are closest to the real situation (Yang, 2006). Various studies describe the benefits of using mobile technologies as a group that can be applied to learning activities that require cooperation (Zurita, Nussbaum & Salinas,

2005). Other researchers focus on the unique potential of tablet devices and their impact on teaching and learning in the context of reading (Eagleton & Dobler, 2007).

Vast resources are invested in the implementation of iPads and in training teachers on their intelligent use in the learning process in the schools. Implementation is carried out on various levels, ranging from the technical level to the didactic level. Nonetheless, the assimilation processes do not guarantee the success of these initiatives to integrate the tablet. The integration of mobile devices has not brought with it a corresponding change in teaching methods and didactic operating strategies (Shamir-Inbal & Blau, 2013).

Studies show that intervention should be based on training that helps teachers to acquire competency in the technological tools, as well as experience in applying new pedagogical ideas in order to understand the relationship between pedagogy and technology (Eyal, 2012; Fishman, Best, Marx & Tal, 2001). Studies indicate that the mastery of different technology skills is not a function of age; instead differences are related to experience with technology (Eshet-Alkalai & Chajut, 2010). However, although there are higher education institutions that provide or loan such instruments to their students, no studies were found examining how these future teachers use these devices in the training process.

3. The Research

The research under discussion studied a pilot programme at a teacher training college, in the framework of which tablet devices were loaned to the students. The subjects were 18 students from the pilot group, who were studying in the college's honours programme in a variety of specialisations. The students received the tablets in their first-year studies, and they are still in their possession. This study examines the students' use of the tablets based on an implementation model that does not include practical training, pedagogical guidance, or support from an ICT faculty expert.

4. Research Questions

How do education students use the iPads? What pedagogical uses of the tablet did the education students implement to advance the learning process as part of their practical training?

5. Research Method

The study was conducted based on a qualitative research paradigm of content analysis and the construction of a grounded theory. Data were collected, and testimonies and pieces of information from a variety of research tools were cross-referenced (triangulation). The research tools included semi-structured personal and group interviews, online questionnaires in Google docs, students' reflective performance reports, lesson plans, observations of practical experience and documentation of discourse on social media.

6. Discussion and Conclusion

The findings show that the students' primary uses for the iPads appear similar to the findings of other researchers (Dew, 2010; Johnson, Levine, Smith & Stone, 2010; Kelly & Schrape, 2010; Melhuish & Falloon, 2010; Valentino, 2010; Mantei, Herrington, Olney & Ferry, 2008; Mouza, 2008). Students' use of the iPads in various contexts: (a) for ongoing personal use, (b) for planning lessons, (c) for active integration in the classroom, which included enhancement of frontal teaching, teaching in groups and active learning – integration of dedicated applications, media stimuli or media support and as a motivational tool, (d) creating and developing content and games using dedicated platforms that enable the teacher to insert the relevant content matter into a genre of games.

There was a change not only in the quality of teaching in the classroom, but also in the students' outlook on their future professional development. The development of learning materials in the form of computerised games is not a routine activity for teachers. For the most part it is time-consuming, and requires high-level planning and thinking and design skills. When the students developed the material, they each brought their own unique talents – academic and professional – to a high level of expression; they had a better understanding of the material to begin studies, greater preparedness for the teaching process and greater satisfaction.

In the unique implementation model tested in this study, students did not receive pedagogical support for planning and implementing lessons using the device. Still, it seemed that the more they experience they gained in school with the device, the more sophisticated and creative the lessons they developed became, to the point where they created open use creative learning materials, simulation and games. The user-friendliness of the device and its intuitive interface require almost no special training.

This finding is consistent with the findings of the researchers, who suggest a link between the duration of experience and the degree of control of the device (Eshet-Alkalai & Chajut, 2010). However, this finding contradicts the findings of other studies that maintain that there is need for a training programme to acquire the technology skills for establishing and implementing innovative pedagogy.

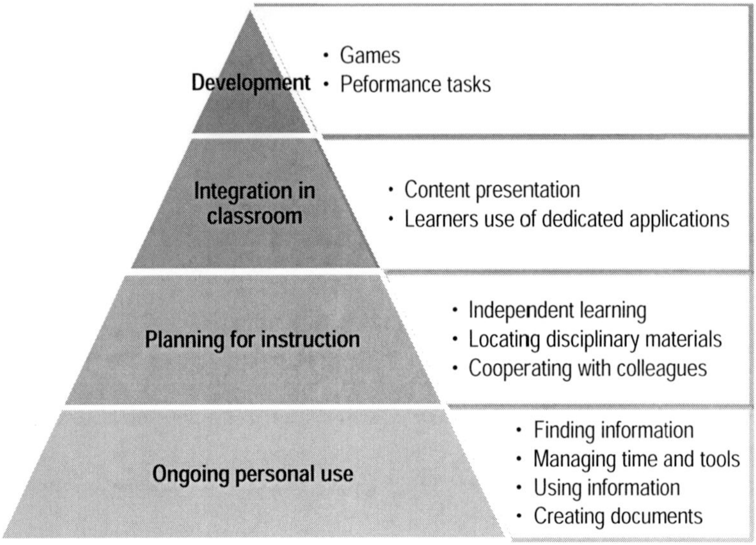

Figure 1. Taxonomy of students' use of the iPads in education

This chart shows the different uses as levels in a hierarchical taxonomy. Each level in the diagram includes the uses of the levels below it. The greater the knowledge and experience of students using the device, the more sophisticated their use (up to the level of development).

In the unique implementation model tested in this study, students did not receive pedagogical support for planning and implementing lessons using the device. Yet, it should address the implications carefully, due to the small group of students, with unique characteristics (honours students). Therefore, it is recommended to conduct a wider study. In addition, it is recommended to analyse the lesson plans and activities, as well as the levels of thinking required of learners in classes where iPads are integrated.

References

Alexander, B. (2004). Going nomadic: Mobile learning in higher education. *Educause Review, 39*(5), 6.

Chen, G. D., Chang, C. K., & Wang, C. Y. (2008). Ubiquitous learning website: Scaffold learners by mobile devices with information-aware techniques. *Computers and Education, 50*, 77–90.

Chen, Y. S., Kao, T. C., & Sheu, J. P. (2003). A mobile learning system for scaffolding bird watching learning. *Journal of Computer Assisted Learning, 19*, 347–359.

Cobcroft, R. S., Towers, S., & Smith, J. (2006). Mobile learning in review: Opportunities and challenges for learners, teachers, and institutions. In *The Online Learning and Teaching Conference 2006*. Queensland: Queensland University of Technology.

Dew, J. (2010). Global, mobile, virtual, and social: The college campus of tomorrow. *Futurist, 44*(2), 46–50.

Eagleton, M., & Dobler, E. (2007). *Reading the web: Strategies for Internet inquiry*. New York & London: The Guilford Press.

El-Hussein, M. O. M., & Cronje, J. C. (2010). Defining mobile learning in the higher education landscape. *Journal of Educational Technology & Society, 13*(3), 12–21.

Eyal, L. (2012). Digital assessment literacy - the core role of the teacher in a digital environment. *Journal of Educational Technology & Society, 15*(2), 37-49. Retrieved December 29, 2014: http://goo.gl/d1ZwBa

Eshet-Alkalai, Y., & Chajut, E. (2010). You can teach old dogs new tricks: The factors that affect changes over time in digital literacy. *Journal of Information Technology Education, 9*, 173–181.

Fishman, B., Best, S., Marx, R., &. Tal, T. (2001). Fostering teacher learning in systemic reform: Linking professional development to teacher and student learning. In *NARST 2001*. St. Louis, MO.

Georgiev, T., Georgieva, E., & Smrikarov, A. (2004). M-learning - a new stage of e-learning. In *International Conference on Computer Systems and Technologies-CompSysTech*, 2004. Rousse, Bulgaria.

Herrington, J., Mantei, J., Herrington, A., Olney, I., & Ferry, B. (2008). New technologies, new pedagogies: Mobile technologies and new ways of teaching and learning. In *The Australian Society for Computers in Learning in Tertiary Education Conference (ASCILITE)*. Melbourne. Australia: Deakin University.

Hutchison, A., Beschorner, B., & Schmidt-Crawford, D. (2012). Exploring the use of the iPad for literacy learning. *The Reading Teacher, 66*(1), 15-23.

Jeng, Y. L., Wu, T. T., Huang, Y. M., Tan, Q., & Yang, S. J. (2010). The add-on impact of mobile applications in learning strategies: A review study. *Educational Technology & Society, 13*(3), 3-11.

Johnson, L., Levine, A., Smith, R., & Stone, S. (2010). *The 2010 horizon report*. Austin, TX: The New Media Consortium.

Kelly, J., & Schrape, J. (2010). 100 days with an iPad: Lessons learnt and apps acquired. Poster presented at The *Australian Society for Computers in Learning in Tertiary Education Conference (ASCILITE).* Sydney, Australia.

Larson, L.C. (2010). Digital readers: The next chapter in e-book reading and response. *The Reading Teacher, 64*(1), 15-22.

Lee, J., Luchini, K., Michael, B., Norris, C., & Soloway, E. (2004). More than just fun and games: Assessing the value of educational video games in the classroom. In *CHI 2004 Connect: Conference on Human Factors in Computing Systems*. Vienna, Austria.

Melhuish, K., & Falloon, G. (2010). Looking to the future: M-learning with the iPad. *Computers in New Zealand Schools: Learning, Leading, Technology*, 22(3), 1-16.

Monahan, T., McArdle, G., & Bertolotto, M. (2008). Virtual reality for collaborative elearning. *Computers & Education, 50*, 1339-1353.

Mouza, C. (2008). Learning with laptops: Implementation and outcomes in an urban, under-privileged school. *Journal of Research on Technology in Education, 40*(4), 447-473.

Naismith, L., Lonsdale, P., Vavoula, G., & Sharples, M. (2004). *Literature review in mobile technologies and learning. Report 11. Futurelab Series*. Bristol: Futurelab.

Peters, K. (2009). M-learning: Positioning educators for a mobile, connected future. In M. Ally (Ed.), *Mobile learning: Transforming the delivery of education and training* (pp. 113-134). Vancouver: Marquis Book Printing.

Price, S., & Rogers, Y. (2004). Let's get physical: The learning benefits of interacting in digitally augmented physical spaces. *Computers & Education, 43*, 137-151.

Rosas, R., Nussbaum, M., Cumsille, P., Marianov, V., Correa, M., Flores, P., Grau, V., Lagos, F., Lopez, X., Lopez, V., Rodriguez, P., & Salinas, M. (2003). Beyond Nintendo: Design and assessment of educational video games for first and second grade students. *Computers & Education, 40*(1), 71-94.

Rossing, J. P., Miller, W. M., Cecil, A. K., & Stamper, S. E. (2012). iLearning: The future of higher education? Student perceptions on learning with mobile Tablets. *Journal of the Scholarship of Teaching and Learning, 12*(2), 1-26.

Shamir-Inbal, T., & Blau, A. (2013). Is the technology ripe: Tablets for learning the elementary school. In *The learner in the technological ear, 8th Chase conference on the research of learning technologies*. Raanana: Open University (in Hebrew).

Speak Up (2010). The new 3 E's of education: Enabled, engaged, empowered, how today's students are leveraging emerging technologies for learning. *Project Tomorrow*. Retrieved December 29, 2014 from: http://goo.gl/HL1AL

Traxler, J. (2007). Defining, discussing and evaluating mobile learning: The moving finger writes and having writ... *The International Review of Research in Open and Distance Learning, 8*(2), 1-12.

Traxler, J. (2010). Will student devices deliver innovation, inclusion and transformation? *Journal of the Research Centre for Educational Technologies, 6*(1), 3-15.

Valentino, D. J. (2010). Using the iPad to connect: Parents, therapists use Apple Tablet to communicate with special needs kids. *The Wall Street Journal*, Oct. 13, 2010. Retrieved December 29, 2014, from: http://goo.gl/5lPZns

Wang, K. T., Huang, Y. M., Jeng, Y. L., & Wang, T. I. (2008). A blog-based dynamic learning map. *Computers & Education, 51*(1), 262-278.

Yang, S. J. H. (2006). Context aware ubiquitous learning environments for peer-to-peer collaborative learning. *Educational Technology & Society, 9*(1), 188-201.

Zurita, G., Nussbaum, M., & Salinas, R. (2005). Dynamic grouping in collaborative learning supported by wireless handhelds. *Educational Technology & Society, 8*(3), 149-161.

The Use of the iPad in a First-Year Introductory Physics Course

Brandon van der Ventel[1]
and Richard Newman[2]

Abstract

We report on a pilot project to investigate the use of the iPad in a first-year introductory physics course. This device has revolutionised the delivery of multimedia content, the nature of social networking and the additional feature of apps. However, it is important to study how it can be effectively used and in a pedagogically sound manner. This is particularly relevant at university level, where there is a higher volume of work (compared to school), much greater class size and a greater demand on student's time. A course in physics offers additional challenges, such as mastery of conceptual issues, algebraic manipulation and numerical implementation. To effectively implement the iPad, we used a four-component model based on: (i) flipped learning, (ii) an interactive classroom, (iii) the use of learning apps, and (iv) the use of e-textbooks. These components were identified, as there are apps available for the immediate implementation in the teaching environment. We discuss each of the apps, which were used, and how they were implemented. We also look at a number of challenges, which are specific to iPad usage at university level, but within an African context. Our findings indicate that the students received the flipped learning aspect and the interactive classroom very positively. Due to the large number of students involved app usage was limited to demonstrations in the formal contact periods.

[1] Stellenbosch University, South Africa. Email: bventel@sun.ac.za
[2] Stellenbosch University, South Africa. Email: rtnewman@sun.ac.za

1. Introduction

The Apple iPad has revolutionised the way in which multimedia content (pictures, sounds, videos) can be delivered. It has also greatly enhanced the use of social media and the mobile delivery of information content. Coupled with this is the app store with a vast landscape of apps for many different areas of application. The question naturally arises if the iPad can be used in a Higher Education (HE) environment in a pedagogically sound manner. This relates to the question posed by Oppenheimer (2003). Is it necessarily so that technology, which works outside of the educational environment, will be successful inside it (Melhuish & Falloon, 2010)? As educators we cannot, however, ignore the advances in technology, since it will ultimately be harmful to the students if 'pedagogy does not keep pace with technology' (Thiruvathukal, 2003). University-level education offers additional challenges (compared to school), such as a higher volume of work, much larger class sizes and a greater demand on student's time. A number of institutions have implemented programmes to investigate the educational benefits of this remarkable device (Schnackenberg, 2013; Valstad, 2010; Gasparini & Culén, 2012). A course in physics requires that students are competent at the following levels: (i) conceptual understanding, (ii) algebraic, and (iii) numerical skills. The key question is if the iPad can be used in the HE environment without it becoming nothing more than a gimmick (Gasparini & Culén, 2012). In other words, we need to address the following: (i) Does the iPad have the potential to positively affect students' performance, in terms of learning, understanding and applying the course content, and (ii) what strategies can be followed at university level to effectively make use of the many extraordinary features of this device (Hoover & Valencia, 2011).

This pilot project was run in the Physics 154 course at the Department of Physics at Stellenbosch University. This is a semester course, which runs from July until the end of October. In the department, Physics 154 is referred to as a 'service course', since the students are mostly registered for a degree in Life Science with majors such as Biology, Physiology, Biochemistry etc. The course is not calculus-based, and they will therefore not be able to continue with the so-called mainstream physics modules. There are approximately 700 students in the course with a very diverse high school background. Due to the demographics of the Western Cape Province, the course is divided into an Afrikaans and English group[1], with

[1] Both these languages are a result of South Africa's colonial past.

roughly equal number of students. Each language group has three formal 50-minute lecture periods per week. In addition, there are alternating practical and tutorial sessions throughout the semester. The topics of electricity and magnetism were covered in this course. It was in this setting that the pilot programme was initiated to investigate the use of the iPad at a HE level.

2. Research Design

There is no doubt that the iPad has tremendous potential in education, and this is already evident at school level. However, there is still the question as to how this device can be used in a pedagogically sound manner in the university environment. As a guide for this pilot programme we used a four-component model, which is graphically illustrated in Figure 1.

The inner part of this figure shows the four components where the iPad can make an immediate impact. These are: (i) the interactive classroom, (ii) flipped learning, (iii) the use of e-textbooks, and (iv) the use of learning apps. The outer part of the diagram shows which apps are available to implement that specific aspect of the model. For the use of learning apps there is the vast app store, or one can do app development using Xcode. We will now discuss each one of these components separately and how it was implemented in this pilot programme.

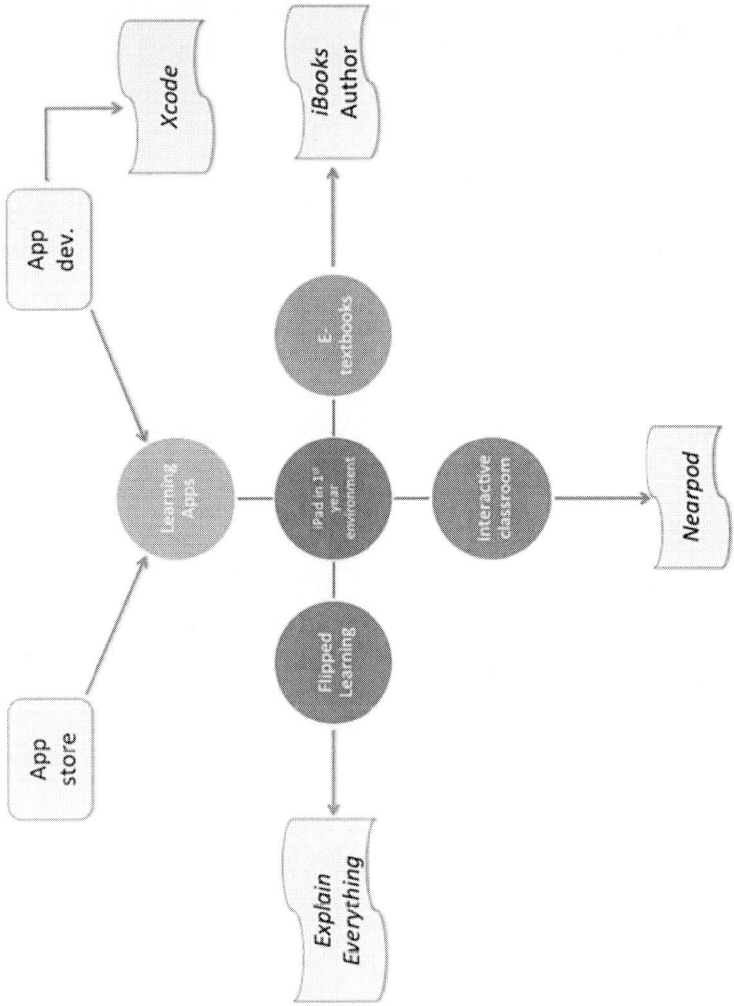

Figure 1. Four-component model for iPad usage

3. Flipped Learning

The concept of flipped learning is based on the idea that traditional classroom activities need not be confined to the physical room where the students and the lecturer meet for a fixed time (Lage, Platt & Treglia, 2000). As discussed by Lage et. al. (2000), the flipped learning model relies heavily on the worldwide web, videotaped lectures and PowerPoint slides with sound. The advantage is that the student now has access to the learning material 24/7 and can study at his/her own pace. A graphical representation of this model of learning is shown in Figure 2.

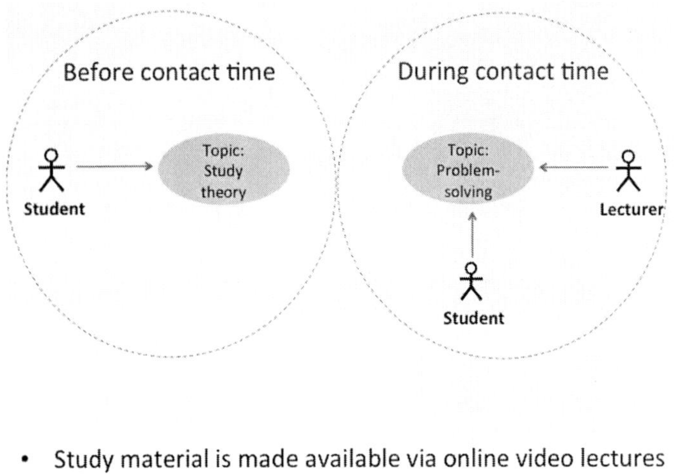

Figure 2. Flipped learning model

The flipped learning model was implemented in this course by making use of the Explain Everything app, available from the app store at a nominal fee. This is a presentation app, where it is possible to insert multimedia effects such as pictures or video with ease. One can also directly record video on a specific slide. The key feature of this app is the fact that one can directly compose handwritten notes with audio on the slide and thus create an entire lesson. The files can then be exported to formats such as mp4 or avi. These media files were then uploaded to our local university server, called WebCT, which is a repository for all the university's educational content. Students that were registered for this course could then have 24/7 access to the learning material. Since this was the pilot programme, we opted to have a traditional lecture in which the

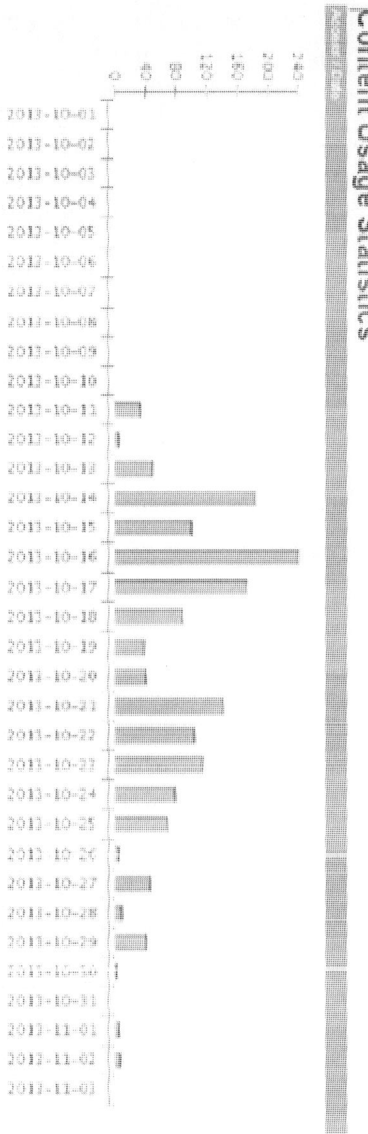

Figure 3. Downloaded statistics for one of the videos created with Explain Everything

fundamentals of the theory was covered, but made available a set of video lectures in which specific problems were solved. Specifically, video lectures were made available for problems on Coulomb's Law, electrical fields, Kirchhoff's loop and junction rules as well as problems related to magnetism. In Figure 3 we show some download statistics from the WebCT server for one of the videos.

4. Interactive Classroom

The traditional lecture period, where the lecturer stands in front of the class, is effectively a one-way flow of information as illustrated in the diagram of Figure 4. The bottom diagram of this figure illustrates the "interactive classroom" approach. Here the flow of information is multi-directional, especially if it incorporates group work as well. This physics 154 course had three tutorial sessions per week, which ran alternatingly with the practical sessions. Due to the large numbers involved, group work was effectively forced onto us.

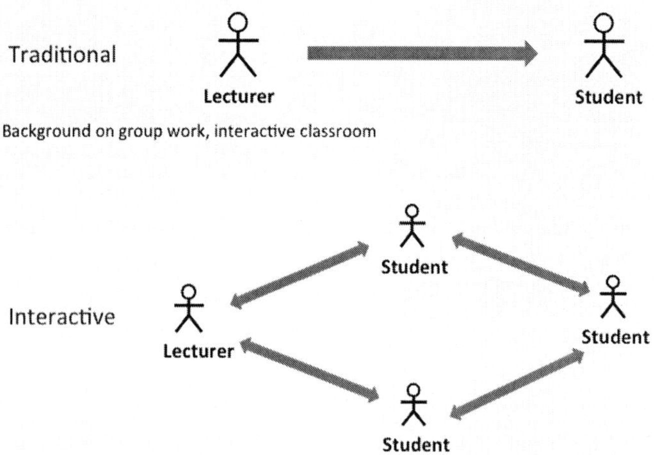

Figure 4. Difference between traditional and interactive classroom model - the red arrows indicate a flow of information

The app which makes this component of the model feasible is an app called Nearpod, available free of charge on the app store[1]. The sequence of steps leading to an interactive classroom session using Nearpod is shown in Figure 5.

One should first create the slides using a traditional presentation creator such as PowerPoint. The next step is to upload these slides to the Nearpod server. In this environment it is then possible to add additional figures, multimedia such as sound or video, multiple-choice quizzes, interactive drawing and polls. To start the Nearpod session the lecturer would sign onto his/her Nearpod account and obtain a unique pin. The students can then become part of the Nearpod session by signing on with this unique pin via the iPad. The presentation to be used in this session is then downloaded onto each iPad and the session can thus begin. The teacher has full control over the session as the teacher can only do the progression through the slides. Whatever is displayed on the teacher's iPad will also show on those who logged in with the unique pin.

Anyone who is part of the Nearpod session can then answer the multiple-choice questions embedded in the presentation and the results are immediately displayed on the teacher's iPad. The multiple-choice question can then be used to investigate each aspect of physics problem-solving namely: (i) conceptual understanding, (ii) algebraic manipulation and (iii) numerical implementation. This app greatly facilitates group work since the results are known instantaneously, and it is possible to exactly pinpoint (with a well-thought out set of multiple-choice questions) where the problems are and what areas need to be addressed. Since the Nearpod session is run via Wi-Fi, the participants need not be in the same physical location and thus it can truly revolutionise distance learning. The success of the session is, however, critically dependent on the speed and carrying capacity of the Wi-Fi connection, and this has to be thoroughly tested before the session is started.

---

[1] The free version allows only 50 participants.

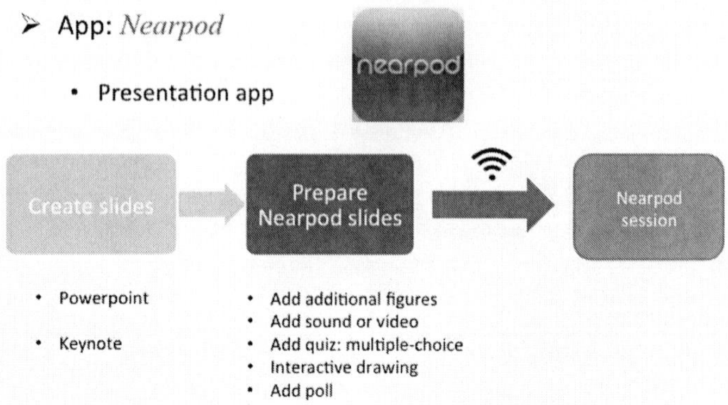

Figure 5. Sequence of steps leading to an interactive Nearpod session

Positive and negative aspects of using the Nearpod app:

1. There were no features of the app that the students had to master. They could immediately focus on the physics questions.
2. Greatly fostered interaction between the students in the group.
3. The nature of the multiple-choice questions allowed students to immediately identify where their problems with the work lay.
4. The lecture hall we used was not optimal for group work.
5. In a group of 4 or more, it became difficult for everyone to see the screen and the device had to be circulated amongst everyone in the group.
6. There is a certain "fun" factor when using the tablet device.
7. Care should be taken when displaying the results as some students felt uncomfortable in being "identified" as submitting the incorrect answers.

5. The Use of Learning Apps

The use of learning apps offers another feature, which could potentially greatly affect teaching with the iPad (Hechter, 2013; MacIsaac, 2012). However, the key challenge is to select apps that enhance the learning process. The following caveats should be taken into consideration:

1. The "less is more" approach should be followed when the iPad and apps form part of the curriculum. In other words, do not clutter the lecture with apps. This can be very distracting for the student, since

a level of proficiency must be attained in the use of the app, before it can add pedagogical value.

2. Do not use the app as a gimmick without any clear educational goal. In the context of this physics course we had to guard against app usage to illustrate a physics principle, when a normal physical set-up would have sufficed. For example, to illustrate the concept of "magnetic field lines" it was more dynamic to use a physical set-up, instead of an app. Firstly, finding apps with clear pedagogical merit is not such an easy task. Secondly, the app we did find could only draw simple field configurations, which were anyway illustrated in the textbook. Since the app basically just provided "pictures" and did not allow for real interactivity, it added no pedagogical benefit compared to the physical experimental set-up we traditionally used to illustrate "magnetic field lines". The other side of this is when we used the app called iCircuit when we studied electrical circuits. This app is fully interactive and allows the user to construct intricate electrical circuits using both active and passive components. The pedagogical benefit of this app is clear in the context of electric circuit theory as we could construct various circuits to illustrate, for example, how the current divides or is shared amongst the electrical components. Investigating such a large number of circuits with arbitrarily varying resistor or capacitance values, for example, would have been impossible if we had been restricted to the use of only physical components.
3. Ensure that the instructor is entirely proficient in the use of the app (Milner-Bolotin & Antimirova, 2010). The following comment by a student in the study of iPads in the classroom at Pepperdine University drives this point home[1]:

> Because there was no training on the apps I had to fend for myself and was confused much of the time. The professor was unable to help as they were just as confused. The iPad was ineffective because no one knew how to use the apps.

It is clear from the discussion above that a judicious choice of apps is critical if they form part of the curriculum. Finding apps, which are suitable for the topic being studied, and which have a level of interactivity, which can enhance the understanding of concepts, is not an easy task. It is for this reason that we also included a component of app development in this project. The program, which enables this part of the iPad-usage model,

[1] http://community.pepperdine.edu/it/tools/ipad/research/results.htm

is called Xcode and can be downloaded free from the app store. Our method was to recruit students who were interested and willing to learn this skill of app development. This allows the lecturer to commission the development of apps, which have very clear and specific goals, leaving out any possible superfluous elements. For example, when analysing electrical circuits using Kirchhoff's loop and junction rules, the last part in the calculation entails the solution of coupled linear equations. To address this part of the calculation an app was therefore written, which can solve a set of linear equations[1]. The point is, however, that we are now able to develop apps, which are focused on what we want in the curriculum.

6. E-Textbook

The fourth component of the iPad usage model is the development of e-textbooks. The app, which makes this possible, is iBooks Author, available free from the app store. This app allows one to create books, which go beyond the normal pdf format. Instead the textbook becomes a dynamic entity enhanced by multimedia such as high-resolution graphics, videos, interactive diagrams and 3D objects. Widgets can be included in the book, which allows setting up questionnaires, multiple-choice questions, interactive graphs and many features that are more dynamic. The book is created on the user's Mac and can then be directly uploaded to the iPad to be viewed with the iBooks app. The final book can be published in the Apple bookstore.

The writing of an e-book using iBooks Author is an ongoing process, and it is important to maintain high standards and quality of presentation. Our first e-book we hope to finish will be based on providing a complete laboratory manual associated with the various experiments done in this course.

7. SWOT Analysis for iPad Usage in an African Context

As a developing country, South Africa faces additional challenges when cutting-edge technology such as the iPad wants to be incorporated into the educational sector. Below we identify some of the strengths,

[1] Not implemented in the class of 2013 since the author of the app (BISvdV) must first register as an App Developer with Apple. There is a process which must be followed, and approval is not necessarily given. In addition, there is a fee involved for paid-apps development.

weaknesses, opportunities and threats when considering iPad usage in an African context.

The high cost of university-level printed textbooks is a major obstacle for African students. The use of the iBooks Author app allows the lecturer to create digital textbooks, which can be distributed for the fraction of the cost or even free to students registered for a particular course. Once loaded on the iPad the student can then personalise these textbooks thus enhancing learning experience. The Nearpod app can positively affect group work and student-lecturer interaction. It can also revolutionise distance learning since all that is needed to be part of the session is a good Wi-Fi connection. This app also allows instant feedback, and both student and lecturer can be fully aware of the level of proficiency on a particular subject. All work can be uploaded to the cloud and synced across devices allowing instant access, and the learning process can thus continue 24/7.

The iPad is, however, very expensive and in an African context, this probably counts as one of the greatest weaknesses of implementing this device. This is not insurmountable as one can always appeal to government or private sponsorships of these devices. Unfortunately, iPads are destructible devices and prime targets for thieves.

Despite the weaknesses mentioned above, it would unwise to disregard the opportunities this device offers for education within an African setting. A sponsorship of these devices will allow under-privileged students to be exposed to the forefront of technology. By including the app development component, students will be taught how to write their own apps. This will create opportunities for entrepreneurship as apps can be sold on the app store (Tiarawut, 2013).

There are, however, a number of things, which threaten widespread iPad usage within the African context. Firstly, there is the large number of students in a classroom. The reality is that we will most probably never reach the stage where each student will have an iPad to use in class. This is because the majority of students do not have the financial means to purchase an iPad. This could, however, be addressed by governmental or private sponsorship. Coupled to the price of the iPad is the fact that a "knee-jerk" reaction might cause faculty or students to settle for lower-end tablet devices, which do not offer the full support as Apple does. For example, it was found that lower-end netbook tablets have a major disadvantage due to the limited computing power they offer (Loch, Galligan, Hobohm & McDonald, 2011). Wi-Fi access and the high cost of Internet usage are also major threats to iPad usage.

8. Summary and Conclusion

In this paper, we have described a pilot project to introduce the use of the iPad in a first-year introductory physics course. Our approach was based on a four-component model consisting of: (i) flipped learning, (ii) interactive classroom, (iii) the use of learning apps and (iv) e-textbooks. These are the four aspects where the iPad can make an immediate impact. There are also apps immediately available to implement any one of these components. The advantage of this model is that once the lecturer has become proficient in anyone of the components, any further work can be delegated to research or teaching assistants.

The use of flipped learning can increase the standard of teaching as the elementary concepts in a course or topic can now be moved to the periphery (in other words, students can study them outside of class hours), while the actual lecturer-student contact time can be devoted to problem-solving. This is particularly important in a course such as physics 154, which is a physics course for life sciences. For example, the theory of the RC-circuit can now be sidelined to an instructional video, while the biological application (for example as membranes) can be concentrated on in the formal lecture period. The "fun" factor of iPad usage must not be underestimated, and group work becomes a more exciting affair when it is used in conjunction with an app such as Nearpod.

The use of learning apps has its place, but the lecturer needs to make a judicious choice to justify its inclusion in the curriculum. App usage as a "gimmick factor" should be avoided at all costs. If the pedagogical benefit of an app is not clear then it should be avoided. By including an aspect of app development lecturers can become proficient in developing apps specifically for their course or curriculum. Not to say that the app should not have wider appeal, but rather that apps should be specific in what they can do or how they benefit the topic. The possibility of entrepreneurship by utilising the skill of app development should also not be overlooked. The use of e-textbooks will also allow the instructor greater control as to what content is included. General-purpose textbooks (especially for a general introductory physics course such as the one discussed here) can now be avoided, and this will have significant financial benefits for the students.

It is clear that the inclusion of the iPad in the teaching environment will in fact place a greater responsibility on the lecturer to ensure that the pedagogical benefit of this remarkable device is identified and exploited.

Acknowledgements

The authors wish to acknowledge: (i) the grant from the Fund for Innovation and Research into Teaching and Learning (FIRLT), (ii) Drs J.P. Bosman and S.C. Strydom from the Center of Teaching and Learning at Stellenbosch University, (iii) teaching assistants, Miss C. Hanekom and Mr J.P. Blanckenberg.

References

Gasparini, A., & Culén, A. (2012). Acceptance factors: An iPad in classroom ecology. In *ICEEE 2012: The International Conference on Elearning and E-Technologies in Education*. Lodz, Poland: Technical University of Lodz.

Hechter, R.P. (2013) Hockey, iPads, and projectile motion in a physics classroom. *The Physics Teacher*, *51*, 346-347.

Hoover, D., & Valencia, J. (2011). iPads in the classroom: Use, learning outcomes, and the future. In *2011 EDUCAUSE Annual Conference*. Philadelphia: EDUCAUSE.

Lage, M. J., Platt, G. J., & Treglia, M. (2000). Inverting the classroom: A gateway to creating an inclusive learning environment. *Journal of Economic Education*, *31*(1), 30-43.

Loch, B., Galligan, L., Hobohm, C., & McDonald C. (2011). Learner-centred mathematics and statistics education using netbook tablet PCs. *International Journal of Mathematical Education*, *42*(7), 939-949.

MacIsaac, D. (2012), iOS physics learning apps (for Apple products iPhone, iPod Touch, iPad). *The Physics Teacher*, *50*, 61.

Manuguerra, M., & Petocz, P. (2011). Promoting student engagement by integrating new technology into tertiary education: The role of the iPad. *Asian Social Science*, *7*(11), 61-65.

Melhuish, K., & Falloon, G. (2010). Looking to the future: M-learning with the iPad. *Computers in New Zealand Schools: Learning, Leading, Technology*, *22*(3), 1-16.

Milner-Bolotin, M., & Antimirova, T. (2010). HP grants for tablet technologies in science teaching: from dream to innovation. In *Proceedings of the 4th International Technology, Education and Development Conference*. Valencia, Spain: INTED.

Oppenheimer, T. (2003). *The flickering mind: False promise of technology in the classroom and how learning can be saved*. Toronto, Canada: Random House.

Schnackenberg, H. L. (2013). Tablet technologies and education. *International Journal of Education and Practice*, *1*(4), 44-50.

Thiruvathukal, G. K. (2013). Who needs tablets? We do. *Computing in Science and Engineering*, *15*(1), 4-6.

Tiarawut, S. (2013). Mobile technology: Opportunity for entrepreneurship. *Wireless Personal Communications*, *69*(3), 1025-1031.

Valstad, H. (2010). *iPad as a pedagogical device (TDT4520)*. Trondheim: Norwegian University of Science and Technology.

BRIDGING THE GAP: PREPARING THE APP GENERATION FOR HIGHER EDUCATION

REBECCA OSBORNE[1] AND SABBA N. QUIDWAI[2]

Abstract

Higher education is a critical need for any country. An educated population places a lower burden on social services and federal and state spending. Moreover, according to the National Center for Public Policy and Higher Education and the Southern Regional Education Board (2004) individuals with more education earn a higher income, resulting in higher tax revenue, increasing the economy. However, there is widespread concern in the United States (US) about the growing number of students failing to graduate high school or complete a university degree. The National Center for Public Policy and Higher Education and the Southern Regional Education Board (2010) reported that nearly 60% of first-year college students must take remedial math and English courses, which do not earn college credit, in order to succeed in the classes in their major. Their high school curriculum, college preparatory courses and standardized testing failed to ensure readiness for their university courses. This paper addresses the growing disparity between the demands set upon students at the university level and the preparation for student success at the high school level, and suggests some strategies for closing this gap.

1. Introduction

Times are changing, and as we find our students in the US falling behind other nations, we now find ourselves in the midst of a learning revolution. Nearly 1.3 million students drop out each year and 7,200

[1] Fairmont Preparatory Academy, Anaheim, CA. Email: rosborne@fairmontschools.com

[2] Fairmont Preparatory Academy, Anaheim, CA. Email: Squidwai@usc.edu

students leave America's secondary education system every school day (Aarons, Maxwell, Zehr, Sawchuck & Swanson, 2010).

If today's generation is going to compete on a global level, educational institutions will have to re-evaluate the role they play. The purpose of our educational system is being called into question, and questions are being asked about how students are readying themselves for the future? Perhaps more importantly, how are students being prepared for higher education?

The initial challenge presents itself in the discrepancy that exists between high school exit requirements and college entry requirements. The ACT (2008) reports that nationally only 22% of high school graduates meet or surpass ACT's College Readiness Benchmarks in English, math, reading and science. With the era of standardized testing that came with No Child Left Behind, students were focusing efforts on passing the exam, and the development of crucial skills such as critical thinking, analysis and technology expertise were being neglected.

With the introduction of the Common Core Standards, an educational initiative in the US that details what K-12 students need to know before they graduate, new expectations are being set. At the forefront of these expectations must be the mastery of 21st Century Learning Skills, identified by the Partnership for 21st Century Learning as critical thinking, creativity, communication and collaboration (Partnership for 21st Century Skills, 2011). While the 4Cs of 21st Century learning are not new, the possibilities and the reality of how ideas can be integrated is more real. The vision of a truly student-centred learning environment where teachers facilitate the learning of students can now be a reality.

The mastery of 21st Century skills allow students to apply their knowledge of core subjects like math, language arts, science and history to contemporary themes of global awareness, finance, health and alternative energy.

In 2008 *The global achievement gap: Why even our best schools don't teach the new survival skills our children need – and what they can do about it* by Tony Wagner produced a chart highlighting this discrepancy (Figure 1).

In order to address the growing divide between college expectations and the readiness of high school graduates, it is important to recognize student and teacher needs. Students in the 21st century live in a world in which they are immersed in digital technology. By their own reports, students spend over 10 hours a day using technology such as cell phones, computers and laptops, and surfing the Web (Rideout, Foehr & Roberts, 2010). This usage represents a considerable increase within the past five years, and is driven largely by use of mobile computing devices with Internet access, like iPod, smartphones, and tablet computers.

High Schools Teach…	Colleges Demand…
Getting the right answer and performing well on multiple choice tests	Figuring out the right questions and using skills to solve new problems
Working alone	Working in teams
Learning with academic disciplines	Learning how to find, communicate and apply information in a ubiquitous environment
Memorizing fixed information	Initiative and leadership in "flat" organisations and taking responsible risks
Complying with hierarchal authority and avoiding risks	Managing time and commitments - prioritizing and flexible time segments
Adhering to external and inflexible time segments	Interacting in a multimedia, graphics-based environment
Sitting passively in a linear, text-based environment	Working with left and right sides of the brain together

Figure 1. This chart adapted from Wagner (2008) contrasts the requirements for college readiness with the preparation provided to students in high school

Don Tapscott (2008), in a series for *Business Week* on the Net Generation, wrote that the old model of pedagogy that is teacher-focused, one-way, and one-size-fits-all, makes no sense to young people who have grown up in a digital world. He argues that members of the Net Generation have different mental habits than their Boomer parents. They expect a conversation, rather than a lecture, and they are used to working in groups, rather than working alone and, he argues, digital immersion has even affected the way they absorb information.

They do not necessarily read a page in a textbook from left to right and from top to bottom. They might instead skip around the page, scanning for pertinent information of interest (Tapscott, 2008). In the report, *Maximizing the impact: The pivotal role of technology in a 21st century education system*, the State Educational Technology Directors Association (SETDA), the International Society for Technology in Education (ISTE) and the Partnership for 21st Century Skills urged renewed emphasis on technology in education (Vockley, 2008). This report recommends using technology comprehensively to develop proficiency in 21st century learning skills, support innovative teaching and learning and create robust education support systems. However, despite federal, state and local investment in technology and Internet connectivity, most schools still use technology sparingly, rather than as a critical component of all educational operations. According to the Technology CEO Council (2007), right now 100 million Americans have broadband access, 219 million Americans use cell phones and the personal computer penetration rate is 73 percent.

It is evident from research studies that the addition of technology into the classroom alone does not improve student performance. As the US Department of Education (2010) suggests, inclusion of technology in classrooms must be done purposefully, with a thought-out plan of what technology will be deployed and how that technology will be utilised in (and beyond) the classroom for instruction. Successful educational technologies depend not only on the tools being used, but the content - digital programmes must have high quality instruction and high quality content if they are going to be effective (Dynarski, Agodini, Heaviside, Novak, Carey, Campuzano, et al., 2008). Successful integration of technology utilises innovative practice and research skills to employ teaching strategies, content, and pedagogical skills that aim to utilise technology as a cognitive tool (Mueller, Wood, Willoughby, Ross & Specht, 2008). It is the combination of this accumulated body of knowledge and skills within an authentic learning context that results in effective instruction and positive student outcomes (Koehler & Mishra, 2010).

Increased access to technology does not necessarily correlate with an improvement in classroom teaching practices (Lim & Chai, 2008; Lowther, Inan, Strahl & Ross, 2008; Ross & Morrison, 2004). Lack of effective teaching practices is frequently correlated with teachers lacking the necessary skills to integrate technology (Baylor & Ritchie, 2002; Ertmer & Hruskocy, 1999; Eteokleous, 2008; Russell, Bebell & O'Dwyer, 2003; van Braak, 2001). A 2000 survey conducted by the National Center for Education Statistics found that only 23% of surveyed teachers felt well prepared to integrate technology in their instruction.

A recent survey conducted by Ithaka S+R shows that "...although many technical barriers to using technology in the classroom have been lowered, there may still exist substantial policy, training, or interest constraints that continue to limit this kind of activity" (Schonfeld, Wulfson & Housewright, 2012). Teacher training is one of the best predictors of technology use (Vannatta & Fordham, 2004). To be effective in schools and classrooms, teachers and administrators need training, tools and proficiency in 21st century skills themselves. Used comprehensively, technology transforms standards and assessments, curriculum and instruction, professional development, learning environments and administration (Vockley, 2008).

Greater collaboration between schools (elementary and secondary) and colleges has, as one of its many possible byproducts, the potential for improving the access and success of underrepresented students through earlier educational intervention, better academic preparation, and more targeted student recruitment (Cuseo, 2008). To better prepare students for the curricular content and 21st century skills needed to succeed in college, communication between high school and college instructors is essential. Indeed, supporting collaboration and increased communication between university and high school educators represents a fundamental commitment to teacher education and student outcomes. These partnerships can result in the formation of long lasting learning communities that benefit both secondary and post-secondary education.

References

Aarons D. I., Maxwell L.A., Zehr, M.A., Sawchuck S., & Swanson, C. B. (2010). Diplomas count 2010: Graduation by the numbers; putting data to work for student success. *Education Week*, *29*(34).

ACT: Resources for education and workplace success. (2008). ACT Press Release: 2008 ACT College Readiness Report News Release.

Baylor, A., & Ritchie, D. (2002). What factors facilitate teacher skill, teacher morale, and perceived student learning in technology-using classrooms? *Journal of Computers & Education*, *39*(1), 395-414.

Cuseo, J. (2008) Collaboration between schools & colleges, aka, school-college partnerships. *Perspectives*, *5*(1), 4A-11A.

Dynarski, M., Agodini, R., Heaviside, S., Novak, T., Carey, N., Campuzano, L., et al. (2008). *Effectiveness of reading and mathematics software products: Findings from the first student cohort*. Washington, D.C.:

U.S. Department of Education, Foundation for Excellence in Education. Digital learning now! Washington D.C.

Ertmer, P. A., & Hruskocy, C. (1999). Impacts of university/elementary school partnership designed to support technology integration. *Educational Technology Research and Development*, *47*(1), 81-96.

Eteokleous, N. (2008). Evaluating computer technology integration in a centralized school system. *Computers and Education*, *51*(2), 669-686.

Koehler, M. J., & Mishra, P. (2010). What is technological pedagogical content knowledge? *Contemporary Issues in Technology and Teacher Education (CITE), 9*(1), 60-70.

Lim, C.P., & Chai, C.S. (2008). Rethinking classroom-oriented instructional development models to mediate instructional planning in technology enhanced learning environments. *Teaching and Teacher Education*, *24*(8), 2002-2013.

Lowther, D.L., Inan, F.A., Strahl, J.D., & Ross, S.M. (2008). Does technology integration "work" when key barriers are removed? *Educational Media International*, *45*(3), 195-206.

Mueller, J., Wood, E., Willoughby, T., Ross, C., & Specht, J. Identifying discriminating variables between teachers who fully integrate computers and teachers with limited integration. *Computers & Education*, *51*(4), 1523-1537.

National Center for Public Policy and Higher Education, Southern Regional Education Board (2004). *The educational pipeline: Big investment, big returns (Rep.).* Retrieved 29 January, 2014 from http://goo.gl/GKvgwv

National Center for Public Policy and Higher Education, Southern Regional Education Board. (2010). *Beyond the rhetoric: Improving college readiness through coherent state policy*. Retrieved 29 December, 2014 from http://goo.gl/9z9eh4

Partnership for 21st Century Skills. (2011). *Framework for 21st century learning*. Retrieved 15 February, 2015 from http://goo.gl/0rHxw

Rideout, V. J., Foehr, U. G., & Roberts, D. F. (2010). *Generation M2: media in the lives of 8—18 year olds*. Kaiser Family Foundation. January 2010.

Ross, S. M., & Morrison. G. R. (2004). Experimental research methods, In D. J. Jonassen (Ed). *Handbook of research on educational communications and technology*, 2nd Ed., (pp. 1021-1043). Mahwah, NJ: Lawrence Erlbaum Associates.

Russell, M., Bebell, D., & O'Dwyer, L. (2003). Use, support, and effect of instructional technology study: An overview of the USEIT study and the participating districts. Boston, MA: Technology and Assessment Study Collaborative. Retrieved 29 December, 2014 from http://goo.gl/rAz3wX

Schonfeld RC, Wulfson K, Housewright R. (2012). *Ithaka S+R US faculty survey 2012*. ICPSR34651-v1. Ann Arbor, MI: Inter-university Consortium for Political and Social Research.

Tapscott, D. (2008, November 10). How digital technology has changed the brain. *Business Week*.

Technology CEO Council. Washington DC: Technology CEO Council (2007). *A great nation: How Americans can lead and prosper in a changing world*. Retrieved 29 December, 2014 from http://goo.gl/Z7g7UY

U.S. Department of Education, Office of Educational Technology (2010). *Transforming American education: Learning powered by technology*. Retrieved 29 December, 2014 from http://goo.gl/LGqfc

van Braak, J. (2001). Individual characteristics influencing teachers' class use of computers. *Journal of Educational Computing Research*, *25*, 141–157.

Vannatta, R. A., & Fordham, N. (2004). Teacher dispositions as predictors of classroom technology. *Journal of Research Technology in Education*, *36*(3), 253-272.

Vockley, M. (2008). *Maximizing the impact: The pivotal role of technology in a 21st ISTE; century education system; SETDA*. Partnership for 21st Century Skills. Retrieved 29 December, 2014 from http://goo.gl/AXIoA2

Wagner, T. (2008). *The global achievement gap: Why even our best schools don't teach the new survival skills our children need – and what can we do about it*. New York, NY: Basic Books.

STUDENT PERCEPTIONS OF THE SUCCESS OF AN IPAD-BASED READING DISCUSSION PROJECT

EMILY SAAVEDRA[1] AND DAWN MURRAY[2]

Abstract

This article presents findings from an action research study that examined student perceptions of an iPad-based, learner-centred reading project for English language learners in a tertiary educational context in the United Arab Emirates (UAE). Students participated in the Reading Discussion Project (RDP), which consists of five discussion events, over the period of one academic semester (approximately three months in length). The RDP was designed to increase the awareness of global and local current affairs in an effort to minimise deficits in general knowledge. The RDP required learners to develop individualised content using the applications "Creative Book Builder" and "iBooks" to create interactive teaching and elearning materials on their iPads for peers in their cohort. These materials were the basis for student-led small group discussions. Subsequent to the discussions, surveys were administered to students to encourage self-reflection of their experiences. All responses were attitudinal and self-reported, with students citing improved reading skills and increased levels of self-confidence as a result of having participated in the RDP. The findings are classified into four main categories: (i) student self-perceived levels of confidence pre- and post-discussions; (ii) perceived value of producing, utilising and discussing peer-created content; (iii) topics selected by students for academic discussion; and (iv) self-recognised improvements in reading skills, namely vocabulary expansion, knowledge of textual organisation and a broader understanding of global and local current affairs. The overall positive trend of responses and the self-perceived growth in skills and abilities indicate that this project is a

[1] Higher Colleges of Technology, Dubai, UAE. Email: esaavedra@hct.ac.ae

[2] Higher Colleges of Technology, Dubai, UAE. Email: dmurray@hct.ac.ae

worthwhile addition to the reading component of the Pre-Bachelors Foundations English Language Preparation Program curriculum.

1. Introduction

Arab learners come from a traditionally oral culture and, at times, lack the impetus to read. The implementation of an iPad-based reading project attempted to motivate students to acquire an interest in developing reading skills and in exploring a variety of topics. Teachers believe students' reluctance to read contributes greatly towards huge gaps in general and world knowledge. This gap adversely affects students' academic performance across skills and as they proceed throughout their tertiary education. It particularly hinders their ability to achieve a band 5.0 in the reading component of the Cambridge International English Language Testing System (IELTS) exam, which is the entry requirement for their subsequent bachelors' courses.

This paper will provide details of the iPad-based reading discussion project (RDP) that has been implemented to address these issues with our students, who are English language learners in tertiary education. It outlines the background and rationale behind the project, followed by a review of current literature on the use of iPads in reading classes. The paper details the research project conducted, with attention to pertinent findings, results born out of the research, conclusions and implications for the future incorporation of the reading discussion project in the reading curriculum.

2. Background

A major federal-led initiative to adopt mobile learning devices (Apple iPads) as the primary teaching and learning method of delivery was implemented in tertiary education across the United Arab Emirate (UAE) in the academic year starting September 2012. This represents, alongside the Trinity College of Foundation Studies iPad implementation (Jennings, Anderson, Dorset & Mitchell, 2011), one of the largest adoptions of iPad tablets for English language learners in higher education institutions and definitely the largest in the Middle East (Gitsaki & Robby, 2013).

The Apple iPad was selected to promote student-centred, active learning methods both in and out of the classroom walls (Hargis, Cavanaugh, Kamali & Soto, 2013), whilst employing emerging technologies that would maximise student motivation and promote collaboration. The iPads were introduced to all new students in the Higher

Colleges of Technology Pre-Bachelors Foundations English Language Preparation Program, totalling over 6,200 students and 360 teachers (Gitsaki & Robby, 2013). Student iPads were loaded with 22 core apps selected on the basis of recommendations made by a small group of “iPad gurus” who ran pilot groups across campuses from April-May 2012. During the initial trials, the app Creative Book Builder (CBB) was identified as a potential ebook writer that would allow students to create and publish their own work in a shareable digital format.

At one of the campuses for women, the RDP was therefore developed to address these issues, whilst exploiting the flexibility and mobility of the iPad. Students were required to select a current news article from a list of online international sources, submit the article electronically to the instructor for approval of newsworthiness, appropriateness and length, and then work on the article to identify the main idea, supporting details, key vocabulary and pertinent discussion points. Students were given the freedom to choose the topic of the article based on their own interests as long as the topics had an academic focal point. Students also had to prepare IELTS type questions (for example true/ false, short answers, multiple choice questions) about their articles. The completed annotated article was checked by the instructor and then shared via iBooks with a group of up to four students from the same class who, after reading the article, discussed the topics and answered the questions in a student-led in-class discussion session, which the instructor monitored and assessed. Students were then asked to reflect on their experiences. A study was then conducted on student responses and reactions to the RDP, the objective being to determine:

- Which topics appealed most to students;
- Whether students' creation and sharing of individualised eReaders was deemed motivating by the students themselves;
- Whether students felt that their reading skills improved over the semester;
- Whether students felt that their confidence improved over the semester.

3. Literature Review

At present there is a substantial amount of information regarding iPads; however, most of it is promotional by nature. Academic research is growing, but it is still in an embryonic phase. Given our interest in promoting general knowledge and encouraging extensive reading, our foci of interest was on maximising the capabilities of the iPads to promote and enhance students' experiences of extensive reading, a skill most students do not consider pleasurable. There are a budding number of studies that have focused on reading and the role that the iPad has played in the classroom. Most of these classroom-based observational studies have highlighted the use of iPads as eReaders, replacements of traditional paper-based texts. They have focused solely on the use of iPads in singular classrooms with a small sample of participants.

Grace (2011) looked at the use of iBooks (on iPads) as opposed to traditional paper-based texts in third grade sustained silent reading classes. She conducted a group comparison of a convenience sampling using switching replications over a two-day period. Her T-tests showed no statistical significance in the differences of comprehension levels between iPads and paper-based texts; however students did comment that they found the iPad easier to use. Similar results have been found with second graders in the USA (Stewart, 2012) and year six students in an Australian primary school (Sheppard, 2011), where the researchers also observed that students were more intrinsically motivated, eager and excited when using the iPad due to the device being intuitive and "fun" to use. This novelty factor alone was seen as a valuable aspect of the device, but sample sizes in all three studies were seen as a limitation. A further limitation of these studies is that they were conducted over a matter of a few hours; therefore, students were not able to experiment much with the device to see if they could utilise iPad-specific applications to improve their reading comprehension results.

Shepherd and Reeves (2011) examined the use of iPads in a tertiary context, at Abilene Christian University, in the USA, to access both etexts and the learning management system (LMS). They noted that iPads allowed readers the ability to read in a non-linear fashion by enabling the reader to interact with texts through the use of hyperlinks to sounds files, definitions and other materials that can enhance the reading experience through a multimodal approach to literacy. Brand, Kinash, Mathew, and Kordyban (2011) also investigated the use of loaner iPads as access points for the same LMS and etextbooks at Bond University, Australia. Attitudes from students were positive with some students preferring to access the etexts to the more traditional printed version. Those students who participated in the study and who borrowed the iPads most over the trial period were found to have higher academic achievement than their counterparts, after controlling for self-management of learning and age.

Also in the tertiary context Eichenlaub, Gabel, Jakubek, McCarthy, and Wang (2011) explored the use of iPads in libraries in Ryerson University, Canada, by lending them out to four students who were then encouraged to use the iPad throughout the semester. Each student was studying a different major, and the intention was to gauge usage and to have students themselves investigate the possible integration of apps in their courses. It was a very small-scale study (n=4) so results are not generalisable. The main finding in this project was that iPads are specifically designed as personal devices so any ideas for making iPads available as short-term library loan items was seen as problematic despite their current laptop loan programme being extremely popular. This study does, however, highlight the potential differences between iPads that are lent to students for a semester and those purchased for individual use. However, longer observations over an extended period of time could have produced quite different results. This would enable us to identify the extent to which the Hawthorne effect, in which novel stimulus can generate better performance (Brand et al., 2011), affected results.

All of these studies looked at native English language mainstream classes, which differ from our context. Also, these studies only focused on iPads as receptive devices, excluding the opportunities for content creation by users. This has left a gap that warrants further exploration as we believe this project embraced "good educational practice involving inquiry-based pedagogy with which students are engaging with real-world content" (Brand et al., 2011). Thus, our purpose was to ascertain student perceptions of the usefulness, or otherwise, of content creation and reading on the iPad.

4. Methodology

This action research study was conducted over a period of one academic semester with a cohort of students (n=18), who were asked to reflect on their experiences participating in the RDP. The RDP is a formative assessment that occurs over five (5) events during a three-month period, each event spaced equally throughout the semester. Thus, students reflected five times throughout the semester on their experiences and self-perceived performance.

All students in the class were asked to answer the survey as part of the self-reflective element of the project. Those students who chose to hand their answers in to the researcher, who was also their teacher, were given the opportunity to do so. All students chose to participate. To eliminate any bias that might affect grades students' reflections were anonymous and participants were actively dissuaded from providing their names.

The surveys contained two question types: Likert 4-point scales and open-ended questions. The latter allowed a wider range of responses. All questions aimed to collect attitudinal responses and were self-reported.

5. Findings and Results

The following section will look at the results of the post-discussion reflection survey. The findings have been divided into four categories.

(i) Student confidence

During self-reflection, students were prompted to indicate their personal levels of confidence prior to, and immediately following, the completion of the discussion. Students were asked to rank on a scale ranging from “very nervous”, “a little bit nervous”, “quite confident” to “very confident”. Prior to the first discussions, 15% of students self-reported feeling “very nervous”, 50% of students felt “a little bit nervous” and the remaining 35% thought they felt “quite confident”. Immediately following the leading of the discussions, students’ self-confidence appears to have improved with a noticeable shift toward the more confident end of the scale: 0% of students reported feeling “very nervous”; 15% were still “a little bit nervous”; 50% were “quite confident”; and 35% now felt “very confident” with their performance.

Three months after the first discussion the same reflections were conducted again. Confidence levels prior to the discussion had improved remarkably. All students had reported an improvement in their perceived level of self-confidence. 0% reported feeling “very nervous”, only 8% reported being “a little bit nervous”, and 92% considered themselves to be “quite confident” (42%) or “very confident” (50%). This shows a noteworthy shift in confidence levels of students in the class, with almost three times as many students perceiving an increase in confidence levels over the three-month period. Likewise, there was an increase in post-discussion confidence levels with 100% of students ranking themselves as “quite confident” (34%) or “very confident” (66%).

(ii) Value of student-created content

Students were asked to rate the RDP for its perceived usefulness value. The findings are itemised in the subsequent table.

The table clearly shows a positive trend increasing throughout the course of this study. The majority of all students deemed the discussions to be useful on all occasions with only a few minor exceptions. It would appear that students, on the whole, found it useful to create and deliver their own content to their peers. The reasons behind students regarding the discussions as "a waste of time" or "not useful", are outside the scope of this study, but are important areas for further investigation.

	RDP 1	RDP 2	RDP 3	RDP 4	RPD 5
A waste of time	0	5	0	0	0
Not useful	5	0	0	0	8
Useful	63	56	59	40	42
Very useful	32	39	41	60	50

Table 1. Student responses in % to the prompt "Today's discussions were..."

(iii) Selected topics

At the end of each event that included 3-5 discussions, students were asked which topic was of most interest to them. Topics had been self-selected on the proviso that there was an academic element to the content. From topics selected as being most interesting, there was a clear emphasis on two main topic areas: health and local interest. Local interest predominantly focused on traffic-related issues such as safety and congestion within the UAE. Discussions regarding health covered issues that are particular relevant to this region including, but not limited to, diabetes, heart disease and thalassaemia.

Of particular note to the researchers was the lack of what could be deemed more traditional age-appropriate female topic areas such as fashion and make-up. They were only mentioned on two occasions over the three-month course as being of most interest. This could demonstrate the division between personal interest and academic interest, but would require further exploration to ascertain the reason behind these topics being rarely selected for academic discussion.

(iv) Improvement in reading skills

As a measure of whether the students felt that their reading skills improved over the semester, the final RDP asked the students to record what they felt they had learnt from participating in the RDPs throughout the semester. 82% of the sample responded to the question, with almost half (44.5%) of these respondents recording a positive improvement in reading skills. With comments such as:

- I learn new words and new information about the role of the UAE.
- I learned about Diwali that is an Indian traditional event and also I learned about communication.
- I learn new voc and new information about reading and diabetes.

- I learned how to explain the idea to the people and organize it.
- I learned how to read articles and I liked all the articles topics.

There were several salient themes that emerged. A perceived increase in vocabulary featured consistently throughout the individual RDPs and also arose in the final survey. Vocabulary was one of the aspects of the iBook development part of the project, and was often overtly discussed so this is not surprising that students would feel that their vocabulary had increased. However, no tests were conducted to see if there was in fact an increase in vocabulary retention. Perhaps this perception of a larger vocabulary contributed towards students' improved self-confidence when discussing academic topics.

Another theme that surfaced was developing an understanding of the organisation of texts. Students were able to identify key organisational markers to pinpoint the main ideas and relevant supporting details of their articles. Enabling students to utilise the Vygotskyian zone of proximal development may have also contributed to the perceived value of creating individualised content for peers.

The final theme that stemmed from the comments collected was that of a broader world view and increased general knowledge base. Two thirds of students referred to having made personal improvements in their ability to express themselves in academic contexts. Just over 30% of these students commented on their engagement in all topic areas.

6. Conclusion

As a result of implementing this project, both reading skills and confidence levels of students improved during the semester. The project encouraged students to take ownership for creating and delivering their own content. This had a motivational effect further demonstrated in the quality of interactive iBooks produced. Students also discussed topics that they would perhaps not have engaged in prior, given their demographic. This is possibly due to parameters set by teachers to include academic, not social, topics and is an area for future consideration. Based on student reflections the RDP has been a highly valuable experience for learners. Thus, given the positive responses received, we intend to continue to include this project as a permanent part of the reading curriculum.

References

Brand, J., Kinash, S., Mathew, T., & Kyordyban, R. (2011). iWant does not equal iWill: Correlates of mobile learning with iPads, e-textbooks, BlackBoard Mobile Learn and a blended learning experience. In *Ascilite 2011 - Changing demands, changing directions*. (pp. 168-178). Hobart: Centre for the Advancement of Learning and Teaching, University of Tasmania.

Eichenlaub, N., Gabel, L., Jakubek, D., McCarthy, G., & Wang, W. (2011). Project iPad. *Computers in Libraries*, *31*(7), 17-22.

Gitsaki, C., & Robby, M. (2013). *iPad project implementation: Year 1 report*. Abu Dhabi: Higher Colleges of Technology.

Grace, K. E. (2011). *Comparing the ipad to paper: Increasing reading comprehension in the digital age* (Doctoral dissertation, Bowling Green State University).

Hargis, J., Cavanaugh, C., Kamali, T., & Soto, M. (2013). A federal higher education iPad mobile learning initiative: Triangulation of data to determine early effectiveness. *Journal of Innovative Higher Education*, *4*(1), 1-2.

Jennings, G, Anderson, T, Dorset, M., & Mitchell, J. (2011). Report of the step forward iPad pilot. Retrieved December 29, 2014 from http://goo.gl/XlrjQ3

Shepherd, I. J., & Reeves, B. (2011). iPad or iFad – The reality of a paperless classroom. Paper presented at the Mobility Conference, Abilene Christian University. Retrieved December 29, 2014 from http://goo.gl/fa2Qc

Sheppard, D. (2011). Reading with iPads – the difference makes a difference. *Education Today*, Term *3*, 12-15.

Stewart, S. (2012). *Reading in a technological world: Comparing the iPad to print* (Unpublished MA dissertation). Bowling Green State University, Ohio, USA. Retrieved December 30, 2014 from http://goo.gl/hC8gZF

iPADS AT THE UNIVERSITY OF WESTERN SYDNEY (UWS): INITIATING INSTITUTIONAL TRANSFORMATION

LYNNAE RANKINE[1]
AND DENNIS MACNAMARA[2]

Abstract

Universities across the globe are embracing the digital world in various forms. Massively open online courses, gamification, flipped classrooms, blended learning and tablet devices offer students the possibility of greater flexibility in how and when they learn, and the continuation of their learning throughout their life and careers. This paper describes the background and rationale for a three-year plan to blend all units and courses and the impact over 12,000 iPads had on transforming the University of Western Sydney (UWS). It includes the hows and whys of the iPad rollout and the impact of one of the largest such implementations in the higher education context. It focuses on the macro institutional ramifications, including pedagogy, professional development and professional practice as well as student learning. The paper seeks to highlight how the iPads are both a symbol and a device for organisation and curriculum transformation.

1. Introduction

Universities are under pressure to innovate and redesign their business to compete in a more global and digital marketplace for higher education that has intensified competition for students and student dollars. Universities not only feel under pressure to "move forward" to maintain market share, they also need to carve out a niche for themselves in a

[1] University of Western Sydney, Australia. Email: l.rankine@uws.edu.au
[2] University of Western Sydney, Australia. Email: d.macnamara@uws.edu.au

market that is increasingly diverse and open (Cutler 2013, Ernst & Young 2013; King 2011). UWS initiated a three year plan in 2012 to transform itself into a blended learning institution that extends the University's "commitment to widening student access to higher education and innovative approaches to curriculum delivery and blended learning will be a hallmark of our program offerings" (UWS Learning and Teaching Plan, 2012-2014). As part of that plan, the university also purchased iPads for all of its first-year students and all staff in 2013.

This paper describes the background and rationale for the three-year plan and the iPad purchase, progress on the implementation, key success factors, the impact on the institution as a whole and the likely future directions at UWS. It includes the hows and whys of the iPad rollout and the impact of one of the largest such implementations in the higher education context. It focuses on the macro institutional ramifications including pedagogy, professional development and professional practice as well as student learning. The paper seeks to highlight how the iPads are both a symbol and a device for organisation and curriculum transformation.

2. Institutional Context

UWS has six campuses situated in Australia's third largest economic region, serving its fastest growing population. UWS has over 40,000 students and up until 2012 teaching was mainly focused on traditional face-to-face campus lectures and tutorials. Many of the institution's full-time students were also juggling significant work or career duties as well as their studies.

In 2010 UWS embarked on a large survey of the student experience in using technology. Nearly all students had access to a range of technologies like personally-owned laptops and computer labs on campus, they were active in their use of technology for study, and rated themselves as technologically literate. However, student ownership and access to mobile technologies was low (5%), and their desire to use these technologies much higher (45%) (UWS Student Experience with Technology Report, 2010). This pointed to the need for:

- A greater use of technology in learning service delivery;
- More flexibility for students in terms of time and place of learning;
- The need to provide technology devices to students as less than 50% had a smartphone or tablet, thus reflecting the socio-economic dynamics of the catchment area of UWS).

During 2012 a radical three-year plan was embarked upon by the University to "blend" every unit of study on offer. The aim is to have all first-year units blended by 2014 and remaining units blended by 2016. Some schools decided to implement some form of blend during 2013. This was no small challenge. UWS has over 350 courses across nine schools representing more than 1600 units.

The University was deliberate in its blended learning strategy to offer the best of on-campus and online learning activities, rather than designing courses that were fully online. This required a blended approach to:

- Creating engaging on-campus classes and vibrant campus cultures;
- Developing accessible online learning materials synchronously and asynchronously;
- Designing learning activities that engaged with the local community;
- Offering both increasing and graduated opportunities for self-directed learning.

To undertake such a bold initiative UWS invested significant monies to: Employ fifty specialist learning design staff embedded mostly closely with academics in schools as well as a small central team (hub and spokes approach); relieve academics from some direct student-facing hours to work with the 50 specialists to redesign/reconfigure their units of study; greatly enhance the IT infrastructure of the institution, especially the wireless network; create new flexible and collaborative learning spaces on campus that are technology-enabled.

3. iPads as a Device for Institutional Transformation

When the iPad was launched by Apple in 2010 it was touted as "revolutionary" (Marx & James, 2010). This device enabled people to download and read books, and look at videos and images together using a vibrant touch screen. That same year, the Australia-New Zealand Horizon Report referred to the "promise of mobiles" in education because of the new ways devices like iPads offered people to connect, communicate, share and access tools for learning (Johnson, Smith, Levine & Haywood, 2010, p. 5). Fast forward two years, and it was predicted that over 665 million tablets would be in use (over 45% of these iPads) by 2016 (Lundren, 2012).

In 2012 at UWS there was a strong institutional focus on blended learning and resources to support the initiatives. Not every academic believed that designing blended learning units for first years by 2014 was really going to happen. The purchase of 14,000 iPads in December 2012 (closer to 30,000 over two years) prompted the response of "Wow, they must be serious". Every new first-year student starting a course in 2013 at UWS and all staff were to receive one. The time frame was extremely short but iPads were in everyone's hands by February 2013. Most of the angst and complaints were around "when will I get mine?" and "what about me?" for anyone who missed out.

There were a number of key success factors driving the potential for a whole-of-institution transformation including: whole-of-university approach, whole-of-student body approach, using practitioners as collegial change agents, multi-tiered approaches to professional development and campus enlivenment (Dawson 2001; Garrison & Anderson, 2003; Scott, 1999; 2008). These changes occurred both at the visible and invisible dimensions of organisational culture (McDermott & Dell, 2001).

4. Whole-of-University Approach

In previous years there had been pockets of elearning initiatives across the University, mostly based on organisational support for enthusiastic staff. This time the blended learning thrust was for all. At the same time, iPads were provided for all full-time academic staff, all first-year students attending UWS for the first time, and gradually iPad pools were established for sessional staff.

The rollout of iPads at rapid speed in January 2013 involved teams of staff from all parts of the university including marketing, student support, academics, security, IT, senior management, policy section, academic registrars units and external consultants such as logistics and device suppliers, including Apple itself. At one meeting held in December 2012 there were about 30 university staff and 15 Apple staff engaged in detailed planning for the rollout. It was necessary for everyone to work closely together to ensure a smooth front-end student and staff experience. This was especially important for staff that were to receive their devices at the same time or even after the students and only weeks before the semester commenced. Many of the UWS team members did not even know each other before the iPad rollout commenced.

The collaborative university-wide teamwork ensured a rollout that was much smoother than anyone could have imagined. Leading the rollout were executives from the university and from Apple and three distinct delivery teams: pedagogy, technology and distribution. The scale of this operation created challenges in the shipment management to campus as well as the management of individual devices.

5. Whole-of-Student Body Approach

Giving all first years a device gave teachers a "licence to thrill". In other words, they had a reason to engage with their students digitally. There were small numbers of students in most classes without iPads (for example, second-year students doing a first-year unit, or repeating students), but in the main this particular cohort of students had alternative devices. So while academics tried to be device-neutral they could at least assume a mobile device. The ubiquity of the devices also drove student behaviour. Anecdotally they spent more time on campus, and early statistics indicated they stayed connected to their course content more frequently.

A series of student events around the iPad collection were organised on different campuses that created a vibrant atmosphere where students and family members came on campus to receive their new device and meet some of the teaching staff. Not only was the distribution of iPads to students symbolic for the university in its commitment to technology-enabled learning experiences, but also it was symbolic for students and families as they were using new technology that they may not otherwise have been able to own.

6. Practitioners as Collegial Change Agents

At a very early stage, the University set up a significant number of staff as key reference points for both blended learning in general and iPads in particular, variously known as "blended learning exemplars" and iPad champions referred to as iPALS (iPad Peer Assisted Learner Supports). There were more than sixty of these in total, who were inculcated into iPad usage for learning through a series of workshops.

The workshops involved a myriad of internal presentations, how-to sessions led by Apple and invited guest speakers, who were already "well-travelled" in the use of iPads in their teaching. Reunion sessions followed during the course of the year to reconnect iPALS and share developments and experiences. Exemplars and case studies have been developed to profile the diverse ways iPads are used at UWS. While iPads are proving to be useful in helping students to feel more confident in their learning, and enabling academics a level of creativity and exploration in designing learning experiences for students, they enable "movement, circulation and close up interactions" and the academic does not need to devote their time and energy to the front of the room to "present" or "lecture" (Morrone, Gosney & Engel, 2012).

7. Multi-Tiered Professional Development

A multi-campus network requires a multi-tiered approach to professional development. Recognising the diversity amongst UWS staff in skills and knowledge in using iPads in teaching, a framework was used to categorise professional development experiences across levels of acquiring, developing and extending.

The centralised team to the whole of institution provided a blend of face-to-face sessions, webinars and fully online course materials. Customised professional development targeted school- or discipline-specific areas and niche areas of interest. Using iPads in various teaching and learning contexts, for example, mind mapping, digital storytelling, accessibility and annotating, were integrated within the whole-of-institution professional development programme for blended learning. A diverse approach to professional development was needed to target early adopters and enthusiasts along with the mainstream academics (Rogers, 1995; Liu, 2012). Adding to the diversity of the whole-of-university approach were monthly blended learning forums. The forums were held on different campuses and featured presenters from all Schools and different departments to share experiences and perspectives in designing for blended learning. They were designed to share experiences in terms of successes and lessons learned, showcase innovations and discuss issues that were relevant to designing learning in higher education. Presenters at the forums included academic staff, professional staff involved in supporting blended learning that are located within schools and in organisational departments. The importance and influence of communities of practice assist with the diffusion of innovation across the University (Rogers, 1995).

8. Enlivening on-Campus Life

It is well established that the disruptiveness of the Internet for businesses that rely on the sale of information is affecting universities across the globe. Increasing prevalence of open and free online education is changing the tertiary landscape, and bricks and mortar institutions such as UWS have advantages over fully online delivery of courses because of a vibrant on-campus life and experience for students (Mazouse, 2013; Harden, 2013). Wireless-enabled learning spaces that are equipped with technology and enable students to plug in their own devices are being cultivated across campuses, and traditional learning spaces like lecture theatres are being redesigned to be more collaborative and flexible spaces where the academics and the students are not “tied” to a single location, either the lectern or the table. Lectures are increasingly using response systems to receive prompt feedback from students and engage even the more quiet students in class discussions. The use of iPads has brought a new level of campus experience into the fray; for example, using augmented reality around landmarks and facilities on campus, or at discipline-related site visits to encourage students to be explorers and discoverers.

9. Conclusion and Future Directions

The University does not seek to be device- or technology-focused per se. The main blended learning thrust is learning design/curriculum design-centric. Nevertheless, the iPad device did sharpen everyone’s focus and drove a whole-of-institution approach. While the iPad did have the potential to push the organisation off track or off message, the introduction of iPads within the blended learning framework and within the context of the introduction of fifty learning design specialists embedded with academics within the schools meant that it in fact enhanced the overall blended learning direction.

In 2014 the blending of all units at UWS will continue with second-year units included in the mix plus those units redesigned in 2013. At the same time another 12,000 iPads will be rolled out to the next batch of first years and last year’s first years are about to move into second year, with unit academics teaching to students with iPads for the first time. The challenges are expected to continue for staff and the university into 2014.

There were a number of lessons learnt in 2013 that can be applied in 2014 and beyond, including:

- The need to make it easier for schools to purchase peripherals and mobile applications to make best use of the devices;
- The need to sharpen the focus on initial learning design of units;
- The need to better consider the assessment of units as an upfront issue;
- The need to retune the balance between personification of materials and re-use of learning objects;
- The need to balance guidelines and standards for consistency and creativity;
- The need to more actively engage with sessional staff.

During 2013 a research and evaluation framework was implemented and data collection commenced. This evaluation is being conducted at both a whole-of-institution basis and at local programme levels. Data emerging from this work will inform future blended learning design and assist with fine-tuning of learning services for units already redesigned.

However, a number of key "learnings" for the future have come out of the work so far including:

1. The value of fostering a teamwork approach across academic teams and academic and professional staff teams. Blending staff as well as blending units seems obvious perhaps.
2. The "hub and spokes" model for allocated specialist learning design staff has worked well, but is a portent of a future distributed model of decision making and support. An institution offering flexible agile services itself must be internally agile. A small central core setting standards and guidelines and providing overall support must become comfortable with less control over day-to-day decision making. Putting iPads in hands has hastened this approach.
3. Significant change management can occur and be well received if key elements are put in place. These include:

- Supporting change with significant resources;
- Rewarding staff who engage with the change process;
- Being consistent with central message and direction of change;
- Explaining the rationale of the change.

At UWS iPads have been both a symbol of and a device or agent for the transformation of the institution to a blended learning future. Stage one has been successfully accomplished. This paper should be seen as no more than a progress report.

References

Cutler, T. (2013). Embracing the future: Innovation and higher education. In *National University Finance and Procurement Conference*. Sydney, Australia: Higher Ed Services.

Dawson, P. (2001). Organisational change. In R. Wiesner & B. Millett, (Eds.) *Management and organisational behaviour: Contemporary challenges and future directions* (Chapter 18, pp. 211-223). Milton, Queensland: John Wiley.

Ernst and Young (2013). *The university of the future.* Retricved December 29, 2014, from http://goo.gl/Bfme0

Garrison, D. R., & Anderson T. (2003). *Elearning in the 21st century: A framework for research and practice*. London: Routledge-Falmer.

Harden, N. (2013). The end of the university as we know it. *The American Interest, 8*(3). Retrieved December 29, 2014 from http://goo.gl/LMnXCV

Johnson, L., Smith, R., Levine, A., & Haywood, K. (2010). *The 2010 horizon report: Australia – New Zealand edition.* Austin, Texas: The New Media Consortium.

King, C. (2011, March 30). Furore over open market. *The Australian.* Retrieved December 30, 2013 from http://goo.gl/a7Edkf

Liu, F., Cavanaugh, C., & Ritzhaupt, A.D. (2013). Leaders of school technology innovation: A confirmatory factor analysis of the change facilitator style questionnaire (CFSQ). *Journal of Educational Administration*, *51*(5), 576-593.

Lundren, I. (2012). Apple of our eye. *TechCrunch.* Retrieved December 29, 2014 from http://goo.gl/tS5YS

Marx, J., James, J. (2010). Apple launches iPad. Retrieved December 29, 2014 from http://goo.gl/mfEU25

Mazoue, G.J. (2013). The MOOC model: Challenging traditional education. *Education Review Online*. Jan/Feb 2013

McDermott, R., O'Dell, C. (2001). Overcoming cultural barriers to sharing knowledge. *Journal of Knowledge Management*, *5*(1) 76-85.

Morrone, A., Gosney, J., & Engel, S. (2012). Empowering students and instructors: reflections on the effectiveness of iPads for teaching and learning. *Educause Review,* April 2012.

Rogers, E. M. (1995). *Diffusion of innovations* (4th ed.). New York: Free Press.

Scott, G., Coates, H., & Anderson, M. (2008). Learning leadership in times of change: Academic leadership capabilities for Australian higher education. *Higher Education Research*. Paper 3. Retrieved December 29, 2014 from http://goo.gl/4UlHyf

Scott, G. (1999). *Change matters: Making a difference in education and training*. Sydney: Allen & Unwin.

iPad Use in Fieldwork: Formal and Informal Use to Enhance Pedagogical Practice in a Bring Your Own Technology World

Brian W. Whalley[1], Derek France[2], Julian R. Park[3], Alice L. Mauchline[4], Victoria Powell[5] and Katharine Welsh[6]

Abstract

We report on the use of iPads and other iOS devices for student fieldwork and as electronic field notebooks and to promote active learning. We have used questionnaires and interviews of tutors and students to elicit their views on technology and iPad use for fieldwork. There is some reluctance for academic staff to relinquish paper notebooks for iPad use, whether in the classroom or on fieldwork, as well as use them for observational and measurement purposes. Students too are largely unaware of the potential of iPads for enhancing fieldwork. Apps can be configured for a wide variety of specific uses that make iPads useful for educational as well as social uses. Such abilities should be used to enhance existing practice as well as make new functionality. For example, for disabled students who find it difficult to use conventional note taking, iPads can be used to develop student self-directed learning and for group contributions. The technology becomes part of the students' personal learning environments as well as at the heart of their knowledge spaces – academic and social.

[1] University of Sheffield, UK. Email: b.whalley@sheffield.ac.uk
[2] University of Chester, UK. Email: d.france@chester.ac.uk
[3] University of Reading, UK. Email: j.r.park@reading.ac.uk
[4] University of Reading, UK. Email: a.l.mauchline@reading.ac.uk
[5] University of Chester, UK. Email: v.powell@chester.ac.uk
[6] University of Chester, UK. Email: k.welsh@chester.ac.uk

This blurring of boundaries is due to iPads' usability to cultivate field use, instruction, assessment and feedback processes. iPads can become field microscopes and entries to citizen science, and we see the iPad as the main "computing" device for students in the near future. As part of the Bring Your Own Device (BYOD) the iPad has much to offer, although both staff and students need to be guided in the most effective use for self-directed education via development of Personal Learning Environments. A more student-oriented pedagogy is suggested to correspond to the increasing use of tablet technologies by students.

1. Introduction

Fieldwork is undertaken in many academic areas; anthropology, biology, geography and geology are obvious fields. Fieldwork may be for a day or for protracted periods of weeks or even months away from "base". A field notebook is traditionally used for this purpose, typically being some form of paper-leaved and bound "notebook". Classic examples are those of Charles Darwin (darwin-online.org.uk/EditorialIntroductions/ Chancellor_field Notebooks.html). Laboratory and theoretical scientists also use such notebooks (for example, Enrico Fermi, www.lib.uchicago. edu/e/ spcl/centcat/fac/fac_img54.html). Indeed, many other areas of investigation use notebooks to record events as an integral part of investigations; journalists, police, social workers and their case notes are other examples. Some of these notes may be used forensically and thus require special treatment of ownership; date, times and locations for example.

Students, in progressing from novice to expert status or accredited practitioner, will almost certainly need training and experience in the compilation and use of notebooks. In geology, for example, field observation is a necessary skill in mapping and the production of a map. A citation for the Oxford Geology Group's Field Notebook competition (oxgg.org.uk/competitions/field-notebook-competition/) suggests that:

> A geologist's field notebook is analogous to the wizard's wand – it is indispensable. Geologists maintain them to keep track of projects, to note interesting geologic features, and as an aide-mémoire. A notebook has the potential for many alternative uses; as a scale for photographs, a weather shield for your head, a swat for midges and most importantly as a vade mecum for the next time you find yourself yomping the same terrain. The Oxford Geology Group Field Notebook Competition (J. M. Edmond's Cup) recognises the importance of a well-kept notebook and aims to promote this aspect of good field practice.

Indeed, a notebook, acting not only as a memory jog but as a virtual revisit, is another view of a notebook. The fragility and fickleness of human memory is well known as well as vision in the "gorilla experiment" where events are not seen because of distraction (Chabris & Simons, 2010). Similarly, students need to be trained in making observations, to know what is important for particular purposes, in geology and other "field sciences". We report here on how iPads can enhance the fieldwork experience for students in a variety of ways, but also show how these devices can further improve investigations and research for all practitioners and beyond fieldwork within pedagogic frameworks. For example, electronic notebooks based on iPads can be used to record date-stamped still and video images directly.

The usefulness of computers for processing student-recorded field data goes at least as far back as "Computers and the field class" by Gardiner and Unwin (1986). The introduction of the iPad in 2010 makes computer use in the field possible. Our project on Enhancing Fieldwork Learning (www.enhancingfieldwork.org.uk) has investigated ways in which iPads are enhancing student experience as well as providing a knowledge base for professional use of iPads. As far as possible we avoid naming specific apps, not only as we do not wish to endorse particular products but because our investigations have applicability for tablet devices other than iPads and Apple's iOS.

As individuals and institutions have taken up iPads, there has been considerable promotion of specific apps that can be used, in our case, for fieldwork. We have shown students and tutors how iPads can be used as meaningful computers in the field and are not just expensive toys. Tutors may take as much convincing as students that iPads can offer more than field notebooks via the affordances of apps. We report on views of iPads and apps in terms of usability, student experiences and questionnaire responses to use and barriers to use. We use the integrating concept of the Personal Learning Environment to look in general terms how educational experiences for students can be enhanced by tablet technologies.

2. Methods and Data Collection

The paper investigates usability of iPads as devices for collection of field data. It works within a basic framework (Figure 1) of usability, and employs responses from a questionnaire to fieldwork practitioners about their use (or not) of technology in student fieldwork. It also views envisaged barriers to using technology, and how students use iPads in practice in the field. Our procedure has been interventionist, by introducing students to iPads in a variety of subject areas, group sizes and locations. The students were almost always using iPads from our project; only rarely did students use their own iPads, although there was some use of "smartphones" (iPhones etc.). We collected students' responses about use and usability by questionnaires. Tutors on the field classes were "early adopters" and showed students the use of appropriate apps for specific purposes.

3. The iPad as a Field Notebook: Facilities and Usability

The model (Figure 1) after Koole (2009) is a useful way of viewing interactions between device, user and social aspects for mobile devices.

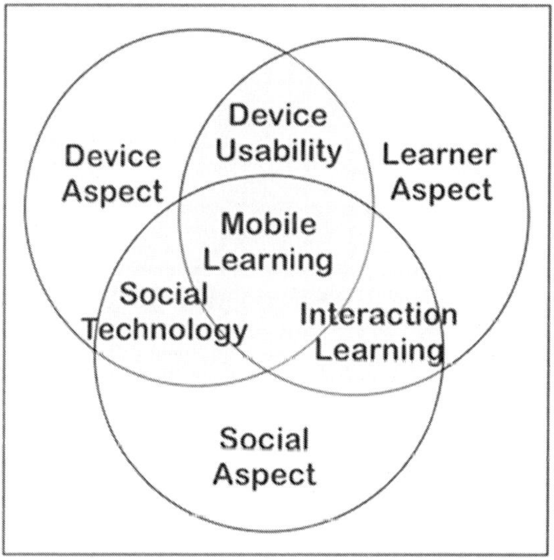

Figure 1. The FRAME model, after Koole (2009), illustrates the potential overlaps of Device, Learning and Social aspects of mobile device use. These apply in general to field use as well as for student learning

The hardware attributes of tablet and smartphone device use, when coupled to their purpose and usability makes it possible to choose the most effective application (app) for particular functions within the areas depicted by Figure 1. The framework is developed on a good psychological basis, involving learner prior knowledge, memory, context and transfer, discovery learning and emotions and motivations (Koole, 2009, Table 2). The three overlapping fields of, Device, Learner Aspect and Social Aspect should operate within a knowledge space of information context and requirement. What these requirements will be may depend upon the subject area and detailed topic and use. Nevertheless, the wide variety of apps already available (and seemingly in ever-increasing numbers) can be viewed within the domains of Figure 1, whether from professional, instructor, or student remits. The pricing structure of apps means that sophisticated, yet workable, apps can be obtained free or at a small cost. Most notably, we have found that some apps may have uses beyond their original, intended audience. Indeed, students may be willing to experiment and find suitable apps to help solve specific problems. At present, in the main it is tutors who make suggestions and recommendations for the use of specific apps in tablet devices.

The FRAME model of Figure 1 is similar visually to the TPCK (Technology, Pedagogy, Content Knowledge) model (Puentedura, 2009). It is one of the aims of our project to include a suitable pedagogic grounding for the use of tablets and apps in fieldwork education.

The first question on usability is practical: "What do you do when it rains?" The answer is, "Put it in a polythene bag". This is actually easier to use than a paper notebook as students can type or draw on the polythene from outside. Specialised waterproof covers can be obtained, and this makes a suitably encased (but bulkier) iPad for note taking in water-proximity situations. iPads will work in extreme fieldwork conditions, for example in very cold conditions where it may be difficult to use a pencil but typing is possible. However, bright sunshine may reduce readability of the screen. For some students with disabilities an iPad may be much easier to use than a conventional notebook, especially if audio recording is used. This usability is the main advantage over a laptop in the field as well as a conventional notebook.

As well as still and video image capture through on-board cameras it is possible to attach devices via wireless/Bluetooth. A field microscope can be shared between large numbers of students and still/video images can again be shared between notebooks and reports. This is difficult for conventional paper notebooks. Field evidence (perhaps with time, data and GPS location) from a tablet's camera can be pasted into a report note directly.

Screen size on the "standard" iPad with "retina" display is about the same as an A5 printed page but the iPad "Mini" has the advantages of being able to pocket the device and is lighter in weight. Although most iPad apps can be used on iPhone (or iPod touch), the screen size of the iPad has benefits for both viewing and writing. Battery life is increasingly improved, and will certainly manage a normal working day of continuous use. Photovoltaic power supplies can be used for remote situations, and rarely will a generator be necessary for recharging.

The basic notebook function can be facilitated by the basic iPad, although Wi-Fi and 3-4G (and Long term Evolution, LTE) connectivity can be useful for backing up information (via the cloud), providing GPS locations and downloading new resources as well as sharing information. Sharing data is frequently a necessity when fieldwork is done in groups. iPads make this possible in the field rather than subsequently exchanging paper-recorded data.

iPads for fieldwork activities tend to be used in groups of 4-5 students. This is mainly a matter of cost and that the majority of students, as yet, do now own their own tablets (although most now use their own mobile "smartphones"). Until shown how apps can benefit their (fieldwork) learning, iPads tend to be viewed as leisure devices for the consumption of media. This applies to tutors as much as students.

4. Examples of iPad Use for Fieldwork Learning Environments

Fieldwork learning can be enhanced by technology, and we know this from students' perspectives (Welsh, Mauchline, Park, Whalley, & France, 2013). We now suggest a few ways to illustrate how this can be done. For brevity, we list below a number of activities that can be accomplished under the general heading of "fieldwork" that provide students with educational experiences and where the use of tablet computers can assist.

4.1 Pre-Fieldwork Preparation

Visualisation of the field site
Explanation of field methods/use of equipment
Explanation of use of field notebooks

4.2 During Fieldwork Capture of Site Context/Sense of Place/Visualisation

Digital storytelling
Vidcasting
Reflective diaries (Evernote)

Familiarisation of place
Geotagging photographs using smartphones (Welsh et al., 2012)
Visualisation of landscape
Podcasting to support student learning
Using video during fieldwork
Using augmented reality for examining new locations or in poster presentations

4.3 Post-Fieldwork Revision/Reflection/Presentations

Access to literature/teaching materials/online resources while in the field
Data management issues in the field
Speed, amount and accuracy of data collection
Storage, security and future access to data
Data collation and analysis
Data sharing

The list shows aspects that are both formal and informal. Note needs to be taken of the way assessment is undertaken for student activities. For example, examination and essays do not align well with experiential education such as fieldwork. Conversely, presenting findings in reports and integrating with digital literacies follow from fieldwork experiences and are also aspects of "employability" (Yorke & Knight, 2007). Fieldwork tasks and immediate reporting of results, even in the field, allow rapid feedback to students on tasks set.

5. Expectations of and Barriers to Field Technology

Although smartphones are becoming more affordable and ubiquitous (Melhuish & Falloon, 2010) a recent study of undergraduate students (Woodcock et al., 2012) found that many who own smartphones were largely unaware of their potential for their own education.

In order to assess the current level of technology being used on field courses, a questionnaire was developed on Survey Monkey (www.surveymonkey.com). Both qualitative and quantitative data and a range of question types were used, including closed multiple choice and Likert scale questions for comparison with earlier research by Fletcher et al. (2007) and open-ended questions, which give the opportunity for participants to share their experiences. Principally, UK higher education practitioners/tutors in biosciences, geography, earth and environmental sciences were targeted. The survey was open to anyone who participated in fieldwork; therefore some responses were obtained from archaeologists, anthropologists and secondary school teachers. The survey had questions which focused on technology used in fieldwork, and why the technology was introduced (if at all) to the fieldwork. Table 1 shows selected responses from this survey relating to reasons for using "technology" in the field. Note that this includes technology as a whole rather than iPads per se. In practice, and despite the practicabilities of modern technologies, there seems to be a rather low uptake of computers for field use or even desire to use technology in the field. Computers may be used after a fieldwork element, to process data and write reports are typical examples. Our survey also showed that technology was not used much in the field, but mainly during the post-fieldwork phase where desktop and laptop computers were mainly used. Pre-fieldwork and field centre technology was again mainly computer usage. This is because of power consumption of laptops as well as impracticality in the field. Some in the field technologies used were portable, such as digital cameras (73), GPS (52), laptops (31), phones (27) and smartphones (20).

Pedagogic reasons for introducing technology	**Frequency**	**Proportion of practitioners (n=76)**
Data processing: - faster/easier data collection (therefore greater amount) - data storage in the field - data security & future access - data analysis in the field - data sharing in the field - greater accuracy in data recording	(Σ=48) 22 2 3 13 5 3	63.2% 28.9% 2.6% 3.9% 17.1% 6.6% 3.9%
Skill development: - development of general ICT skills - development of subject-specific skills using specialist field technologies/equipment e.g. GPS - learning up-to-date methods - development of employability skills - dynamic, multi-mode, hands-on learning - enable students to evaluate pros/cons of different methods	(Σ=37) 9 8 7 8 3 2	48.7% 11.8% 10.5% 9.2% 10.5% 3.9% 2.6%

Post-fieldwork revision/reflection/reporting	9	11.8%
Enhancing the learning experience	8	10.5%
Facilitate communication - between students in the field - between different countries/places - contact between field and "base" - for safety	(Σ=8) 1 3 1 3	10.5% 1.3% 3.9% 1.3% 3.9%

Table 1. The main reasons for introducing technology to fieldwork Practitioners often responded to the open question with more than one reason (total responses =146), 81% were from the UK

Table 2 provides more detail from the participant/tutor survey as to the barriers perceived as difficulties with tablet technology. Since this general survey, the iPad allows most of these attributes in Table 1 to be practised in the field. iPads have major usability advantages over laptops in the physical attributes mentioned above, especially by virtue of their size, power consumption and general capabilities.

Barriers	Frequency (total = 168)	Proportion of practitioners (n=79)
Cost - general - availability of kit/cost to buy & maintain kit - risk of losing/damaging equipment - high roaming charge for smartphones - insurance of kit	 24 19 6 1 3	 30.4% 24.1% 7.6% 1.3% 3.8%
Reliability of kit/durability in rugged conditions	17	21.5%

Staff competence/confidence/imagination	16	20.3%
Student concerns - reluctance/competence of students - reluctance to use own equipment - don't all have same phones/devices - need simplified software/interface	 10 1 1 1	 12.7% 1.3% 1.3% 1.3%
Staff preparation time/keeping up to date with technology	10	12.7%
Power supply/battery life	10	12.7%
Practicality/portability of some devices	9	11.4%
Web access at field centre/in the field (inc. costs)	8	10.1%
Technology doesn't seem useful/just don't need it	4	5.1%
Unreliable/Need technical support when problems arise	4	5.1%
Shipment abroad (inc. costs)	4	5.1%
Need to teach the fundamentals behind the process	3	3.8%
Gadgets can be a distraction to the students	3	3.8%
Screen readability of gadgets	3	3.8%
Lack of institutional support/poor IT infrastructure	3	3.8%
Access to technology for large groups at field centre	2	2.5%
Unwelcomed by interviewees	1	1.3%
Mobile phone coverage	1	1.3%
None	4	5.1%

Table 2. Possible barriers to the use of technology in fieldwork. Practitioners often responded to the open question with more than one barrier (total responses =168)

Table 2 highlights two main types of barrier to using technology in fieldwork. First, physical impediments such as cost and durability were deemed significant. Secondly, human perceptions of technology were considered important. This applied to both undergraduates and students, with low levels of digital literacy deemed to be a barrier. The cost is a decreasing inhibitor, especially if students are likely to bring their own devices.

6. Student Experiences on Field Trips

The project has used iPads (series 2) to improve and extend the use of technology to aid participation and effectiveness in fieldwork. Undergraduates are generally working in small groups (4-5) in the field. We supplied one iPad per group for fieldwork sessions of 4-6 days in the UK, Italy and New York with both physical and human geography modules and in Iceland with international students on a biology field course. The FRAME model (Figure 1) shows where mobile devices such as the iPad can fit within the range of requirements of Table 1.

Although there were concerns that the equipment might get broken (which did not happen); the students' feedback was very positive. One student summed up the experience: "The iPad was exceptionally useful for the fieldwork; instant note-taking; recording and manipulating data instantly." Another noted that "the tablet, brings together several useful applications in one place, for example, GPS, photo/video/Internet, so we don't need 3-4 pieces of equipment."

In practice, we have had to show how iPads can be used educationally in the field, for recording data as well as using them to record short videos of their activities, as in digital storytelling (France & Wakefield, 2011). Students may have to be shown how to use a clinometer app and thence more complex geological recording and subsequent incorporation of field data into a digital notebook. However, once the principles are illustrated students themselves as a means of problem-solving in general can explore the usability features of iPads. Data recording and analysis is also easy to achieve. Although sharing is easy it would be useful for each student to have their own device and be familiar with them before going into the field.

7. Generalising Learning Experiences

We have taken the view that fieldwork (as indeed other out of classroom activities such as work in archives or laboratory) benefits students by presenting them with experiential opportunities for their education. Tablets, such as the iPad, allow them to take full advantage of truly personalised computing. Table 1 shows some of these educational attributes that could be used widely for a range of academic disciplines. Figure 2 suggests that these attributes can be placed within an educational or pedagogic framework. Moreover, it is a structure that centres on learning activities. Fieldwork clearly provides one such activity although laboratory work is often an extension of fieldwork as well as an independent activity.

Our fieldwork experience shows that students, once directed to specific apps, quickly become enthusiastic users of iPads. This enthusiasm could be taken to classroom/lecture theatre activities if students possessed their own devices. However, lecturers/tutors need to be prepared to use them for experiential education.

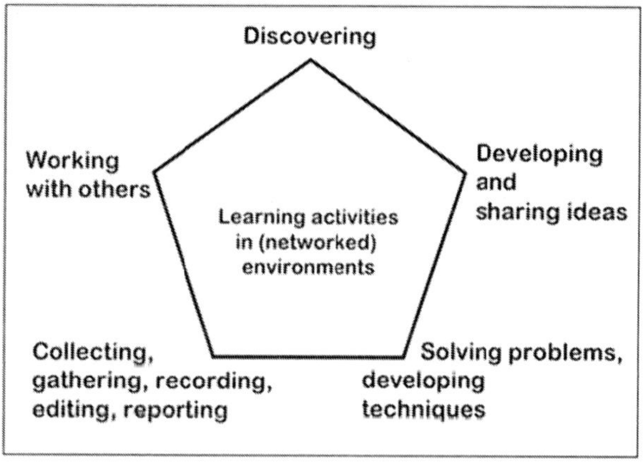

Figure 2. Five types of learning activity after Beetham (2013)

We would relate the activities and circumstances in fieldwork (or any out-of-classroom activity) that can be accomplished by the use of tablets such as iPads to Figure 2. We do not necessarily require networked activity for these activities. Communication can be asynchronous, according to local conditions and connectivity. The "reporting" (that is, communicating and writing notebooks) aspect has also been added to Beetham's (2013) schema as we view that, especially in fieldwork, this is an important activity for students.

It is important that students benefit from iPad and Cloud technologies, because they are simple devices and concepts in practice, but can be used to help solve difficult questions. However, for any problem-solving approach, students need to be guided initially, not just in the field, but by tutors in designing meaningful questions and structures for investigation.

Figure 2 is a generalised example of structures to enable this. Further support for design practices has, amongst others, been suggested by Agostinho et al. (2013). We suggest that appropriate learning designs should be used in all forms of education to enhance student capabilities from novice to expert. iPads can assist this progress greatly but staff involvement is most important rather than students following a few early adopters (Welsh & France, 2012). In general, mobile technologies "are increasingly a user's first choice for Internet access (L. Johnson, et al., 2012). However, the gap of "Moore's Chasm" in technology uptake between early adopters and early majority of users (Ebner et al., 2007) needs to be tackled.

8. Personal Learning Environments and Personal Learning Networks

We define a Personal Learning Environment (PLE) simply as a location where a learner happens to be. We include anyone who is learning about something, whether expert or novice. Thus, "learners" will be moving within educational spaces as in Figure 3. Any activity, not just fieldwork, can be incorporated within this framework. Addition of an iPad, as a vade mecum, enhances the educational environment for students.

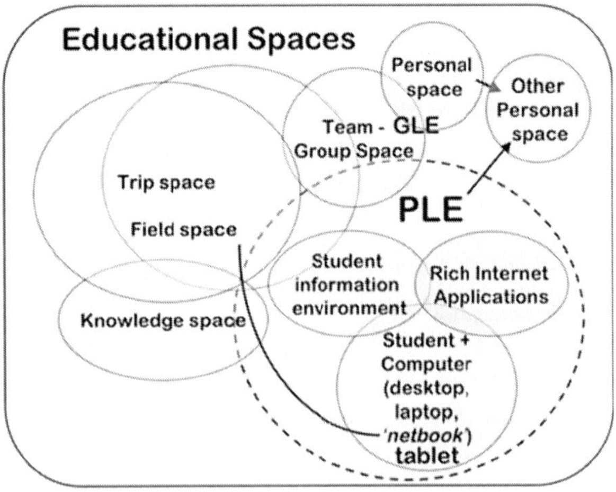

Figure 3. A generalised view of the domains in which personal learning environments (PLE) may exist

Different PLEs can be configured for various situations and incorporate appropriate workflows. For fieldwork, "desktop, laptop, netbook" computing power can now be substantially replaced by "tablet computing", and "Rich Internet Applications" can include apps as much as web-located facilities.

The implications of using iPads and smartphones within the domains of Figures 1, 2 and 3 can now be viewed as the ability for anyone to use these versatile devices. That they are versatile, for smartphones e.g Welsh and France (2012) and iPads (Bedall-Hill, et al., 2011) is now well established. We suspect students will soon buy their own tablets for leisure and social activities, possibly as well as smartphones. How well these will be supported by institutions, especially in terms of Wi-Fi provision, remains to be seen. Importantly, students are likely to be purchasing them for educational purposes as well as social, as they maximise the advantages of cheapness, usability and adaptation to a wide variety of requirements (Figure 1). As such, students will increasingly be prepared to Bring Their Own Devices (BYOD), not only for fieldwork, but as replacements for bigger, less convenient laptops with a shorter battery life and so on. The BYOD movement is already gaining pace in education (Johnson, 2012) with specific calls for tablet usage (Thirvathukal, 2013). Educators, at all levels, need to be aware of designing educational materials with this in mind.

9. Conclusion

Our experience is that students, whether they have used iPads before or not, readily appreciate the use of tablet computers in the field to help record data, images and audio and to use these assets in a meaningful way to present reports via some form of field notebook. That such devices and attributes can be used under difficult field-based situations promotes tablet use under a wide variety of personal learning environments. These student experiences promote reaching the digital shoreline (McHaney, 2011). On the way, they will learn new skills about dealing with the digital world on their own account by integrating their own learning experiences. Not least is the importance of understanding the nature of knowledge and the importance of digital literacies (Hess & Ostrom, 2011). We believe that the ease of use of iPads and software (apps) will make them increasingly common in everyday use and thus as part of education and subsequent employment via the Bring Your Own Device/Technology (BYOD) movements, especially as prices fall (Welsh, et al., 2011). Integrating this involvement is necessary on a day-to-day basis by educators. In particular, learning activities and tasks need to be brought into play in designing better educational experiences for students, as students themselves will be using tablet technologies to their advantage.

References

Agostinho, S., Bennett, S., Lockyer, L., Jones, J., & Harper, B. (2013). Learning designs as a stimulus and support for teachers' design practices. In H. Beetham & R. Sharpe (Eds.), *Rethinking pedagogy for a digital age* (2nd ed.), (pp. 119-132). New York, London: Routledge.

Bedall-Hill, N., Jabbar, A., & Al Sheri, S. (2011). Social mobile devices as tools for qualitative research in education: iPhones and iPads in ethnography, interviewing, and design-based research. *Journal of the Research Centre for Educational Technology*, *7*(1), 67-89.

Beetham, H. (2013). Designing for active learning in technology-rich contexts. In H. Beetham & R. Sharpe (Eds.), *Rethinking pedagogy for a digital age* (2nd ed.), (pp. 31-48). New York and London: Routledge.

Chabris, C., & Simons, D. (2010). *The invisible gorilla, and other ways our intuition deceives us*. London: Harper Collins.

Ebner, M., Holzinger, A., & Maurer. H. (2007). Web 2.0 technology: Future interfaces for technology enhanced learning?, In C. Stephanidis (Ed.), *Universal access in human-computer interaction. Applications and services* (pp. 559-568). Berlin: Springer.

Fletcher, S., France, D., Moore, K., & Robinson, G. (2007). Putting technology into fieldwork education: A pedagogic evaluation. *Journal of Geography in Higher Education*, *31*(2), 319-330.

France, D., & Wakefield, K. (2011). How to produce a digital story. *Journal of Geography in Higher Education*, *35*(4), 617-623.

Gardiner, V., & Unwin. D. J. (1986). Computers and the field class. *Journal of Geography in Higher Education,10*(2), 169-179.

Hess, C., & Ostrom, E. (Eds.). (2011). *Understanding knowledge as a commons: From theory to practice*. Cambridge, MA: MIT Press.

Johnson, D. (2012). On board with BYOD. *Educational Leadership*, *70*(2), 84-85.

Johnson, L., Adams, S., & Cummins, M. (2012). *The NMC horizon report: 2012 Higher Education edition*. Austin, TX: The New Media Consortium.

Koole, M.L. (2009). A model for framing mobile learning. In M. Ally (Ed.), *Mobile learning: Transforming the delivery of education and training* (pp. 25-47). Edmonton, Canada: AU Press.

McHaney, R. (2011). *The new digital shoreline*. Sterling, VA: Stylus.

Melhuish, M., & Falloon, G. (2010). Looking to the future: M-learning with the iPad. *Computers in New Zealand Schools: Learning, Leading, Technology*, *22*(3), 22(3), 1-16.

Puentedura, R. R. (2009). SAMR and TPCK: intro to advanced practice. As we may teach. Retrieved December 29, 2014 from: http://goo.gl/eeUHtc

Thiruvathukal, G. K. (2013). Who needs tablets? We do. *Computing in Science & Engineering 15*(1), 4-6.

Welsh, K. E., & France, D. (2012). Smartphones and fieldwork. *Geography*, *97*(1), 45-51.

Welsh, K. E., France, D., Park, J. R., & Whalley, W. B. (2011). Technology in fieldwork: It doesn't have to cost the earth. *Bioscience Bulletin*, *33*, 10.

Welsh, K. E., Mauchline, A. L., Park, J. R., Whalley, W.B., & France, D. (2013). Enhancing fieldwork learning with technology: Practitioner's perspectives. *Journal of Geography in Higher Education*, *37*(3), 1-17.

Woodcock, B., Middleton, A., & Nortcliffe, A. (2012). Considering the smartphone learner: An investigation into student interest in the use of personal technology to enhance their learning. *Student Engagement and Experience Journal*, *1*(1), 1-15.

Yorke, M., & Knight, P. (2007). Evidence-informed pedagogy and the enhancement of student employability. *Teaching in Higher Education*, *12*(2), 157-170.

STUDENT TEACHING WITH IPADS: INCORPORATING MODERN DIGITAL TOOLS IN TEACHER PREPARATION

KIMBERLY L. TOHILL[1]

Abstract

Technology provides infinite and exciting opportunities to improve both teaching and learning when it is integrated into authentic learning experiences in meaningful ways. In an effort to explore and evaluate new technologies, world language teacher certification candidates in a university teacher preparation programme were provided with iPad 2 devices for use during their final year of academic study, which included student teaching. Because of the in-depth and longitudinal examination of data, document collection and analysis, participant interviews, and small sample size, this research agenda is presented as a case study using phenomenological thematic analysis. Examination of the participants' experiences resulted in the emergence of four main themes that characterised their use of technology: students and technology, teachers and technology, affordances of technology, and infrastructural issues of technology. A significant finding of this study is that participants did not use the iPad 2 devices nearly as much as expected. This study highlights the need for further research in the area of educational use of iPads for both pre- and in-service teachers in addition to how attitudes towards technology affect classroom integration.

1. Introduction

Technology provides infinite and exciting opportunities to improve both teaching and learning when it is integrated into authentic learning experiences in meaningful ways. This study builds on and contributes to

[1] The Pennsylvania State University, United States of America. Email: ktohill@gmail.com

work regarding the integration of cutting-edge technology into teacher preparation programmes and identification of how technology can improve teaching and learning. The ever-increasing ubiquity of technology demands that teacher education programmes re-evaluate the ways in which they train teachers. As Steinweg, Williams, and Stapleton (2010) noted: "To prepare our teacher candidates for schools of tomorrow, we must continue to explore, model, and evaluate new technologies" (p. 54). In an effort to explore and evaluate new technologies, world language teacher certification candidates were provided with iPad 2 devices for use during their final year of academic study, which included student teaching.

Although studies have examined the use of iPads by students in K-20, to the best of my knowledge there has not been a study that examines the use of iPads by teacher certification candidates during their student teaching experiences – particularly in the area of world languages. As such, this study provides insight into how world language teacher certification candidates use iPads and how these digital devices can support them during their student teaching.

This paper begins with a review of literature that explores the fundamental components of this study, including technology in teacher education programmes, mobile technology transforming pedagogy, and iPad affordances. It continues with the research questions and methodology, which details the process of phenomenology utilised. Following is the presentation of findings separated by four themes extracted from the data: students and technology, teachers and technology, affordances of technology, and infrastructural issues of technology. Findings are summarised in the discussion section and implications for further research are addressed. The paper finishes with study limitations and general concluding remarks.

2. Review of Literature

2.1 Technology in Teacher Education Programmes

Despite the fact that most teachers complete their training and education at a university, research studies indicate that beginning teachers still feel unprepared to adequately and effectively integrate technology into classroom instruction (as cited in Jayachandran, 2009; as cited in Luke & Britten, 2007; as cited in Sutton, 2011). At present many teachers and teacher candidates use technology as a resource for locating information and as a medium for creating things such as lesson plans, communications, classroom materials, instructional documents, and the occasional digital presentation (Stobaugh & Tassel, 2001, as cited in Sutton, 2011). They are, however, unaware of how modern digital tools can be leveraged to improve and enhance learning both in and out of classrooms.

Producing beginning teachers who are able to craft technology-rich learning experiences necessitates the inclusion of technology instruction and learning experiences throughout teacher preparation programmes including field experiences (Chesley & Jordan, 2012; Golas, 2010; Hixon & So, 2009; Luke & Britten, 2007; Sutton, 2011). Unfortunately, technology courses have not been prioritised in teacher preparation programmes. According to Betrus' (2012) 10-year study, the number of institutions offering an introductory technology course for teacher education students decreased from 80% in 2000 to 64% in 2010. The same study also noted that while more than half of the topics taught had changed over the ten-year period, the emphasis remained on office suite applications rather than emerging technology (Betrus, 2012).

Technology courses encourage teacher education students to increase the integration of technology into their lessons, which in turn follows them into their teaching careers (Steinweg et al., 2010). In a study by Frazier and Sadera (2013), 78.2% of the surveyed teacher candidates cited "training provided by the teacher education programme" while 70.6% cited "previous experiences as a student in classes which incorporated technology" as factors that influenced their decisions about technology integration (p. 3154). Another study found a strong relationship between increased technology skills and increased self-efficacy for the use of these skills during classroom instruction (Southall, 2012).

2.2 Mobile Technology Transforming Pedagogy

Because of their unique affordances, mobile devices have the potential to revolutionise teaching and learning in 21st Century classrooms. Advantages such as ubiquity, level of personalisation, accessibility and intuition all contribute to a pedagogical paradigm shift when incorporating mobile technology into instruction. These devices encourage and foster the use of social constructivist and collaborative pedagogical techniques, and consider context as an influential factor for instructional integration (Manuguerra & Petocz, 2011; Rossing, Miller, Cecil & Stamper, 2012; Sharples et al., 2009). The collaborative and social aspects of mobile technology are propelling the shift from traditionally cognitive or constructivist paradigms of educational technology integration towards a social constructivist paradigm that emphasises synergistic interaction among learners, teachers, devices, and content. Not only is there a physical social environment that impacts learning, but now there is also a virtual social environment to consider.

Mobile devices change interactions that occur among learners, teachers, and content (Amador-Lankster & Naffziger, 2013). Social aspects of mobile technology pervade these interactions, necessitating a paradigm shift to account for them. Furthermore, a social constructivist approach offers more flexibility to accommodate the often spontaneous and capricious nature of mobile learning (Kukulska-Hulme, 2009; Lally et al., 2012). Technology integration into classroom settings has traditionally fallen in line with existing institutional and pedagogical practices without breaching any boundaries or redefining any norms. However, mobile technology and "its digital affordances to enhance creativity, collaboration and knowledge generation, or to radically reconstruct curriculum or assessment processes" challenge preconceived and long-standing conceptions and practices regarding educational technology integration into 21st century classrooms (as cited in Lally et al., 2012, p. 220).

Teachers often utilise and rely on the same tools and technologies as their students do for everyday tasks. However, while they may have sound understanding of these tools for personal use, they may not be willing or able to integrate them into classroom instruction. Incorporating mobile technology into educators' technology dossiers begins with teacher preparation programmes that impart pedagogical knowledge infused with mobile-specific elements (Kukulska-Hulme, 2009; Wakefield & Smith, 2012). Simply providing teachers with powerful digital tools does not predicate their usage, much less appropriate and meaningful usage. Incorporating mobile technology into classroom instruction requires training and preparation that begins with teacher preparation programmes and continues as teachers challenge traditional paradigms and practices.

2.3 iPad Affordances – Super Powers or Super Hype?

The iPad has been lauded for its portability, convenience, usability, battery life, collaborative capabilities, and general ubiquity (Crichton, Pegler & White, 2012; Geist, 2011; Rossing et al., 2012; Wong, 2012). The iPad often fits the bill as a "one-stop-shop" device that provides multi-functionality in one powerful package, thus dissolving the need for several devices to perform specific tasks. Nevertheless, one of the most common criticisms of the iPad for educational use is its focus on consumption – as opposed to creation – of content (e.g. Amador-Lankster & Naffziger, 2013; Henderson & Yeow, 2012). Features that make iPads so desirable for content consumption may hinder content creation. The small size does not detract from the sharp resolution and high quality images that make the iPad a convenient option for on-the-go movie viewing or flipping through a photo slideshow. However, the small size does make it difficult to input text, for example, since the on-screen keyboard demands nearly half of the screen real estate when utilised. Furthermore, many people find the virtual keyboard cumbersome to use (Amador-Lanskter & Naffziger, 2013; Rossing et al., 2012), and often attach an external keyboard thus defeating the purpose of the all-inclusive tablet. The inability to split the screen to view more than one window simultaneously also frustrates content creation. The fact that there are no built-in apps that facilitate creation further impedes using the iPad as a tool that incites students and teachers alike to produce artefacts.

Portability and convenience seem to overshadow the iPad's educational dearth where active learning is paramount. Students can easily pass the devices to each other or gather around one to view content due to the lack of attachments and need for location stability. Some applications even allow for multiple touch input, which enhances collaboration (Murray & Olcese, 2011). The iPad's portability further encourages informal learning as students seamlessly transition among multiple contexts without disruption. These unique and ubiquitous devices facilitate the anytime, anywhere learning expected by today's students (Geist, 2011; Lee, 2011). While iPads have been popularly touted as the next best thing in education, it may be too soon to reach any conclusions considering the paucity of evidence to support this assertion.

Since the iPad was introduced in 2010, there is still much room for research surrounding this device. However, few studies have examined either pre- or in-service teacher use of iPads with students. This study demonstrates the inclusion of modern digital tools – iPad 2s – into an established teacher preparation programme; it also serves to examine the ways in which teacher certification candidates utilise them in both their personal and professional lives.

3. Research Questions

This study's principal thrust was to examine how world language student teachers used and integrated iPad 2 devices into their student teaching experiences.

A secondary aspect was to explore how the student teachers used the devices in their personal lives and how these two patterns of usage intersected and overlapped. These research questions framed the direction of this study:

1. What is the classroom experience of student teaching like for world language teacher education students with iPads?
2. What is the personal experience of student teaching like for world language teacher education students with iPads?

4. Methodology

Because of the in-depth and longitudinal examination of data, document collection and analysis, participant interviews, and small sample size, this research agenda is presented as a case study using phenomenological thematic analysis. The underlying motivation was to learn about the experiences of world language student teachers using technology in their classrooms - specifically the iPad – and provide a rich description of these experiences.

5. Context

This study involved world language teacher education students from a large, northeastern public university during their university-required student teaching experiences. Observations of the student teachers took place in two different high schools in the same geographic area; both districts are comparable in terms of student demographics and socioeconomic status. Students simultaneously enrolled in a course entitled "Practicum in Student Teaching – Secondary Education", which encompassed the student teaching field experience in addition to on-campus seminar meetings and required assignments.

6. Participants

In the fall of 2012, participants were identified among world language teacher education students, who were in their final year of study and who would be engaging in the student teaching experience in the spring of 2013. From this group, three female students – Elizabeth, Kara and Molly – agreed to participate. Participants were provided with iPad 2 devices that they were permitted to fully personalise. All participants had completed equivalent courses of study in the world language education programme at the same university. Each participant completed a 15-week student teaching experience in world languages at one of three local high schools.

Observation times were coordinated based on weekly teaching schedules with concerted efforts to observe different class periods each visit. Information and artefacts gleaned from interviews, course-required documents and assignments, and observations serve to inform conclusions and recommendations surrounding the use of iPads to support the student teaching experience. Pseudonyms have been used to protect the identity of the participants.

7. Data Collection

Several types of data were collected for this study. Field observations of approximately one hour in length were conducted on three separate occasions for two participants, resulting in five hours of video recordings. During the observations, I recorded field notes using a laptop computer, resulting in 14 single-spaced pages total. Due to school district policy, I was unable to observe the third participant in the field, so there is no video recorded data or field notes regarding her classroom activities.

Throughout the semester, the participants met weekly with their student teaching supervisor, typically in an on-campus classroom to discuss relevant information regarding their teaching activities as well as course assignments. The six sessions that were held on campus were video recorded, resulting in approximately eleven (11) total hours of video recordings, which were subsequently analysed. I wrote notes and transcribed relevant conversation while viewing the videos. Evidence of the iPads' role in the student teaching experiences was extracted from these notes and recordings.

Furthermore, I interviewed each participant upon conclusion of her student teaching experience. The interviews were conducted one-on-one via Skype or in person and were video recorded, resulting in approximately four hours of conversation. Furthermore, throughout the semester, participants contributed various assignments and documents to the student teaching course wiki space. From these assignments, I collected the technology journals, weekly summation journals, and teaching philosophies of all three participants.

8. Data Analysis

Prior to analysis, I transcribed the interviews and relevant aspects of the weekly seminar video recordings. I then engaged in "horizonalization" as a way of identifying all expressions that were relevant to this particular experience (Moustakas, 1994). I read through the data, and began to assign codes that reflected the structures of the student teachers' lived experiences (Van Manen, 1990). After passing through all of the data once, I made a second pass to code anything I may have missed and to revisit my previous codes.

After coding all of the data, I made a list of the codes in an effort to cluster them into themes. Asking myself whether or not the codes were essential to understanding the lived experience of student teachers using technology in their classrooms, I eliminated two codes because I did not feel they were integral components of this experience. Having identified the invariant constituents, I began to cluster them and entertain preliminary themes as a way of capturing and describing "aspect(s) of the structure of lived experience" (Van Manen, 1990, p. 87). Through reading and reflecting upon the invariant constituents, I began to see connections from which four main themes emerged: students and technology, teachers and technology, affordances of technology, and infrastructural issues of technology. These themes represent "the stars that make up the universes of meaning we live through. By the light of these themes we can navigate and explore such universes" (Van Manen, 1990, p. 90). The emergent themes illuminate the lived experiences of world language student teachers using technology in their classrooms and provide insight into this phenomenon.

9. Findings

Examination of the participants' experiences resulted in the emergence of four main themes that characterised their use of technology: students and technology, teachers and technology, affordances of technology, and infrastructural issues of technology. While the interweaving and intersecting of the main themes are what synergise to create the luminescence of each experience, the smaller components texturalise the themes to draw out the multi-faceted nature of each. However, it is important to note that participants did not use the iPads nearly as often as other modes of technology for various reasons.

10. Students and Technology

When incorporating technology into classroom learning, teachers must adequately prepare ahead of time and plan for how implementation will occur, how students will engage and learn with the technology, and how its use will be authentic rather than contrived. All participants exhibited behaviours and expressed thoughts that suggest the theme of students and technology was the principal focus of their technology efforts, which upholds constructivist beliefs that are prominent in teacher preparation programmes today. Three strands that comprise the main theme emerged from the data: engaging students with technology, preparation for technology integration, and authentic use of technology.

Engaging students with technology involves them becoming active participants in their own learning. Molly's classroom came equipped with an interactive whiteboard that she utilised frequently. She recalled:

> I've been trying to use the [Promethean] board more so that students can come up and actually write on it and do things because I've noticed when we're just showing PowerPoint, it's like using a projector. But then when students volunteer to come write on the [Promethean] board, everybody is suddenly more interested. (Personal communication, April 11, 2013)

Due to software and hardware compatibility issues, Molly was unable to connect her iPad to the interactive whiteboard. Demonstrating her commitment to engaging the students, Molly added:

> I wanted to really utilise it [iPad] and make the best of it. But there were just some things like the software for example. It's either iPad or have the kids write on the [Promethean] board, and because of how they get to interact with it, I'm going to pick the board. (Personal communication, April 11, 2013)

Though she tried to incorporate using the iPad with available technology, Molly was unsuccessful and ultimately prioritised engaging students with active learning over the new device.

Elizabeth also encouraged active learning in her classroom where she incorporated the iPad into a learning experience during which two students used websites and apps to locate travel information for visiting Spain. She noted that having students share one device worked well though having a device for each student would be ideal. Engaging students with technology not only facilitates active learning, but also encourages students to take greater ownership of their learning.

Engaging students with technology requires careful planning and preparation on the part of the student teachers. Both Elizabeth's and Kara's planning and preparation efforts were evident in the technology-rich lessons they presented to their classes. In one instance, Elizabeth experienced difficulty with a video that she intended to show; she demonstrated her preparedness for technology problems by swiftly correcting the issue while maintaining the flow of the class. She further expressed evidence of preparation by ensuring access to various websites and videos through the school's firewall and having a backup plan for failed technology ventures. The amount of available time for planning and preparation also affected how often and how extensively the participants used technology. All three participants expressed their desires to use more tools, apps, and technology devices more frequently if only they had more time to explore, tinker, and prepare.

The third facet of students and technology theme is the authentic use of technology. Beyond merely using technology for the sake of using it, utilising technology in ways that people within the targeted community actually use it contributes to the authenticity of the learning experience. Kara incorporated a target language video from YouTube in her lesson to teach students how to ask where objects are in a room. The choice of media contributes to its authenticity – students already use YouTube in their daily lives; in addition, this particular video was created by same age peers further demonstrating a project that her students could feasibly complete. Molly used her iPhone to videotape herself doing a cooking demonstration, which she narrated in the target language. Relevant and authentic use of technology engages students and enhances learning.

While the positive outcomes of students interacting with technology are touted and praised, the negative ones are less often noted or even recognised. Molly's experience illuminated an issue that bears careful consideration. Many of the students in her school district came from socio-economically challenged backgrounds. Hailing from a middle class family and graduating from a high school with a one-to-one laptop initiative, Molly never felt out of place among her friends and classmates with her iPhone. Receiving an iPad to use during her senior year of college felt like a logical extension of technology interest. However, as she utilised both the iPhone and iPad in her teaching, she became increasingly uncomfortable with her apparent device fluency. Molly noticed that students acted differently towards her when she used the devices, and most times the reactions were not positive. She felt that her devices put a barrier between her and students she was trying to reach by using them. Students whose parents were worried about paying the rent watched as this seemingly affluent teacher flashed an iPhone and an iPad. As a result, Molly hesitated to use the iPad and often relied on technology that was already in place.

11. Teachers and Technology

To use technology with students, teachers must also be active technology users. This simple fact raises various issues, including learning how to use devices, striving to integrate technology meaningfully into lessons, and the crossover between personal and professional technology usage. All participants expressed initial difficulty in learning how to complete tasks using the iPads, especially typing. Participants noted that they preferred to use a laptop or desktop computer for any tasks that were typing intensive, including creating lesson plans, exams, and other classroom materials. They also mentioned that file-sharing, formatting, and storage were difficult – if not impossible – using the iPad. Participants expressed frustration at spending long stretches of time trying to figure out how to do something on the iPad only to learn they could not do it or that it was incompatible with their school's technology infrastructure. Unfamiliar applications and interfaces proved cumbersome while the small screen size also inhibited usage. As a result, participants frequently abandoned the iPads in favour of more "reliable" and familiar technology that was easier to use. Time was also a consideration, as the sheer amount of applications and programs available for use far exceeded the amount of time participants could devote to learning when accounting for other professional and personal responsibilities.

Meaningful technology integration was an issue with which participants struggled. While students may expect teachers to use technology, it is not something that should be used simply for usage sake. There must be sound reasoning and motivation propelling its incorporation. Molly expressed:

> It shouldn't be all lecture, it shouldn't be all technology. It should be a good combination of both and you should use whatever is most fitting to what you're trying to teach. If you're trying to teach conversational skills, you're not going to stand there and lecture. You're going to have the students talking to each other or maybe listening to a podcast…using it [technology] to enhance the content in whatever way that is, and sometimes it might be better to just lay off the technology. (Personal communication, April 11, 2013)

Patterns of technology use for professional and personal tasks were similar among all participants. Professionally, Kara, Molly, and Elizabeth all used the iPads to create presentations for classroom lessons and to read and highlight articles for their seminar class. However, none of the participants actually used the iPads to play the presentations that they created on them. Molly used an online program on her iPad to track attendance and grades; Kara and Elizabeth both had access to applications to complete similar tasks but did not use them. Participants utilised the iPads for personal use more extensively than for professional. Elizabeth downloaded several language learning applications, Kara enjoyed the social networking capability, and Molly often used the Twitter and

YouTube applications. Participants preferred using the iPads for personal use, mainly due to institutional and infrastructural barriers that restrained use in their classrooms.

12. Affordances of Technology

Participants noted the main affordances the iPad provided were ubiquity, personalisation, and convenience. Elizabeth lauded the seemingly "always appropriate" nature of the iPad. She remarked:

> I was able to take it [iPad] places and use it when it would have been awkward to use my laptop. When I was travelling, I would take it along, and when on the bus, it's kind of awkward to have your laptop sitting on your lap. But it wasn't a problem to be holding my iPad with one hand and using it. It just seemed more appropriate to use in a lot more situations than a laptop. (Personal communication, April 4, 2013)

Molly also appreciated being able to discreetly pass the iPad to students who had missed class so that they could review the material she had covered without disrupting the other students.

Personalisation allowed each individual to custom tailor the iPad in a way that was most appropriate for the ways in which she used it. Kara synced her iPad with her iPhone to improve her productivity by having applications and files available on both devices. Elizabeth found self-study applications to be personally beneficial; she also remarked about the possibility for students who could use them for remediation or advancement if they had their own iPads. Because all participants had their own iPads, they were able to configure them individually, and all noted the potential for personalised learning to impact their future classrooms.

Convenience was perhaps the most acclaimed attribute of the iPad. Smaller and lighter than a laptop yet larger than a smartphone, the iPad fits easily in a purse and provides a dazzling visual display. Kara remarked:

> It [iPad] made things a lot easier because it's not like I have to get it out and turn it on. It's not such a hassle. It's super simple to carry around with me everywhere…I always had it with me because it was so easy for me rather than lugging around a laptop. (Personal communication, April 16, 2013)

Kara often used her iPad in the faculty room as a quick reference or to enter grades; when the bell rang, she effortlessly packed the iPad in her bag and headed to her classroom. Molly found the iPad well suited for taking attendance and completing homework checks as she circulated throughout the room; the portability made it the perfect option rather than trying to carry a laptop with her. All participants agreed that convenience was the biggest affordance of the iPad.

13. Infrastructural Issues of Technology

The factors that limited professional usage of the iPad within the high school environment mostly dealt with the infrastructural issues, including available technology and incompatibility with systems already in place. The three districts in which the student teachers were placed were comparable in terms of available technology and support. All student teachers had access to a wireless Internet connection, laptop computers, and LCD projectors as well as standard devices such as CD players, DVD players, and televisions; two of the student teachers also had access to interactive whiteboards and the accompanying software. Kara was unable to connect her iPad to the interactive whiteboard, because the district did not have the necessary hardware to do so; while Molly was able to connect to the hardware, the software was incompatible with her iPad rendering it impossible to use. Connecting the iPad physically to the interactive whiteboard also defeats the mobility affordance as Molly noted.

Similarly, connectivity issues and outdated hardware resulted in participants being unable to print from their iPads, which also influenced their motivation to create materials using the iPads. Knowing that they would not easily be able to print, share, or store what they created detracted from the desire to utilise the iPads as a content creation or presentation tool. Many times it was simply easier for the student teachers to use district-provided equipment that was fully compatible with and connected to the current system to enhance their lessons or complete professional tasks during the school day. Despite the limitations they faced in the high school settings, the student teachers did not experience these issues in the university settings in which they used the iPads. Student teachers seamlessly connected to the hardware and software systems, resulting in increased professional usage of the iPad in this setting.

Conversely, infrastructural issues minimally affected personal iPad usage. Because patterns of personal usage differed as previously described, the student teachers did not face the same barriers that impeded professional usage such as hardware and software compatibility.

14. Discussion

Though the precise experiences of the three student teachers varied, four common themes related to technology integration emerged: students and technology, teachers and technology, affordances of technology, and infrastructural issues of technology. The importance that the participants placed on the interaction between students and technology upholds the strongly constructivist beliefs that permeate current educational thought and teacher preparation programmes. Considering how students and technology interact also involved how implementation would occur, how students would engage and learn with the technology, and how its use would be authentic. This theme was the most prominent throughout the student teachers' experiences, and highlights the need for support and professional preparation in this area.

There were several issues that inhibited the student teachers' use of iPads, including the technology learning curve, the inadequacy of the device for specific tasks, infrastructural considerations, and incompatibility. Contrary to expectations, the student teachers used the iPads in their classrooms infrequently for professional reasons and only intermittently outside their classrooms for professional reasons. The majority of iPad usage was for personal reasons both within and outside their classrooms. The student teachers noted that it was often easier and more convenient to utilise the technology that was already in place and functional rather than trying to incorporate new devices. This is consistent with the literature that acknowledges that mobile technology integration challenges traditional paradigms, and that technology integration often falls into line with current practice. In these cases, integrating iPads challenged the current system and ultimately failed against its influence. It is imperative that teacher preparation programmes address this disconnect between pedagogy and practice; student teachers engage with new ideas and pedagogy during their teacher preparation programmes that they are unable to realise when they enter real life settings such as field experiences and student teaching.

15. Implications for Future Research

This study highlights the need for further research in the area of educational use of iPads for both pre- and in-service teachers. Because of the current infrastructure in many K-12 school districts, iPads may not yet have the place in education that many would like them to have. Therefore, research is needed to identify how iPads can improve teaching and learning in an effort to encourage schools to revise their current technology plans – if findings indicate that iPads really do supersede the capabilities of such commonly used tools as laptops and interactive whiteboards.

If iPads are to have a place in teacher education programmes and in K-12 schools, researchers must strive to identify best practices that provide evidence of improved teaching and learning that result from affordances not otherwise available through traditional means. Furthermore, research into teacher attitudes toward technology and school technology climate may produce findings that would advise teacher educators as to how they might effectively integrate technology into teacher preparation programmes in ways that will positively affect future teachers with the ultimate goal of improving the K-12 school technology climate.

16. Conclusion

The goal of this study was to examine pre-service teachers' experiences with technology during their student teaching experiences – specifically, the use of an iPad 2 device. Although the study did not show significant professional use of the iPads by student teachers, it did illuminate four common themes that affected technology use during student teaching: students and technology, teachers and technology, affordances of technology, and infrastructural issues of technology. This study was limited by the small sample size and the restriction of observing one of the three participants. Findings support previous research studies that suggest technology education must be an integral part of teacher preparation programmes in an effort to improve teaching and learning with modern digital tools. Teacher preparation programmes must continue to encourage pre-service teachers to innovate and explore with technology in ways that support both personal and professional development and that improve learning experiences for students.

This study was limited by the small sample size and the fact that the school districts were relatively homogenous in terms of student population. Similarly, different participants may have yielded different results based upon their willingness to persist or not through the various obstacles these participants faced. A further limitation was the inability to observe one of the three participants in her classroom due to school district regulations.

References

Amador-Lankster, C., & Naffziger, L. (2013). Power of using iPads during clinical practice with teacher candidates. In R. McBride & M. Searson (Eds.), *Proceedings of Society for Information Technology & Teacher Education International Conference 2013* (pp. 2534-2539). Chesapeake, VA: AACE.

Betrus, A. (2012). Historical evolution of instructional technology in teacher education programs: A ten-year update. *TechTrends*, *56*(5), 42-45.

Chesley, G. M., & Jordan, J. (2012). What's missing from teacher prep. *Educational Leadership*, *69*(8), 41-45.

Crichton, S., Pegler, K., & White, D. (2012). Personal devices in public settings: Lessons learned from an iPod touch/iPad project. *The Electronic Journal of elearning*, *10*(1), 23-31.

Frazier, L., & Sadera, W. (2013). Technology use in teacher candidate internship experiences and factors affecting this use. In R. McBride & M. Searson (Eds.), *Proceedings of Society for Information Technology & Teacher Education International Conference 2013* (pp. 3152-3154). Chesapeake, VA: AACE.

Geist, E. (2011). The game changer: Using iPads in college teacher education classes. *College Student Journal*, *45*(4), 758-768.

Golas, J. (2010). Effective teacher preparation programs: Bridging the gap between educational technology availability and its utilization. *International Forum of Teaching and Studies*, *6*(1), 16-18.

Henderson, S., & Yeow, J. (2012). iPad in education: A case study of iPad adoption and use in a primary school. *Proceedings from HICSS 2012: 45th Hawaii International Conference on System Sciences*. Maui, Hawaii.

Hixon, E., & So, H. (2009). Technology's role in field experiences for preservice teacher training. *Educational Technology & Society*, *12*(4), 294-304.

Jayachandran, A. (2009). Technology integration practices of foreign language preservice teachers: A case study. (Doctoral dissertation). Retrieved from ProQuest, (3383142).

Kukulska-Hulme, A. (2009). Will mobile learning change language learning? *ReCALL*, *21*(2), 157-165.

Lally, V., Sharples, M., Tracy, F., Bertram, N., & Masters, S. (2012). Researching the ethical dimensions of mobile, ubiquitous and immersive technology enhanced learning (MUITEL): A thematic review and dialogue. *Interactive Learning Environments*, *20*(3), 217-238.

Lee, M. J. (2011). Web 2.0 technology meets mobile assisted language learning. *The International Association for Language Learning Technology Journal*, *41*(1), 161-173.

Luke, C. L., & Britten, J. S. (2007). The expanding role of technology in foreign language teacher education programs. *CALICO Journal*, *24*(2), 253-267.

Manuguerra, M., & Petocz, P. (2011). Promoting student engagement by integrating new technology into tertiary education: The role of the iPad. *Asian Social Science*, *7*(11), 61-65.

Moustakas, C. E. (1994). Phenomenological research analyses and examples. In C. Moustakas (Ed.) *Phenomenological research methods* (pp. 103-119). Thousand Oaks, CA: Sage.

Murray, O. T., & Olcese, N. R. (2011). Teaching and learning with iPads, ready or not? *Tech Trends*, *55*(6), 42-48.

Peluso, D. C. C. (2012). The fast-paced iPad revolution: Can educators stay up to date and relevant about these ubiquitous devices? *British Journal of Educational Technology*, *43*(4), 125-127.

Rossing, J. P., Miller, W. M., Cecil, A. K., & Stamper, S. E. (2012). iLearning: The future of higher education? Student perceptions on learning with mobile tablets. *Journal of the Scholarship of Teaching and Learning*, *12*(2), 1-26.

Sharples, M., Arnedillo-Sanchez, I., Milrad, M., & Vavoula, G. (2009). Mobile learning: Small devices, big issues. In N. Balacheff, S. Ludvigsen, T. Jong, A. Lazonder, & S. Barnes (Eds.), *Technology-enhanced learning* (pp. 233-249). Dordrecht: Springer Netherlands.

Southall, S. P. (2012). *Digital native preservice teachers: An examination of their self-efficacy beliefs regarding technology integration in classroom settings* (Unpublished Doctoral dissertation). Longwood University, United States.

Steinweg, S. B., Williams, S. C., & Stapleton, J. N. (2010). Faculty use of tablet PCs in teacher education and K-12 settings. *TechTrends*, *54*(3), 54-60.

Stobaugh, R. R., & Tassell, J. L. (2011). Analyzing the degree of technology use occurring in pre-service teacher education. *Educational Assessment, Evaluation & Accountability*, *23*(2), 143-157.

Sutton, S. R. (2011). The preservice technology training experiences of novice teachers. *Journal of Digital Learning in Teacher Education*, *28*(1), 39-46.

Van Manen, M. (1990). *Researching lived experience: Human science for an action sensitive pedagogy*. Albany, NY: State University of New York Press.

Wakefield, J., & Smith, D. (2012). From Socrates to satellites: iPad learning in an undergraduate course. *Creative Education*, *3*(5), 643-648.

Winslow, J., Dickerson, J., Lee, C., & Geer, G. (2012). Mobile technologies: Tools for organizational learning and management in schools. *International Education Studies*, *5*(4), 188-195.

Wong, W. (2012). Tools of the trade. How mobile learning devices are changing the face of higher education. *Community College Journal*, *82*(5), 54-60.

EXPLORING HOW EDUCATORS INCORPORATE IPADS IN LEARNING AND INSTRUCTION: EXPECTATIONS, EXPERIENCES, AND REFLECTIONS OF EDUCATION STUDENTS AND FACULTY IN A DIGITAL MEDIA MASTER'S PROGRAMME

BENJAMIN BAAB[1] AND JOHN BANSAVICH[2]

Abstract

The provision of iPad 2s to students and faculty in a Digital Media and Learning Master's programme afforded a unique opportunity to investigate holistically the iPad usage patterns of pre-service and in-service educators. The purpose of this two-year, descriptive, mixed methods case study was to explore student and faculty iPad use expectations, experiences, and reflections. Approximately fifty-six (56) graduate education students and seven (7) faculty participants reported their iPad use in school, professional, and personal activities via online surveys, in-person interviews, focus group discussions, and classroom observations. Thematic content analysis of participant responses and observations identified usage clusters, such as e-document reading, communicating, collaborating, Web browsing, and note taking. Over the two-year period, observations revealed how these educators developed their iPad-related knowledge and skills, and increasingly relied on the iPad to accomplish school, work, and personal tasks. Participants reported that their initial expectations about iPad use were met, and suggested continuation and expansion of iPad use in the programme. Investigating participant expectations, use and reflections

[1] University of San Francisco, United States of America. Email: baab@usfca.edu
[2] University of San Francisco, United States of America. Email: bansavich@usfca.edu

provided a framework for understanding the technology implementation project.

1. Exploring how Educators Incorporate iPads in Learning and Instruction

The popularity of mobile devices and tablets/iPads in particular (Gawelek, Spataro, & Komarny, 2011; Griffey, 2012; Hill, 2011; Massé, 2012; Waters, 2010) and their increasing use in education (Barnes & Herring, 2011; Duncan, 2011; Enriquez, 2010; Geist, 2011; Hall, 2011; McConnell, McConnell, & McConnell, 2011; Murphy, 2011; O'Loughlin, 2011; Ostashewski & Reid, 2010; Perkins, Hamm, Pamplin, Morris, & McKelvain, 2011), provides an opportunity to explore how educators learn to incorporate new forms of technology in learning and instructional activities. Tablets, specifically iPads, fill a space between laptops and smartphones and provide access to a new set of software tools (Massé, 2012; Stager & Brenner, 2013). Observing how higher education students and faculty incorporate iPad use into their regular suite of tools can provide educators with insights about usage patterns that are not wholly predetermined by specific instructional directives (Peluso, 2012). After a brief overview of the literature, the design of this study and its setting will be described, followed by the insights that emerged and their implications for educational practice.

2. Literature Review

Laptop use in university settings has been widely researched to the point where a model explaining laptop use has been developed (Simonaitiene & Kutkaityte, 2013). The laptop use factors that have been identified by these researchers include both aspects of usefulness as well as obstacles. Although not as widely studied as laptop use, smartphone use has received recent attention from researchers (e.g., Mueller, Wood, De Pasquale & Cruikshank, 2012), who reported similar complexities involving benefits and challenges related to smartphone use (i.e., Blackberry Curve) by graduate business students in Canada. Positioned between laptops and smartphones, iPads might combine the functionality of laptops with the mobility of smartphones. Initial studies of higher education iPad use (e.g., Geist, 2011; Gosper, Malfroy & McKenzie, 2013; Griffey, 2012; Hall, 2011; Kukulska-Hulme, 2007; Murphy, 2011; O'Loughlin, 2011; Pegrum, Howitt & Striepe, 2013; Penny, 2011; Perkins et al., 2011; Pettit & Kukulska-Hulme, 2007) identify potential benefits, particularly those involving the reading and annotation of electronic documents.

Several theoretical perspectives inform this study, including theories of learning related to mobile devices (e.g., Keskin & Metcalf, 2011; Traxler, 2007), theories of innovation diffusion in schools (e.g., Frank, Zhao, Penuel, Ellefson & Porter, 2011) and technology implementation (e.g., Hazen, Wu, Sankar & Jones-Farmer, 2011; Kukulska-Hulme, 2012; Lewis, Fretwell, Ryan & Parham, 2013), and theories of teacher concerns development (e.g., Mackey & Evans, 2011). Key elements in these theories include the classroom social context, experimentation and risk, constructed knowledge, and connected learning.

The purpose of this mixed methods case study was to explore student and faculty expectations, experiences, and reflections of iPad usage in a two-year Master's programme in digital media and learning. The central question focuses on the student and faculty experiences using the iPad in scholarly, professional, and personal activities. The specific research questions were:

1. What were student and faculty expectations regarding iPad use for scholarly, professional, and personal activities?
2. What were student and faculty iPad uses for scholarly, professional, and personal activities?
3. What were student and faculty reflections about their iPad use?

Technology tools and apps include directions for use, but with educational tools and apps, students and faculty need supplements that explain why and when to use them. Understanding this need and the approaches students and faculty take to incorporate new tools can help instructional planners and app developers focus their work to support the needs of those who use their products.

This study has clear delimitations and limitations. Among the delimitations is the selection of the location, institution, and programme with which both researchers are closely connected. This study is a description of a phenomenon by insiders, the study's main limitation. Researcher bias can never be eliminated, but triangulated data collection and multiple sources attempted to reduce potential bias.

3. Method

Because the study's intent was to understand iPad use from multiple perspectives, the research design involved a mixed methods case study approach (Creswell, 2012; Stake, 1995). The case involved the provision of iPads to graduate education students and faculty for instructional and personal use. Descriptive, quantitative data helped to illustrate iPad usage patterns and participant characteristics, while participant views of iPad use provided rich, qualitative insights into their experiences.

The setting for the study was the Digital Media and Learning (DML) Master's programme at the University of San Francisco's School of Education. Graduate students enrolled in DML courses over a two-year period were invited to participate. Participant selection involved opportunistic, purposeful, convenience sampling. Of the 56 student participants, just under two-thirds were female and over half were Caucasian and in the 25-40 age range. Half of the students were employed full-time, mostly as K-16 teachers, and just over 30% were employed part-time. Students rated their level of technical expertise on a 5-point scale from Novice (1) to Expert (5) – see Table 1. Students rated their general computer expertise highly, while their assessment of iPad expertise was closer to the centre of the rating scale. As indicated in Table 1, less variability was associated with general computer expertise and expertise with a non-iPad tablet. The variability among the other ratings illustrates the diversity of the student expertise.

Technology	Mean[1]	Standard Deviation
Computers, in general	3.9	.70
iPod	3.3	1.42
iPhone	3.0	1.53
iPad	2.4	1.40
Another smartphone	2.1	1.39
e-Book reader (e.g., Kindle, Nook)	2.0	1.37
Another tablet	1.6	1.01

[1] Novice = 1; Expert = 5

Table 1. Self-reports of student technical expertise (n=56)

In an initial 60-minute group session, the researchers provided the participants with a brief introduction, assurances of ethical practices, and basic iPad use instruction. The researchers obtained informed consent from all participants. A wiki (http://ipad2.wiki.usfca.edu) was also created to support collaboration among participants. Participants were encouraged to share apps and relevant articles and resources. Data collection methods included entries into online journals for student participants and one-on-one interviews with programme faculty, using researcher-developed, open-ended prompts. First-hand observations supplied additional data about classroom integration activities. Four end-of-semester focus group meetings with student participants were also conducted.

Participants shared their expectations, experiences, and reflections about iPad use in four ways: initially bimonthly and then monthly journal entries by student participants using Moodle's survey feature, monthly one-on-one interviews with faculty, faculty surveys at the beginning and end of each semester, and quarterly classroom observations of 12 different courses. The variety of data sources allowed the researchers to triangulate evidence and thus gain a more holistic understanding of the phenomenon.

After transcribing the interview and focus group data, the researchers employed an iterative, constant comparative data analysis process (Creswell, 2012) to code the data. By combining initial open codes into more general categories through axial coding (Creswell, 2012), themes and trends in participant responses emerged. The researchers conducted the data analysis independently initially, and then audited each other's work to improve the quality of the analysis process by identifying and reducing potential bias and generally strengthening the rigour of the process.

4. Findings

The purpose of this mixed methods case study was to explore student and faculty expectations, experiences, and reflections of iPad usage in a two-year Master's programme in digital media and learning. Student participation (Table 2), reflects patterns related to the programme. For example, most students enter the programme in the fall, resulting in larger numbers of initial expectation entries during those semesters. Students only entered their expectations once during the study. Totals shown in the table represent unique individuals. Both journal entries and reflections represent multiple entries per participant.

Term	Expectations[1]	Journal (Usage)	Reflections
Year 1, Semester 1	26	20	3
Year 1, Semester 2	6	17	11
Year 2, Semester 1	16	16	5
Year 2, Semester 2	8	10	3
Total[2]	56	49	21

[1] Expectations were collected only during the first term of a student's participation.
[2] Totals represent unique individuals. Some students participated during multiple terms.

Table 2. Number of student participants by term and submission type

5. Participant Expectations

The two most frequently mentioned expected iPad uses identified by students were reading electronic documents (n = 20, 35.7%), and using the iPad in class as either a student or a teacher (n = 19, 33.9%). Students also indicated that they expected to use their iPad to take notes or record classes (n = 13, 23.2%) and communicate with others (n = 10, 17.8%). Students expressed the goals of developing basic skills with the iPad and iOS and learning about iPad apps, particularly educational apps (n = 13, 23.2%). In addition to these shared expectations, students identified over 20 other specific iPad uses that reflected their diverse interests. For example, one student noted interest in testing apps and websites, while several others mentioned game development and drawing. Convenience, portability, and ease of use (n = 9, 16.1%), and speculation about completely replacing laptop usage (n = 5, 8.9%) represented other iPad use expectations.

Faculty had similar expectations for iPad use in the classroom, including using the device for reading and annotating, research, collaboration with students, and delivering presentations. They also noted examples of using the iPad for content creation versus content consumption. Learning more about iPad apps for education and knowing what other educators have done with the iPad in their courses was desired. Faculty wanted to learn about the trends of iPad use and apps that would be helpful for them and their students' learning.

6. Student Participant iPad Use

Student participants completed online journal entries via Moodle throughout the duration of the study. Four questions prompted them for descriptions of iPad use related to their DML courses, other academic pursuits, professional activities, and personal use. Additional questions probed the extent of use, their process of learning, and a general comparison with other technologies. The extent and type of iPad use is shown in Figure 1. Notice the limited reporting of work-related iPad use.

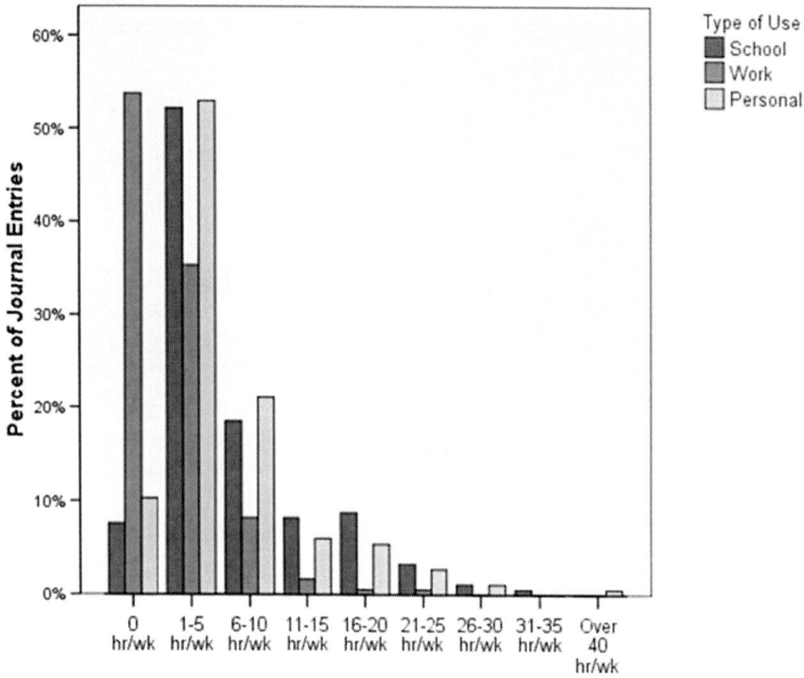

Figure 6. Self-reported extent of student iPad use by type of activity

7. iPad Use in DML Courses

Fifty-one student participants submitted 186 journal entries about their iPad use in DML courses. Approximately half of the student participants reported using their iPads to read and annotate course material, explore educational apps for use in teaching, take notes, search or browse the Web, and design lesson plans and instructional content. Nearly a third of the student participants indicated uses related to accessing course learning management sites, collaborating and communicating with others, sharing and managing files using cloud-based services, preparing and delivering presentations, and testing educational apps. In contrast, a quarter of the students reported little or no iPad use over the reporting period. The students mentioned less frequently a wide range of other uses, including research activities and multimedia-related uses (e.g., viewing videos, taking pictures, recording audio, making movies).

They described their diverse experiences by categorising their iPad use as "information consumption" and expressing the goal of "using it as much as possible for both of my courses." This use was not without challenges, however, as indicated by about 10% of the students who shared these sentiments: "I am finding that typing on it is uncomfortable" and "I'm frustrated that there doesn't seem to be a 'folder' structure that lets me organize my notes." They followed these accounts with later journal entries that indicated changes in their iPad use, such as "I did find that using the keyboard almost brought the iPad to the level of a laptop in terms of usability when needing to do a lot of typing" and this observation:

> The other day I forgot the iPad at home and I had to download the Blackboard App for my iPhone in order to get the assignment I needed. That was a pain! I realized that I have already grown accustomed to having the iPad with me.

8. iPad Use for Other Academic Pursuits

When asked about other academic uses of their iPads, 48 student participants posted 176 journal entries, with over half of the students indicating that they used their iPad to read and annotate material related to their scholarly pursuits. A third of the students mentioned note taking and word processing, exploring and testing educational apps, conducting literature search activities, and web browsing/searching. About a quarter of the students reported using the iPad for communication (e.g., email). Notably, almost half of the students reported no other academic use of their iPad beyond what they reported related specifically to their DML courses.

Student responses indicated their generally positive experiences with reading materials with their iPad. In fact, one student used the journal entry as an opportunity to advocate for digital materials throughout the academic programme. A similar sentiment is evident in this response: "I haven't used it in my other classes... my other class at USF does not allow phones, laptops, iPads to be used in class." The students described the convenience and benefit of e-reading in a variety of ways: "I enjoy reading in digital formats. My books are synced with my iPad phone and computer so I can read anywhere without loosing [*sic*] my spot."

9. iPad Use for Professional Work Activities

Accounts of iPad use for professional activities generally illustrated two themes – no professional use, often due to unemployment or theft concerns, or use of the iPad in teaching. Of 51 student participants who posted 172 entries about their professional use, over half of the students and nearly half of the entries represented no use of the iPad in their professional work activities. The iPad uses reported by student participants in their teaching activities included taking attendance, presenting, testing and using educational apps, preparing lessons, documenting student work, and grading. A quarter of the students identified work-related note taking during meetings. One participant commented that increased iPad familiarity encouraged her to no longer prohibit in-class iPad use by her students. Those preparing to be teachers described their use as important preparation for their future work. Again, although work-related use was generally positively described, this quote illustrates a contrasting view of the iPad's utility: "I need a computer to do my job. The iPad is just a toy."

10. iPad Use for Personal Activities

Fifty-two student participants submitted 182 journal entries describing a rich variety of personal iPad use. Communication use was mentioned the most, with two-thirds of the student participants and over 40% of the total entries indicating uses such as email and Skype or FaceTime communications.

General entertainment pursuits, including game-playing, web surfing, video viewing, news/magazine/blog reading, social networking, music listening, general reading, and video or picture taking, were reported by 25-40% of student participants. About 20% of the students reported using the iPad to pay bills, bank online, or shop online. Approximately 10% of the students mentioned iPad use for travel-related activities, personal organisation (e.g., calendar, task management, note taking, file sharing), cooking activities, and homework assistance. About 15% of the student participants reported no personal use of their iPads. These two quotes represent shared reactions: "I found out, to my utter surprise, that I like reading books with iBook!" and "It's almost as though my iPhone has 'dumbed-down'- I'm not plugging into it as much for media and using it more as a phone and messenger device - and doing more of this [media access] on the iPad."

11. Learning How to Use an iPad

Student journal entries about their learning illustrated further rich diversity in both their learning achievements and their learning processes. The students reported many discoveries of specific apps, covering a very wide range of uses. Among specific iPad skills, students learned how to adjust system settings, lock the screen orientation, "split the keyboard," capture screen images, connect to presentation devices, take and view pictures, manage and switch between apps, and work with the iPad's accessibility features.

Learning processes and sources involved teachers, classmates, friends, family, and colleagues: "Many of this has been word of mouth...", "I have a friend who is an iPad nut, she shows me cool applications and where to find them" and "I recently learned from my parents about the Apple TV functionality that is possible with iPads." Students also acknowledged that their learning proceeded from "trial and error exploration," setting "aside time each day to 'explore' the iPad," and employing "hands-on exploration to learn the various functions on these apps." Online resources facilitated learning as noted by this student: "I watched their one-minute tutorial online to get my bearings, and then began experimenting with the app." This student's response illustrated the combination of advice and exploration:

> Many features and functions are by accident, but I am surrounded by a lot of savvy iPad users at work who are "geeked" out to teach me another cool, functional, efficiency-increasing app. I have also tried to google "best iPad apps/tricks" and many of these blogs give great tips. Mostly, I've been trying to observe others and… ask as many questions as possible.

Personal contact aided initial learning, as shared by this student: "When I have questions and problems, though, I need to talk with people about these, before I consider going to any online self-help tutorials."

12. Comparisons With Other Technologies

The student responses comparing iPad use to other technologies illustrated complexity. Of the 41 student participants who posted 151 journal entries, two contrasting comparisons were evident. Almost half of the students noted more laptop/desktop and smartphone use than iPad use.

About 20% ranked their iPad use higher than laptop/desktop or smartphone use. Reasons given for preferred laptop/desktop use included the benefits of a keyboard, a larger monitor, and more processing power. Alternatively, the reasons supporting iPad use mentioned convenience, portability, ease of use, and startup speed. This summarisation obscures the complexity of responses, because preferences and opinions changed during the study, with the same participant relating opposing observations at different times.

The following quotes illustrate the nature of this complexity:

12.1 Favouring Laptop/Desktop

"Also storage is another big concern, I don"t know a good way to organise files within iPad, so it is just much easier for me to keep my files on the computer."

"Right now my laptop is still the better tool."

"I still like my laptop more but the iPad is growing on me."

"I have not found it to be a replacement for my other devices. So, far it is just fun. I am investigating ways I can use it instead of my laptop, and I find it takes discipline to make the shift from laptop to iPad, but I will keep trying to integrate it into my routine."

"I've noticed my iPad use decrease (in terms of time spent) compared to other IT. I think the iPad is a 'nice to have', certainly lighter and more convenient to carry than my laptop, but I view my phone and laptop as 'must haves'."

"iPad is not my 'go-to' technology. I prefer my laptop and I just don't need to be technologically mobile at this point in my life."

12.2 Favouring iPad

"I'm definitely starting to use my iPad way more than my laptop at home. It is way more convenient to power up and just hop on the Internet."

"With more and more apps I have downloaded, I have grown to become less dependent on my desktop."

"The iPad is truly like having the world within the reach of my fingertips."

"iPad has been used about 90% of the time compared to other devices."

"iPad is the go-to device for anything information-consumptive."

"I am able to carry it without much difficulty. I also don't have to worry about the power source as iPad can last for a longer period of time than a laptop. It is incredibly fast. I am just amazed by it."

"We even purchased one for use after the study."

"The iPad is now overtaking my iPhone as the 'go-to' equipment of choice."

12.3 Mixed Views

"It's useful but is more of a consumer of content than a creator."
"I like the iPad for Light Duties - a quick check of email, brief Light reading, websurfing for fun... For productivity, I still much prefer my PC's. Better screen size, better keyboard comfort, better access to printer, and fully loaded with software productivity tools."
"I use the iPhone and my Desktop more. But now I use my iPad more than my laptop, which is starting to seem obsolete."
"I still use my laptop as the primary device in my home, but I think that the iPad is superior in many respects when it comes to classroom use. I like the portability and simplicity of it and it's something that my middle school students aren't intimidated by."

13. Faculty Participant iPad Use

Faculty use of the iPad was communicated during monthly interviews. Faculty used the iPad in a variety of ways, including using apps to help them with their productivity (e.g., GoodReader, Evernote, and Dropbox) and communication with students, such as WebEx and Skype to allow them to conduct teaching outside of class, connecting students and guest lecturers.

In Year 2 of the study, there was an obvious shift towards greater iPad use for students. Faculty noted that the students felt much more comfortable using the iPad and even preferred it to their laptops in the classroom. The increased level of comfort with the iPad during the second year of the study suggests that the integration of the iPad into the programme supported greater use of the device.

One faculty member explained the students' uses of the iPad as follows:

> Primarily the students have been using their iPad in the class. Students use the iPad for searches, classroom activities; they will usually use their iPad. They might do a presentation on their iPad. It has become the appliance de jour.

This instructor confirmed her beliefs the following month:

> The point is that the iPad was replacing the laptop. Whereas in the past the students preferred laptops, now I see the students using the iPads as many of the apps they preferred were on iPads."

Another instructor validated this finding by stating:

> The iPad is used by virtually every student in the course. It is being used as a presentation tool to share with one another. They even share together in small groups. With the iPad, …as a tablet, they work in small groups.

Another instructor noted that the iPad is changing the ways that students prepare for their projects. "We are using them in a number of ways. We are designing all of our lessons using the iPad…"

AirServer was installed in the classrooms in Year 2, and appeared to make a difference in how faculty and students shared content on the iPad. Airserver uses AirPlay on the iPad, along with a host Mac or PC, to allow for wireless projection of anything on the iPad. Faculty and students could demonstrate apps and share presentations from anywhere in the classroom.

The faculty consistently reported that the students' response to the use of the iPad in their course was very enthusiastic. One instructor noted her students' response as "Very positive, pretty much off the charts. I've been teaching in this program for many years. This is the first time I have really felt like this is transformative."

Another instructor noted that:

> The iPad facilitates a type of cooperative-based learning for the class. I have designed activities so that students perform searches together. If we are going to promote continued iPad use, I would encourage the faculty to do more discovery based learning. Because the class relies on a lot of collaborative based learning. The iPad is a little bit superior for activities in the classroom. I think that tablets are on the verge of making a bigger impact on the K-12 classroom.

14. Participant Reflections

Approximately twenty (20) students submitted final reflections about their iPad use. Overwhelmingly, students reported that their expectations were met. The examples and reasons given by students mentioned reading and annotation, browsing, portability, app familiarity and variety, note taking, collaboration, video viewing, quality of device, and usefulness. One student reported that iPad use "changed the way I look at the written word." The few negative responses referred to lack of opportunity for work-related iPad use, failure to develop comfortable use, and continued dependence on a laptop or desktop computer.

Examples where student expectations were exceeded included learning about the variety of apps, ebook reading, ease of use (e.g., quick boot, long battery life), learning/sharing among classmates, note taking, multimedia uses (e.g., camera, video, sound – ease of capturing/documenting), annotating articles, traveling with the iPad – described as the "perfect in-between" (phone/laptop), and online shopping/leisure activities. Apps mentioned explicitly as exceeding expectations included AirSketch, AirServer, Subtext, Dropbox, iTunes U, and Goodreader. The shared sentiment was summarised by this statement: "I am going to miss the niche that my iPad filled in my life!"

Difficulty typing was the most frequently mentioned reason that the iPad failed to meet expectations. Other reasons for unmet expectations included a lack of laptop functions (e.g., media manipulation, file system), superficial or less robust apps than on laptop/desktop, lack of Flash support, and a desire for a trial period for non-free apps. Three students offered general assessments of their experiences. One stated that an iPad would be "nice to have", but it is not essential and is too expensive. Another student indicated that the iPad was expected to be a "game-changer" like the iPhone, but was not. A third student expected the iPad to be a "ticket to getting on-board with social networking" – but did not achieve that goal.

For some of the faculty the need to purchase apps and vetting through the large number of apps were both daunting. Faculty were satisfied with the device, especially during Year 2 of the study. As students became more comfortable with the iPad they began to make greater use of the device during class time and for class projects and presentations.

15. Discussion

The central findings identified how students and faculty used the iPads, how they learned about iPad features, apps, and uses, and how they decided which technology to use. The student participants read and annotated electronic documents and took notes with their iPads, illustrating their active construction of knowledge. Communicating and collaborating with other people constituted another frequently reported iPad use, employing elements of social learning (Keskin & Metcalf, 2011). Accessing Web resources quickly and conveniently exemplified the role of the iPad in supporting some of the elements of connectivism (Siemens & Conole, 2011).

Equally important to understand was their learning process. By Year 2 of the study, both student and faculty participants demonstrated greater comfort and use of the iPad. The three factors of "focus, fiddle, and friends" identified by Frank et al. (2011, p. 142) were clearly evident in the accounts of participant learning. For example, initial expectations were occasionally vague due to a reported lack of awareness. Increasing focus on iPad use addressed this need. Accounts of hands-on, trial-and-error experimentation illustrated the "fiddle" factor. Opportunities to take risks without negative repercussions allowed the students and faculty to extend their learning and use. The third factor, "friends," was evident particularly in the use of AirServer, or more generally, wireless projection, which significantly aided the use of the iPad during class for presentations and app sharing. Both the student and faculty participants valued the open, honest sharing of iPad experiences.

Preferences related to technology use revealed several dimensions of influence. Participants identified technological reasons (e.g., convenience/ portability/ease/speed vs. power, familiarity, large screen) for choosing a device to use, but they also reported that their device selection was driven by location and by the needs of the task at hand. Understanding the benefits and limitations of the iPad helped the participants make more informed choices when completing a task.

Some study limitations have been noted, but another arose during the course of the study. Final participant reflections were collected at the end of each semester. This time period is not the best for data collection in school settings. As a result, less than half of the students submitted final reflections about their iPad use.

The reported participant experiences lead to further questions about technology adoption and use. For example, observed differences in use patterns could be investigated by considering adopter and environment characteristics identified by Hazan et al. (2011). Likewise, the predictor and moderator influences included in the Unified Theory of Acceptance and Use of Technology (Lewis et al., 2013) could be observed systematically to predict iPad use.

The participants provided specific suggestions for the DML program, which might be considered by other educators. Specifically, they urged the continuation of open, informal, and frequent sharing of iPad experiences. The opportunity to build knowledge and skill with the iPad should also continue by lending iPads or other devices to students as needed. The participants encouraged systemic iPad use throughout the DML programme and beyond to other programmes in the school. More frequent opportunities for student and faculty collaboration and in-class demonstration of iPad apps were also suggested as enhancements to the programme.

16. Conclusion

This mixed-methods case study explored iPad use by education students and faculty. The findings indicated that subsequent iPad use met participants' initial expectations and resulted in positive experiences within the classroom and beyond it. As participants learned about iPad features and apps and shared their learning with others, they developed an understanding of iPad strengths and limitations. This understanding motivated them to consider and experiment with iPad use for a wide range of academic, professional, and personal tasks. The investigation of student and faculty expectations, actual use, and subsequent reflections illustrated a framework to inform other technology implementation projects.

References

Barnes, J., & Herring, D. (2011). Learning their way: Mobile devices in education. In *Proceedings of Society for Information Technology & Teacher Education International Conference 2011* (pp. 127-129). Chesapeake, VA: AACE.

Creswell, J. W. (2012). *Educational research: Planning, conducting, and evaluating quantitative and qualitative research* (4th ed.). Boston: Pearson.

Duncan, D. (2011, May 26). For Seton Hill students and professors, iPads open new paths. *Pittsburgh Post-Gazette*. Retrieved December 29, 2014, from http://goo.gl/1Uf8gg

Enriquez, A. G. (2010). Enhancing student performance using tablet computers. *College Teaching, 58*(3), 77-84.

Frank, K. A., Zhao, Y., Penuel, W. R., Ellefson, N., & Porter, S. (2011). Focus, fiddle, and friends: Experiences that transform knowledge for the implementation of innovations. *Sociology of Education, 84*(2), 137-156.

Gawelek, M. A., Spataro, M., & Komarny, P. (2011). Mobile perspectives: On iPads, why mobile? *Educause Review, 46*(2), 28-32.

Geist, E. (2011). The game changer: Using iPads in college teacher education classes. *College Student Journal, 45*(4), 758-768.

Gosper, M., Malfroy, J., & McKenzie, J. (2013). Students' experiences and expectations of technologies: An Australian study designed to inform planning and development decisions. *Australasian Journal of Educational Technology, 29*(2), 268-282.

Griffey, J. (2012). The rise of the tablet. *Library Technology Reports, 48*(3), 7-13.

Hall, O. (2011). iPad: Assessing the impact of mobile learning technologies on graduate management education. *Global TIME 2011*, 2011(1), 19-20.

Hazen, B. T., Wu, Y., Sankar, C. S., & Jones-Farmer, L. A. (2011). A proposed framework for educational innovation dissemination. *Journal of Educational Technology Systems, 40*(3), 301-321.

Hill, R. A. (2011). Mobile digital devices. *Teacher Librarian, 39*(1), 22-26.

Keskin, N. O., & Metcalf, D. (2011). The current perspectives, theories and practices of mobile learning. *Turkish Online Journal of Educational Technology - TOJET, 10*(2), 202-208.

Kukulska-Hulme, A. (2007). Mobile usability in educational contexts: What have we learnt? *International Review of Research in Open and Distance Learning, 8*(2), 1-16.

Kukulska-Hulme, A. (2012). How should the higher education workforce adapt to advancements in technology for teaching and learning? *Internet and Higher Education, 15*(4), 247-254.

Lewis, C. C., Fretwell, C. E., Ryan, J., & Parham, J. B. (2013). Faculty use of established and emerging technologies in higher education: A Unified Theory of Acceptance and Use of Technology perspective. *International Journal of Higher Education, 2*(2), 22-34.

Mackey, J., & Evans, T. (2011). Interconnecting networks of practice for professional learning. *International Review of Research in Open & Distance Learning, 12*(3), 1-17.

Massé, D. (2012). iPad and tablets are hot but not yet a laptop replacement. *Microwave Journal, 55*(6), 62.

McConnell, S., McConnell, B., & McConnell, K. (2011). Mobile devices in a project-based physics classroom: Developing NETS-S in students. In *Proceedings of Society for Information Technology & Teacher Education International Conference 2011*, (1), 1561-1565.

Mueller, J., Wood, E., De Pasquale, D., & Cruikshank, R. (2012). Examining mobile technology in higher education: Handheld devices in and out of the classroom. *International Journal of Higher Education, 1*(2), 43-54.

Murphy, G. D. (2011). Post-PC devices: A summary of early iPad technology adoption in tertiary environments. *E-Journal of Business Education & Scholarship of Teaching, 5*(1), 18-32.

O'Loughlin, A. (2011). The use of iPads for educational purposes: A study of lecturer and student engagement within mobile learning environments. *Global Learn Asia Pacific 2011,* (1), 1196-1198.

Ostashewski, N., & Reid, D. (2010). iPod, iPhone, and now iPad: The evolution of multimedia access in a mobile teaching context. In *Proceedings of World Conference on Educational Multimedia, Hypermedia and Tele-communications 2010*, 2862-2864.

Pegrum, M., Howitt, C., & Striepe, M. (2013). Learning to take the tablet: How pre-service teachers use iPads to facilitate their learning. *Australasian Journal of Educational Technology, 29*(4), 464-479.

Peluso, D. C. C. (2012). The fast-paced iPad revolution: Can educators stay up to date and relevant about these ubiquitous devices? *British Journal of Educational Technology, 43*(4), 125-127.

Penny, C. (2011). Slide to unlock: An iPad pilot project for higher education faculty. In *Proceedings of Society for Information Technology & Teacher Education International Conference 2011*, 1931-1932.

Perkins, S., Hamm, S., Pamplin, K., Morris, J., & McKelvain, R. (2011). Exploring learning with the iPad: ACU connected and the future of digital texts. In *Proceedings of Society for Information Technology & Teacher Education International Conference 2011*, 1640-1642.

Pettit, J., & Kukulska-Hulme, A. (2007). Going with the grain: Mobile devices in practice. *Australasian Journal of Educational Technology, 23*(1), 17-33.

Siemens, G., & Conole, G. (2011). Editorial. *The International Review of Research in Open and Distance Learning, 12*(3), i-iv.

Simonaitiene, B., & Kutkaityte, K. (2013). Model of the research on the expression of laptop computer use factors in university studies. *Nešiojamųjų kompiuterių naudojimo veiksnių universitetinėse studijose raiškos tyrimo modelis, 79*(1), 36-45.

Stager, G., & Brenner, D. (2013). *Laptop vs tablet. Scholastic Administrator, 12*(4), 42-44.

Stake, R. E. (1995). *The art of case study research*. Thousand Oaks, CA: Sage Publications.

Traxler, J. (2007). Defining, discussing, and evaluating mobile learning: The moving finger writes and having writ... *International Review of Research in Open and Distance Learning, 8*(2), 1-12.

Waters, J. K. (2010). Enter the iPad (or not?). *T.H.E. Journal, 37*(6), 38-40.

USING IPADS TO INCREASE THE LEVEL OF STUDENT ENGAGEMENT IN THE PEER REVIEW AND FEEDBACK PROCESS

ANITA BACKHOUSE[1], IAN WILSON[2] AND DANIEL MACKLEY[3]

Abstract

This investigation explored the use of iPads in a Higher Education (HE) setting in order to evaluate how and if they could enhance an already established approach to peer review and feedback. The context centred on a cohort of 140 pre-service teacher education students engaged in small-group assessed activities in one of their modules. Although some aspects of the existing formative assessment process worked well, the level of student engagement in peer review was felt to need improvement. An opportunity to explore the use of iPads in group work and collaborative learning environments arose as part of the York St John University (YSJ) iPad Project. The management and deployment of the iPads was based on Apple's "institutional" model (Apple Inc., 2013a), and was informed by the YSJ technology-enhanced learning quality framework. A practitioner research methodology involved collaboration between the tutors, students and technology-enhanced learning adviser. Qualitative analysis of student and tutor verbal and written feedback and reflections, questionnaires and observations provided an insight into the level of enhancement attained. Following the eight-month investigation, a number of findings emerged that highlighted that the use of iPads significantly increased the level of student engagement. Both tutors and students became critical reflectors of the technology as well as formative assessment practice. Although the institutional management and deployment model played a significant part in the adoption of the technology for the tutors and in the level of student

[1] York St John University, United Kingdom. Email: a.backhouse@yorksj.ac.uk
[2] York St John University, United Kingdom. Email: i.wilson@yorksj.ac.uk
[3] York St John University, United Kingdom. Email: d.mackley@yorksj.ac.uk

engagement it also contributed to a level of disruption. The tutors and students were able to critically evaluate the effectiveness of the iPads in terms of time, workload and enhancement of the peer assessment and feedback process for the future.

1. Introduction

The project is set in the context of a second-year undergraduate teacher education programme where two tutors carried out an investigation into whether the use of iPads would enhance the peer review and feedback components of small-group assessed activities. The cohort (n=140) was organised into five teaching groups, based on whether they are training to teach very young children (age 3-7 years) or older, primary-age children (5-11 years). As part of their formal assessment within the teaching and learning in science module the students work together in groups of six, on average, to participate in three assessed group activities across the eight-month period of the module.

A well-established and well-received aspect of the group assessments is peer review and feedback coupled with tutor-mediated self-assessment by each of the small groups. The value of peer assessment is well-documented (Divaharan & Atputhasamy, 2002; Nicol Macfarlane-Dick, 2006), and the work of Sluijsmans and Prins (2006) further confirm its value in a teacher education environment because of the authenticity and wider professional attributes that it brings.

The model for peer review and feedback has been employed in the module for a number of years, and is firmly underpinned by the work of Black and Wiliam (1998a and 1998b) in terms of formative assessment or assessment for learning and is further reinforced by the work of Black et al., (2003). The students' enthusiasm appears to stem from the authenticity of the group activities – the production and mounting of an interactive classroom display, a 30-minute practical-based mini-lesson delivered to their peers and a 10-minute science-focused assembly, again delivered to peers.

These activities all relate to everyday occurrences that might be found in any mainstream primary school in the United Kingdom. Together with the authenticity of the activities, previous module evaluations and ongoing feedback from the students confirm that they value the opportunity to enter into a dialogue about their activities and to receive prompt and meaningful feedback. The focus of the feedback contains some summative judgements, but is always aimed at "feeding forward" (Duncan, 2007) into any future activity of a similar nature the students might encounter at university or in school-based settings.

The self-assessment and tutor mediation aspect was felt to work well. Careful tutor questioning during the mediated self-assessment opportunity resulted in a meaningful dialogue that drew on the students' experiences not only during the activities, but also on their experience during school-based practice. This was felt by the tutors to strengthen the students' ability to reflect and evaluate on their practice that is an essential component in their development as reflective practitioners (Schon, 1983), and supports the findings of Vu and Dall'Alba with regard to students' peer assessment experiences (2007).

The tutors had established that dialogue as part of the assessment process improved engagement and critical evaluation, but felt that the element of peer engagement in the review and feedback process was an issue and in need of improvement. Vu and Dall'Alba (2007, p. 552) highlighted the need for research that "strikes a balance between enhancing the benefits of peer assessment for student learning, while reducing the tension experienced by students". This project aimed to do that.

When 20 iPads became available as part of the university's focus on mobile technologies as part of the Technology Enhanced Learning Quality Framework (York St John University, 2012), the tutors took the opportunity to investigate how and if mobile technology might play a part in enhancing the quality and level of engagement in peer review and feedback.

This paper details work in progress, and illustrates how the iPads were used within the project, and how they were received and evaluated as an intended enhancement to an already established peer review and feedback process. Analysis of the responses from student questionnaires have been themed and discussed to illustrate how these outcomes have gone on to inform subsequent work involving student perceptions and values with regard to assessment pedagogy.

2. Background to the York St John University (YSJU) iPad Project

The aim of the YSJU iPad Project is to provide opportunities for staff to increase student engagement in the university classroom through the use of mobile/tablet technology. The focus of the project is on exploring the benefits of using iPads in group work and collaborative learning activities and the impact they have on teaching, learning and assessment.

The teacher education proposal for the use of iPads satisfied the aims of the University's iPad project well, and both tutors were encouraged and supported by the iPad Project team in identifying suitable applications that might be appropriate for peer assessment and feedback. The iPad Project Teaching Enhanced Learning (TEL) Adviser played a significant role in the research process.

3. Methodology and Data Collection

The research method adopted in this investigation was based on action research. The problem under investigation had been identified by both tutors and students, and the solutions or improvements were likely to benefit both. In this respect, the method was more participatory in nature and the exploratory approach might more accurately define the methodology as practitioner research (Fuller & Petch, 1995).

In line with the work of Kemmis and McTaggart (1992) opportunities for review and reflection were frequent, built into the ongoing assessment process and initially based on separate small-group collaborations. Evidence was collected and evaluated throughout the process and, in so doing, the scope of the investigation increased.

The initial investigation involved tutors, the full cohort of students and the TEL adviser. The data that was collected via the questionnaires was coded into themes and analysed. Following an evaluation of the data collection method and data analysis the outcomes were used to inform and enhance the following year's assessment procedures.

4. Description and Use of Applications

4.1 eClicker Presenter

The application is made up of two parts: the Presenter and the Audience. Teachers and presenters use the eClicker Presenter app to enter questions and begin the polling. Participants use the free eClicker Audience app, or their device's web browser, to view and answer the questions, right on their smartphone, tablet or laptop.

The tutors designed statements that the student audience could use to feed back their opinions on the quality of the small group presentations. Nine statements relating to the assessment criteria for the group presentations were loaded into the eClicker Presenter application. Each statement was graded with four response options: strongly agree, agree, disagree and strongly disagree.

At the end of the presentations the students were able to access the statements through eClicker Audience either on the iPads or through their mobile phones via a Wi-Fi connection within the teaching space. The eClicker Presenter application enabled the iPad to act as a hub for the "audience" iPads in the room. As the results were fed back to the presenter iPad they appeared as bar charts providing an overall picture of the audience responses for each statement. The bar charts on the presenter iPad were then used as prompts in the post-presentation discussion between the tutor and the presentation group.

4.2 Socrative

Following feedback from the students about the suitability of eClicker (Findings – section 3.2), an alternative application was found, which they felt to be more appropriate for their needs.

Unlike eClicker, Socrative is a web-based application, and has the facility for students to add comments to their statement response choices. In other aspects Socrative operated in a similar way to eClicker via teacher and student log in. Teachers log in through their device and select an activity that controls the flow of questions and games. Students simply log in with their device and interact real time with the content.

Student responses are visually represented for multiple choice, true/false and Short Answer questions. For pre-planned activities a teacher can view reports online as a Google spreadsheet or as an emailed Excel file (Socrative, 2013a, b).

The most significant difference that favoured eClicker was the instant analysis of the results into bar charts. This was overcome in Socrative by opening the feedback in a spreadsheet and the comments were easily viewed within there.

4.3 Notability (Ginger Labs, 2012)

This application is primarily designed as a note taking application for use with iPads. This application was used by the students to provide feedback on the quality of the classroom displays that their peers had created. The students captured images of a display, and then handwrote or typed text directly onto the image. It is possible to "zoom-in" on specific areas of the display and take additional images. The annotated images were saved anonymously as PDF documents and uploaded to a cloud-based storage facility, in this case a Dropbox (2013) account from within the Notability application. The PDFs were stored in group folders within

Dropbox and a link was emailed to the students who had created the display; they were then able to download and view all of the feedback ready for discussion with the tutor.

5. Findings

5.1 Extent of Use

Notability, eClicker and Socrative were used in the module over an eight-month period. Each student had the opportunity to use Notability to provide feedback five times, to use eClicker five times and Socrative three times. Feedback via Notability generated approximately 450 PDF files over the period of the investigation. eClicker provided an opportunity for approximately 35 feedback sessions and a further 15 feedback sessions took place using Socrative.

5.2 Feedback

Following informal responses from the students about their use of eClicker and Notability they were invited to complete an online questionnaire about their experiences. They were asked to comment on the ease of use of each of the applications and what they liked in particular, and what features they would like to see to improve that experience. There were twenty-two respondents to the questionnaire and, in general, these mirrored the informal comments that the tutors had received during the sessions.

5.3 eClicker

Detailed responses to the question "What do you like most about giving feedback using eClicker?" were analysed into the following categories:

- Simplicity and ease of use;
- Anonymous;
- Quick;
- Multiple choice/set statements.

Responses to the question, "what features would you like to see that eClicker does not have and why?" revealed that the students felt there should be the option to include comments with the feedback judgements. There was a need for more detail about what the students had done well or what the suggestions for improvement might be.

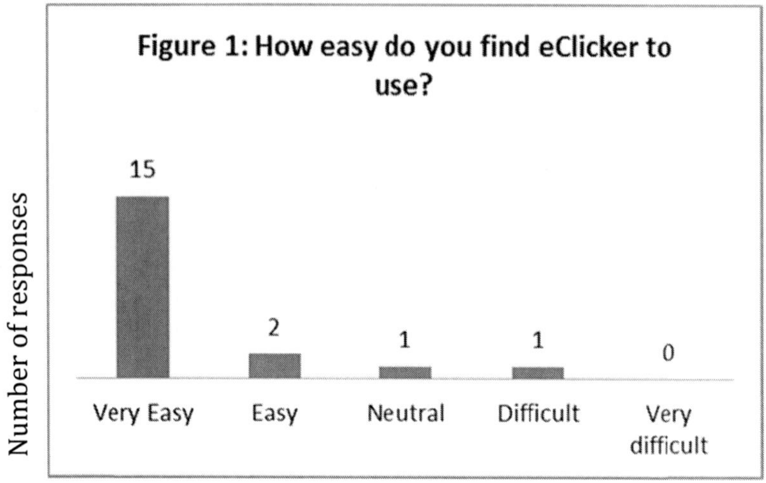

Figure 1. Student responses for eClicker (n=19)

6. Tutor and TEL Adviser Observations During eClicker Feedback Sessions

6.1 Positive Outcomes

- Students quickly adapted to the use of eClicker;
- All students participated in the peer feedback and some students downloaded eClicker Audience to their mobile phones in order to provide their feedback;
- Students responded well to the feedback statements and felt that this helped them to focus on the assessment criteria;
- Students appreciated the anonymity of the peer feedback;
- eClicker feedback took less time than the previous written comments;
- The students felt that the instant analysis and presentation of the overall judgements was clearly presented and understandable.

6.2 Considerations

- Students receiving the peer feedback felt that they needed more detail about why certain feedback had been given and wanted to know the justification, particularly for the more negative responses.

7. Notability

Following informal responses from the students about their use of Notability they were all invited to complete an online questionnaire about their experiences. They were asked to comment on the ease of use of each of the applications and what they liked in particular and what features they would like to see to improve that experience.

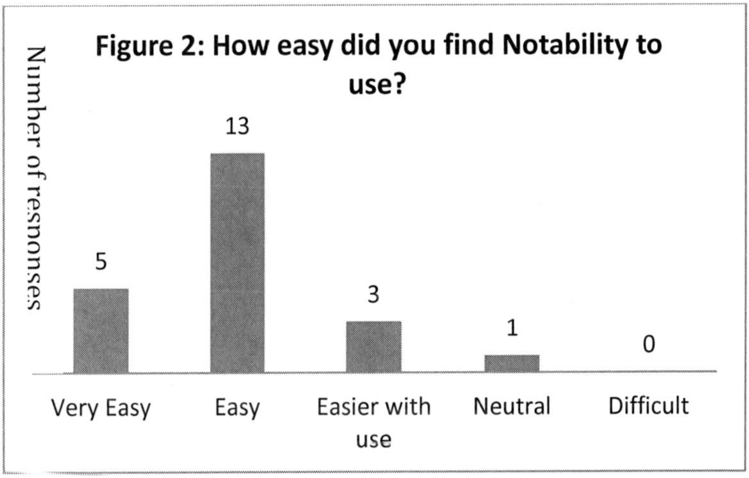

Figure 2. Student responses for Notability (n=22)

Detailed responses to the question, "what do you like most about giving feedback using Notability?" were analysed into the following categories:

- Ease of use;
- Able to focus on exact areas of the display and give targeted feedback;
- Flexibility in terms of how much or how little to write;
- Time to think and consider feedback.

Other responses included:

"It feels very modern and hi-tech to give feedback this way."
"The software is versatile and the system seems to be quick and effective."

There were very few suggestions for additional features in response to the question, "what features would you like to see that Notability does not have and why?", but one student felt that the upload procedure to Dropbox could be more straightforward.

8. Tutor and TEL Adviser Observations During Notability Feedback Sessions

Observation and discussion notes revealed:

8.1 Positive Outcomes

- All students in all teaching groups were keen to provide feedback;
- The speed and confidence in the use of Notability increased with use, in general;
- There was an increased level of peer/peer and peer/tutor discussion about the qualities of the displays as the students constructed their feedback;
- The quality of the annotations improved over time to become more detailed and focused, which was indicative of a deeper level of thinking;
- The students began reflecting on the process of peer feedback as a means of assessment;
- The groups of students were very positive about the amount of feedback received – this could be between 12 and 20 separate PDF files;
- The groups of students always accessed their peer feedback in advance of the tutor discussion meetings and came ready to discuss it.

8.2 Considerations

- The time taken to provide feedback in this way impacted on the time available for other activities in the session;
- Although some students became proficient very quickly others were much slower to gain confidence and still required reassurance and guidance in using Notability.

9. Management of the iPads and Applications

The iPad project adopted the "Institutional Ownership model" (Apple Inc, 2013). Prior to each teaching session the iPads were prepared by the

TEL Adviser with the relevant settings and applications. This involved ensuring that the devices were connected to the institution's Wi-Fi network, that the relevant and most up-to-date versions of the applications were installed, and that access to certain features of the device was restricted.

To ensure anonymity during the learning activities each iPad was assigned a generic name. The name was placed on the lock screen of each device and was used by the students when they saved their feedback on the classroom displays to Dropbox. Previously, students had used their initials when saving the files to Dropbox. The tutor later deleted these before the feedback was shared with the relevant group.

The management of the iPads continually evolved throughout the eight-month period they were used with students. Initially, students were asked to sign into Dropbox and select the correct folder to save their feedback. After the early sessions it was clear that this was likely to lead to confusion due to the number of students and the need to access specific folders. The most significant change to the process was, therefore, the set-up of the Dropbox account prior to the session before the classroom display activity.

Regular updates to both the iOS (the iPad operating system) and the applications were required throughout the duration of the project. Occasionally, the reduced quality of the Wi-Fi connection in the teaching room meant that the Notability PDF files needed to be uploaded to Dropbox after the session rather than during it. Connectivity between eClicker Presenter and eClicker Audience was also affected by the quality of the connection meaning that on occasion reconnection was necessary and previous feedback data from that session was lost. After each session the iPads were collected by the TEL Adviser and synchronised with the Apple Configurator (Apple Inc, 2012). This removed all content that had been created on the device.

10. Positive Outcomes

- Setting up the folder structure in Dropbox prior to the teaching session gave for a more streamlined and straightforward upload procedure. This prevented students from saving feedback files in the wrong location.
- The ability to disable the App Store and in-app purchases and other iOS features prevented students from being distracted whilst engaging with the learning activity.

- Apple's Volume Purchasing Program (Apple Inc., 2013b) allowed us to purchase apps (in quantities of 20+) at a discounted rate. Currently, app developers have the option to make their app available at a reduced rate (up to 50% off) for educational institutions.

11. Considerations

- The preparation and management of the iPads became resource intensive. Prior to each session the TEL adviser had to sign into Dropbox on each device (20 in total) and set up the connection with Notability.
- Occasionally, the reduced quality of the Wi-Fi connection in the teaching room meant that the Notability PDF files needed to be uploaded to Dropbox after the session rather than during it. Connectivity between eClicker Presenter and eClicker Audience was also affected by the quality of the connection, meaning that on occasion reconnection was necessary and previous feedback data was lost.
- Although there are clear advantages to an institutional model for managing the iPads this does limit access to them and, as such, limits spontaneity and creativity in their use; all sessions needed to be pre-planned and booked on the system.

12. Post-School Experience Questionnaire

The purpose of the questionnaire was to establish whether using iPads for a sustained period for peer feedback had any impact on the students' awareness of their own assessment practice with the children in their school placements. This deeper level of inquiry had been prompted by students commenting on the impact of the iPads in the way they approached peer feedback during the workshop sessions and in some of the initial questionnaire responses.

It is worth noting that the response rate for the questionnaire was much higher than for the previous questionnaire. This questionnaire was carried out using the Socrative application using the iPads.

13. Analysis of Student Responses

Whilst the responses paint a positive picture about the apparent impact of the iPads on the students' engagement with peer assessment and feedback the text responses after each statement revealed some interesting additional insights. The responses that were of particular significance, in terms of providing a focus for future investigation, were in Tables 2, 3, 4 and 5. Students' attitude to peer review and feedback meant that whilst they valued the giving of feedback almost 40% did not value, or trust the feedback they received from their peers. There are implications here both for the use of peer feedback within our own modules and equally from a pedagogical perspective in the classroom. These findings concur with the work of Nicol and McFarlane-Dick (2006), but are nonetheless important with regard to the developing pedagogical practice and values of our students.

Table 5 suggests that almost 42% of students will tailor their own feedback to reflect the type of feedback they received. This meant that if students received negative feedback about their work they would respond in kind and also give negative feedback regardless of the quality of their peers' work. This was a concern for the module tutors and brought into question the value of peer review and feedback.

Positive comments	Number of responses
Quick and easy	11
Motivating	7
Feedback is anonymous	8
Helped to raise awareness of the assessment process	34
Visually appealing	5
Total	65

Negative comments	Number of responses
Need more detail in eClicker responses	12
Time-consuming	6
Total	18

Table 1. Student comments with regard to the use of iPads for peer assessment and feedback

Types of comment	Number of responses
Important because people have different feedback preferences	40
I am just happy to receive feedback – I do not mind how it is given	7
Important because I prefer to get more justification about the marks I am given	8
Important because I like to feel I have control over the assessment process	11
Total	66

Table 2. How important do you feel it is to have a say in how you receive feedback on your work?

Types of comment	Number of responses
I like to compare other people's work with my own	8
It helps me to clarify and understand the assessment requirements	7
It helps me to reflect and improve my own work	49
I like to see alternative perspectives	11
I am concerned about other students being biased in their feedback on my work	10
I find it useful for getting ideas	6
Total	91

Table 3. Giving feedback to peers on their work helps you to reflect on your own work

Types of comment	Number of responses
Disagree – I prefer tutor only feedback	5
Disagree – I do not trust peer judgements	32
Agree – it helps me to think about what I need to do to improve my own work	29
Agree because I like alternative perspectives	23
Agree because it helps to develop empathy for the feedback process	4
Total	93

Table 4. Receiving feedback from peers helps you to improve your work for next time

Types of comment	Number of responses
The type of feedback I give depends on the feedback that I receive	25
I give the type of feedback that I would like to receive	9
It helps me to think about the whole feedback process	7
It helps me to be more reflective about my work	10
No, it has no effect on the type of feedback I give	9
Total	60

Table 5. The quality of feedback you receive helps you to think about how you give feedback to other people

	Number of responses
Yes, but need more detail in the voting app	12
Yes, it is quick and easy	11
Yes, it is motivating	7
Anonymity is important	8
Yes, raised my awareness of assessment process	34
Only that it is time-consuming	6
Visually appealing	5
No impact	4
Total	87

Table 6. Working with iPads in the science sessions helped you to think about the value of peer assessment and feedback

14. Discussion

What we all hoped was that the iPads and the applications we used were appropriate, met everyone's needs and enhanced the previous methods. The desire for success was, however, not necessarily driven by the same goals for tutors and students; the tutors' goal was a deeper level of critical engagement from the students, whilst the students, in the initial stages, were more concerned with the novelty of being able to use the iPads on a regular basis. The tutors felt that the opportunity to use iPads within sessions led to a greater level of motivation on the part of the students to participate in the feedback process.

With increased familiarity and confidence in the use of iPads came an increase in the quality of the peer feedback. With regard to Notability, the level of detail in the feedback improved, and comments became more developmental and forward-focused. We cannot underestimate the importance of regular use of technology in order to embed it fully within pedagogical process. Making access to feedback flexible for the students was well received, and supported the findings of Conole, de Laat, Dillon and Darby in their study that looked at the role of technology in changing study patterns in higher education contexts (2008). Flavin discusses the lack of engagement with new technologies or superficial use within classrooms (2012). His work goes on to identify a reluctance to exploit the true potential of technology with a focus on the disruptiveness of the technologies as they interrupt established routine. Deegan and Rothwell (2010) identified a range of potential barriers with regard to either the perceived or actual issues associated with the fitness for purpose of technology hardware and applications. Interestingly, though, work by Liu, Li and Carlsson (2010) suggested that ease of use (or lack of it) was not an indicator of likelihood of adoption of m-learning methods and technology. In our study, some students did feel the iPads were a distraction at times, and felt they were time-consuming and not part of the learning process. These students were in the minority but nevertheless, this may have implications for their future practice in the classroom and this is worthy of further study.

Furthermore, the presence of technical support within the classroom, certainly in the initial stages, was advantageous to the effective and productive use of the technology for the students and tutors alike. What we should not assume is that all students are "digital natives" (Prensky, 2001), and we should be mindful that according to Bennett (2012, p. 4) this does not apply across a whole population but to certain subgroups, and we should address equally the potential for a "digital divide".

15. Conclusion

In terms of the outcomes of the study, the students did engage more with peer review and feedback when the iPads were used and the approach did enhance established practice. However, this increased level of engagement revealed issues in terms of the students' level of understanding about formative assessment that can now be addressed within the module. A direct consequence of the iPads has, therefore, been a raised awareness of students' attitude towards peer assessment, which will then inform module design and assessment procedures. The next steps are to further explore the technology and applications in order to help engage students more in setting their own assessment criteria and making the links between their own assessment values and pedagogical practice.

References

Apple Inc. (2013a). Institutional iOS ownership deployment model.

—. (2013b). The Apple volume purchasing programme. Retrieved December 29, 2014 from: http:// goo.gl/lD5LRD

—. (2012). Apple Configurator (version 1.3) [Mobile application software] Retrieved December 30, 2013 from: http://itunes.apple.com

Bennett, S. (2012). Digital natives. In Z. Yan (Eds.), *Encyclopedia of cyber behavior* (pp. 212-219). Hershey, PA: IGI Global.

Big Nerd Ranch (2012a). eClicker audience (Version 1.0.4) [Mobile application software] Retrieved December 30, 2013 from: http://itunes.apple.com

—. (2012b). eClicker presenter (version 1.0.13) [Mobile application software] Retrieved December 30, 2013 from: http://itunes.apple.com

Black, P., & Wiliam, D. (1998a) Assessment and classroom learning. *Assessment in Education*, *5*(1), pp. 7-73.

Black, P., & Wiliam, D. (1998b) *Inside the black box*. London: NFER Nelson.

Conole, G., de Laat, M., Dillon, T., & Darby, J. (2008). "Disruptive technologies", "pedagogical innovation": What's new? Findings from an in-depth study of students' use and perception of technology. *Computers and Education*, *50*(2), 511-524.

Deegan, R., & Rothwell, P. (2010). A classification of m-learning applications from a usability perspective. [Internet] *Journal of the Research Center for Educational Technology (RCET)*, *6*(1), 16-27.

Divaharan, S., & Atputhasamy, L. (2002). An attempt to enhance the quality of cooperative learning through peer assessment. *Journal of Educational Enquiry*, *3*(2), 72-83.

Dropbox (2013). Dropbox [Internet] Retrieved December 30, 2013 from https://www.dropbox.com

Duncan, N. (2007) 'Feed-forward': Improving students' use of tutors' comments. *Assessment & Evaluation in Higher Education*, *32*(3), 271-283.

Flavin, M. (2012). Disruptive technologies in higher education. *The Journal of the Association for Learning Technology*, *20*. Retrieved December 29, 2014 from: http://goo.gl/wef514

Fuller, R., & Petch, A. (1995). *Practitioner research; Reflexive social worker*. Oxford: Oxford University Press.

Gingerlabs (2012). Notability (Version 4.42) [Mobile application software]. Retrieved December 30, 2013 from: http://itunes.apple.com

Kemmis, S., & McTaggart, R. (1992). *The action research planner*. Geelong: Deakin University Press.

Liu, Y., Li, H., & Carlsson, C. (2010). Factors driving the adoption of m-learning: An empirical study. *Computers & Education*, *55*, 1211-1219.

Nicol, D. J., & Macfarlane-Dick, D. (2006). Formative assessment and self-regulated learning: A model and seven principles of good feedback practice. *Studies in Higher Education*, *31*(2), 199-218.

Prenksy, M. (2001). Digital natives, digital immigrants. *On the Horizon*, *9*(5), 1-6.

Schön, D. (1984). *The reflective practitioner: How professionals think in action*. New York: Basic Books.

Sluijsmans, D., & Prins, F. (2006). A conceptual framework for integrating peer assessment in teacher education. *Studies in Educational Evaluation*, *32*, 6-22.

Socrative (2013a). Socrative student [Mobile application software] Retrieved December 30, 2013 from http://www. socrative.com

Socrative (2013b). Socrative teacher [Mobile application software] Retrieved December 30, 2013 from http://www. socrative.com

Vu, T., & Dall'Alba, G. (2007). Students' experience of peer assessment in a professional course. *Assessment and Evaluation in Higher Education*, *32*(5), 541-556.

York St John University (2012). iPad Project [Internet] York, York St John University. Retrieved December 29, 2014 from: http://goo.gl/Va58eu

IMPLEMENTING IPADS AS PERSONAL LEARNING DEVICES: MAKING THE PAPERLESS MBA POSSIBLE

SHARON ALTENA[1]

Abstract

In 2011 Queensland University of Technology's Graduate School of Business formulated a digital learning strategy, and embarked on a three-year journey to transition the Executive MBA from a paper-centred learning environment with paper-based study guides, timetables, forms, textbooks and notebooks to a fully paperless environment by the end of 2014. This paper reports on how iPads have been implemented as Personal Learning Devices (PLD) to achieve the paperless MBA. It discusses the challenges faced, how these have been overcome, key learnings, and recommendations applicable for others considering a paperless classroom through the use of iPads and other tablet technologies. An action research methodology using focus groups, observations, open-ended informal discussions with students and student surveys has been used to guide the transition to a paperless learning environment. Although this research is still ongoing, preliminary findings indicate that as long as adequate, targeted iPad learning interventions and ongoing support is provided to students, the iPad can be used effectively as a PLD.

1. Introduction

The Graduate School of Business is a commercial arm of the Business School at Queensland University of Technology (QUT). It currently offers five postgraduate programmes, one of which is the Executive Master of Business Administration (EMBA). The Graduate School also designs and

---

[1] Queensland University of Technology, Australia. Email: sharon.altena@qut.edu.au

delivers a number of customised short executive education programmes that are tailored to the specific needs of corporate and government clients.

The students studying the EMBA program are predominantly male, mid-career professionals, aged between 32-50 years of age, which means that our cohort of students includes both digital natives and digital immigrants (Prensky, 2000). Entrance into the EMBA programme requires students to have an undergraduate degree and a minimum of five years experience, with two of those years being at a supervisory level. The students attend classes one weekend per month over twenty-two (22) months, with many students flying to Brisbane to attend classes from across Australia, close Pacific nations and Asia. As business executives, a large percentage of our students is mobile and undertakes significant travel as part of their work.

Traditionally, the learning materials provided to EMBA students consisted of printed learning guides, paper-based textbooks, printed timetables and paper-based forms, all of which were supplied to students as part of their course fees. Blackboard, our learning management system, was used to provide access to readings and other materials that students would typically download and print. Students studying an EMBA were required to have a laptop, which was used in lectures for sending and receiving mail, making notes on PowerPoint slides, accessing websites and for reading and printing documents.

In May 2011, some twelve (12) months after the iPad1 was released in Australia, the Executive Director of the Graduate School of Business recognised that the iPad was a game-changer for student learning, in fact what Christensen refers to as a disruptive innovation (Christensen & Overdorf, 2000). He made a decision that the Graduate School of Business should lead the university in the move towards mobile learning through the implementation of iPads for the next intake of EMBA students, commencing in January 2012. This implementation was not to be a trial of the iPad, but a full implementation across all 24 units in the EMBA program.

The initial driver for this implementation was the desire to become a more environmentally sustainable programme by eliminating the use of paper and reducing the substantial costs associated with printing. Other key drivers included the desire to explicitly demonstrate to students that we truly live up to our tagline of being a university for the "real world". In a similar way to Illinois Institute of Technology and other early adopters of the iPad, "we are a university of technology" and therefore needed to be at the forefront of technological advancements (Rath, 2010), to explore the potential of the device to support student learning and to do things differently.

Furthermore, as a school within a university of technology that is developing current and future business leaders, we have an obligation to develop the digital literacy of students for learning and to develop skills that can be transferred across into their working life.

As a programme committed to and highly valuing face-to-face classes and the important networking opportunities an MBA offers students, this initiative was also being implemented to allow us to skip the eLearning phase and leapfrog ahead to mobile learning, drawing on the learning from early pilots happening globally.

Issued with an iPad 2 and a $100 iTunes Gift Card, I was tasked with the responsibility of implementing iPads into the EMBA and asked to "make it happen".

The objective of this paper is to report on how the paperless MBA has been made possible through the introduction of iPads as a PLD. It discusses the challenges faced, how these have been overcome, key learnings, and recommendations applicable for others considering a paperless classroom through the use of iPads and other tablet technologies as PLDs.

2. Creating a Plan

It was important to have a clear goal and plan for the implementation of the iPad. Kha suggests that:

> Without a specific goal and plan, the iPad has no more impact on the classroom than a cellular phone. Students will use it to chat or to surf. You have to have an explicit plan. (Fuch, 2011)

From the outset, we viewed the iPad as a PLD rather than a learning technology. This is an important distinction. We were interested in investigating three key questions: How could students use the device to assist them with their studies and learning? Can an iPad replace a laptop in the classroom? Is it possible to achieve a paperless learning environment for postgraduate learners? The iPad as a technology for the lecturer to use in the classroom for teaching was a secondary consideration. This implementation was to be a bottom-up, student-centred innovation that in time would gain traction and momentum and begin to influence up and eventually the classroom practice of academics.

We took a long-term view of the implementation of iPads with the development of a three-year plan that identified a key focus for each year.

This does not mean that it precluded other experimental and development activities relating to iPads, but they were not the main focus. This plan was divided into four phases, and in keeping with an action research methodology, the learning from each phase was reflected upon and built into and extended into the next phase of the project (Figure 1).

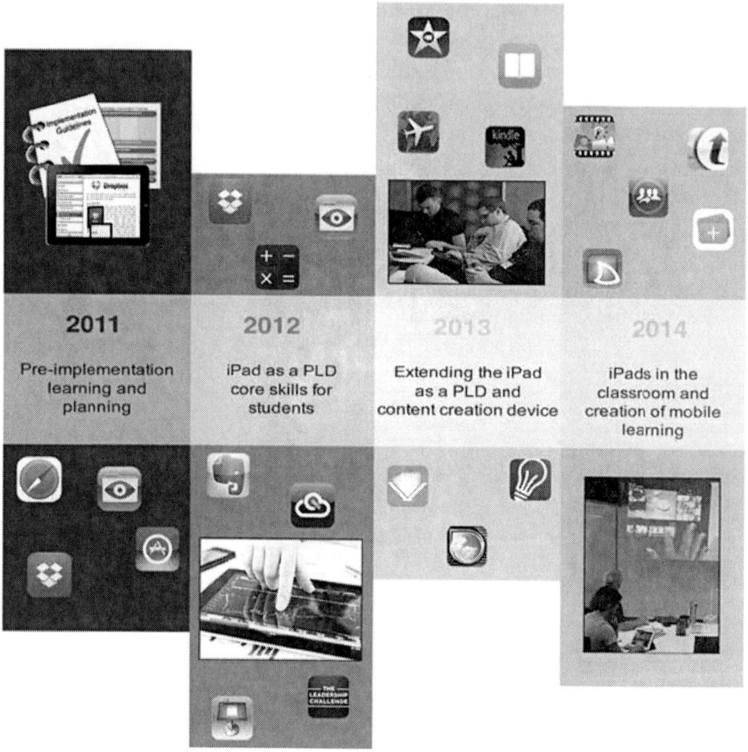

Figure 1. iPads implementation plan

3. Phase 1: Pre-implementation Learning and Planning

3.1 Exploring the Possibilities

Now, some years on, it is easy to forget that the iPad represented a significant change in the way we interact with learning materials and create learning. The iPad was unlike any other device we had previously used. We had become accustomed to PCs, mice and USB sticks, and were now moving to what Murphy refers to as a post-PC era (Murphy, 2011) with a device that relied on touch and used the cloud rather than physical means to transfer files. The iPad required a rethinking of familiar workflows to access, transfer and store files, read and make notes on documents, access information and interact with the device.

Initially we examined how students studied and identified three key activities:

- Access to information and research;
- Communication, collaboration and knowledge construction;
- Management of learning (Figure 2).

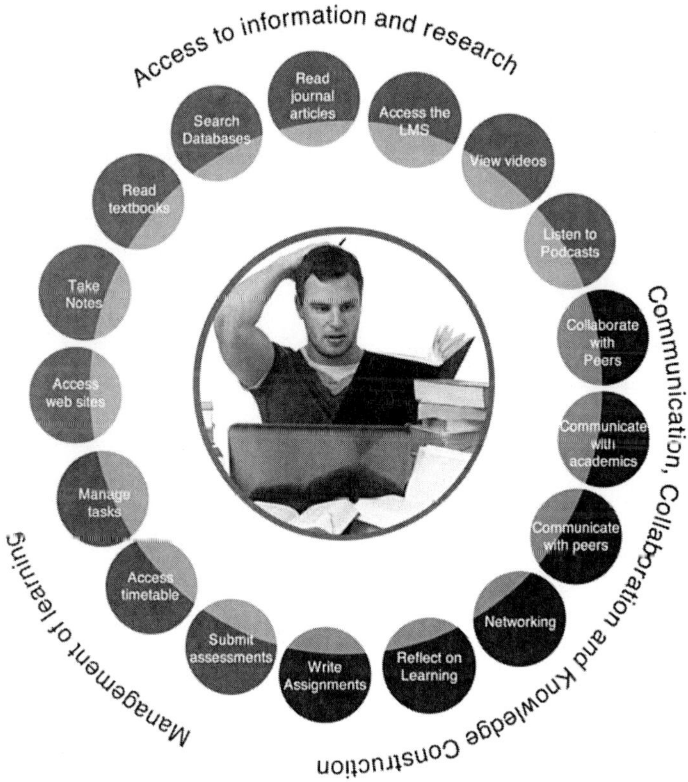

Figure 2. Student study activities

These are similar to the activities identified by Fischer, Smolnik and Galletta (2013) in their study of tablet use in higher education. We explored how these activities could be replicated or extended on an iPad using the new affordances the iPad offers students.

3.2 Student Trial

In preparation for the implementation of iPads in 2012, a small pilot programme, as recommended by Chester (2010) and Fuch (2010) was established. The pilot, consisting of six EMBA students (two previous iPad users and four non-iPad users), was established in July 2011 to allow us to investigate the potential of the iPad from a student perspective. The trial lasted for three months with focus group sessions held on two occasions to get feedback on the iPad, the apps we had recommended and the apps students had discovered for themselves. The trial was supported by an initial student workshop, where they were introduced to the device, including setting up email, connecting to the QUT Wi-Fi network, purchasing apps using the iTunes card, cloud-based storage, iPad security, the apps we wanted them to evaluate and the scope of the project. Additionally, a student iPad website was created to provide support to students. This contained FAQs, reviews of apps and tip sheets for using selected apps.

4. Findings From the Trial

This trial provided us with four key insights that would be incorporated into the implementation phase.

1. Need for ongoing student training and support
   It was clear that we needed to provide ongoing student training and support if we wanted to change postgraduate student habits. For example, all students in the trial had reported that they experimented with annotating documents using the GoodReader app, however, when pushed for time, they reverted back to their old pen and paper habits. Although the trial students saw the benefit in being able to electronically annotate documents, they were not skilled at this and needed to invest more time, which they did not have, to learn these skills.
2. Cloud-based storage
   Students indicated that Dropbox was the most valuable app they used. Some commented that cloud-based storage provided through

Dropbox had revolutionised the way they work at university and in their work life.

3. PDF formatted documents
The trial identified that providing materials in PDF format enabled students to read and annotate documents and PowerPoint presentations on the iPad. We discovered that the iPad did some strange things to some PowerPoint presentations including reversing diagrams or making some slides appear upside down.
4. Blackboard
Blackboard by default opens document in the same window, which prevents documents from being downloaded into the GoodReader app on the iPad. We discovered that we needed to ensure documents uploaded to Blackboard opened in a new window.

At the end of the trial students indicated that in order for the implementation of the iPad to be deemed as successful, we needed to "go hard". They recommended that we take away all paper and expose students to as many apps for learning as possible. This advice was the direct opposite of the thoughts of the faculty, who felt that many of the EMBA students were, in the main, not particularly technologically savvy and that we needed to proceed slowly and with extreme caution with our executive students.

5. Establishment of a BYOD Policy

A number of other universities within Australia and overseas, such as University of Adelaide, Trinity College at Melbourne University, IMD, IESE, Wharton, Illinois Institute of Technology, Stanford, Ohio State University and Seton Hill University (Jennings, et. al., 2010; Herrick, 2011; Rice, 2011) were giving commencing students iPads upon their enrolment. We took a different approach, based on our view of the iPad as a PLD and introduced a BYOD policy. Consequently, students were required to purchase an iPad in addition to the laptop that had been a requirement of the programme for a number of years.

6. Issue of Staff iPads

Although the use of iPads by staff was not the main focus of the initial implementation, it was important to provide academics and administration staff working within the Graduate School of Business with an iPad and an iTunes card to enable them to begin to explore the device and new ways of working. Staff were provided with instructions on how to set up and maintain security of their iPad, and were invited to attend a number of workshops designed to highlight the features of the device and some key apps that they might be interested in exploring further. A staff support website was also established to provide just-in-time learning and support. Staff were encouraged to use the iPad for work and personal purposes and to explore the possibilities it provided, but were not put under pressure to use the iPad.

7. Implementation Guidelines

Many academics were nervous and some openly expressed concern about the use of iPads in the program. These concerns included:

- Fear that the students would be seduced by the technology;
- Students would no longer read as it is too difficult to read online;
- It is a high-pressure and intensive programme and we are now adding another level of complexity for students who struggle with computers;
- Costs to students of purchasing apps could be quite considerable;
- There may be an expectation for faculty to change their approach.

In response to these concerns, a set of guidelines for implementing iPads was developed with the assistance of programme directors. These guidelines clearly set out the apps that could be introduced to students, how iPads could be used, the pace of this change and support that would be provided to students and staff. These guidelines were communicated to all staff at a meeting where feedback and input was encouraged.

8. Preparation of Student Workshops

In preparation for the implementation, a survey was sent out to commencing students to gauge their previous experience in using iPads. The data collected from this survey was used to tailor student workshops to meet the specific needs of students.

9. Phase 2: iPad as a PLD Core Skills Development

9.1 Student iPad Orientation

As part of the 2012 Orientation program, two iPad training sessions were included, one in the first weekend and one in the second weekend a month later.

The first workshop focused on getting iPads configured for QUT systems, exploring the apps that come standard with the iPad, setting up email, introducing and setting up cloud-based storage, downloading documents onto the device, transferring files from iPad to computer and computer to iPad, subscribing to the iCloud calendar, iPad security including passcodes and Find my iPad, and backing up data via iCloud and iTunes.

The second workshop focused on teaching students how to use the full features of the GoodReader app and also provided students with a range of tips, tricks and shortcuts for using their iPads.

9.2 iCloud Calendar

The iCloud calendar allowed us to create a student timetable of scheduled classes, assessment due dates, two-week and one-week reminders about assessment due dates, details of networking events and reminders about when course fees were due. Once this calendar was created in the cloud we sent students an email with a link inviting them to subscribe to the calendar. Once subscribed, any updates to assessments or classes were automatically synced to their devices through the Calendar app. This ensured that students and staff always had the latest information. Students are also able to subscribe to the iCloud calendar on their PC or Mac, and Android users were able to subscribe through their Gmail account.

9.3 Accessing and Annotating Documents Using GoodReader

Students were taught how to download their academic readings, PowerPoint slides and learning guides from Blackboard using the GoodReader app, as well as how to navigate downloaded documents, search documents, bookmark pages, read, annotate and share annotations with others. The sharing of annotations has been particularly helpful to students when working on collaborative assignments. Additionally, students were taught how to use GoodReader to manage and organise files on the iPad, including being able to manually or automatically sync updates to documents to either Dropbox or their computer networks.

9.4 Dropbox

Students used Dropbox for cloud-based storage and as a mechanism for transferring files from PC/Mac to the iPad. Some students working in groups set up shared folders within their Dropbox as a cloud-based central repository for storing and sharing group files.

9.5 Communicating Using Mail, Yammer, FaceTime and Skype

At orientation students set up their QUT email accounts on the iPad, and were shown how to manage their email, including the use of multiple email accounts on the one device. Students were also provided with access to Yammer, a private social networking tool used to create a learning community, facilitate knowledge construction and communication amongst students when they were off campus, and to also facilitate communication with staff. During the year, as the need arose, students were introduced to both FaceTime and Skype to facilitate communication and collaboration with their peers and as a mechanism for allowing team members to join face-to-face meetings remotely.

9.6 Self-Publishing

In the process of transitioning to a paperless MBA, we began exploring how to self-publish our own learning guides for student use on the iPad. Initially we explored the use of iBooks Author, which is a robust, easy-to-use tool with many additional third-party widgets available to further increase the interactivity of eBooks. However, at the time, eBooks developed using iBook Author could only be read on an iPad, not even on a Mac, hence we decided we could not use the tool.

We also explored the use of InDesign and Adobe's Digital Publishing Suite, but found that the learning curve was significant, and required specialist skills that academics and administration staff did not have. A number of iPad eBook authoring apps such as CBB were tested, but we found that the books generated were not ideal for our purposes. Other free or low-cost applications that allow the creation of eBooks such as Calibre and Nameo were tested, but they did not allow the creation of fixed layout eBooks. As a graduate programme for executives, it was important that the eBooks we produced were high quality and visually appealing.

Although the creation of PDF documents using Adobe Acrobat Professional does allow for including interactivity and embedded videos, the underlying engine is based on Flash, which of course does not work on an iPad. After evaluating the range of options, we eventually settled on creating PDF versions of learning guides generated from Microsoft Word. By combining standard Microsoft Word tools such as bookmarks and hyperlinks we were able to include navigation within the eBook, as well as interactivity such as videos, quizzes and links to external documents. These interactive PDF documents, combined with the power of the GoodReader app, have allowed us to create fixed layout eBooks that have all of the typical features of eBooks.

9.7 Evaluation of the First Year

Over the course of the first year we learned a great deal about the iPad through informal feedback from students and our own observations. Six months into the programme all students were invited to participate in an EMBA review forum to provide feedback on their experiences of the EMBA programme. As part of this forum, students had the opportunity to provide initial feedback on the use of iPads. Students indicated that most of them were using the iPad, and they certainly appreciated the portability of the device, but feedback indicated that progress was too slow and that we needed to use it more for them to get the benefit of their investment in the device. One student quoted that "it was like having a Ferrari and only being able to drive it in first gear". Essentially, our implementation guidelines had put the brakes on what we could do in the first year. Bottom-up innovation driven by students required us to use a revised approach for the second year of implementation.

10. Phase 3: Extending the iPad as a PLD and Content Creation Device

10.1 New Approach to Student Orientation

Student feedback from the first year of implementation required us to re-evaluate how we introduced iPads to students. It was Everett Rogers (2003) who said "people are more likely to adopt an innovation if they see the advantage of the new strategy relative to what they currently use" (Roblyer, 2005, p. 197). With this in mind we set about identifying the WIFM (What's in it for me?) factor. What is it that the iPad does really well that computers do not? For us, in our context, that factor was introducing eBooks to replace paper-based textbooks.

10.2 Early Bird Clinic

An early bird clinic was added to the orientation programme for the second year that was supported by QUT IT Help Desk staff. The purpose of this early bird clinic was to get the iPad set up before the workshops.

This included setting up email, Apple IDs, Dropbox accounts, Amazon accounts, connection to the QUT network and the purchasing of key apps to be used in the workshops. We provided students with a checklist of tasks they needed to complete with systematic self-paced instructions for how to accomplish the tasks.

10.3 Student Workshops

The first workshop still focused on the iPad as a PLD, but now we had more time available to demonstrate the power of the iPad through the introduction of eBooks and the Kindle app - this created the WIFM factor. Students were able to see how they could highlight and make notes in their eBook, have their notes backed up to the Amazon website, share notes, search their book to locate quotes for assignments, and showed how the eBook, notes and highlights were synced across their iPad and computer. They could immediately see the affordances that eBooks offered them that were not available in paper books (p-Books).

The Bump app was also used as a “fun” activity for students to share their contact details with others, and certainly created a buzz in the room. We also integrated a number of activities using QR Codes to show students how to use their devices to read codes that gave them access to task descriptions, we sites and surveys.

The second workshop again focused on the GoodReader App, since this is a core app used in our programme. Students were introduced to the Vbookz PDF app that reads PDF documents aloud, enabling students to listen to their PDF documents when travelling or exercising. For the busy executives in our programme this created the WOW factor. The second workshop also allowed us to introduce students to FaceTime and Skype, where they could see immediate uses in their studies, business and personal lives.

10.4 eBooks

The second year of the project has really been the year of the eBook. We have managed to negotiate with publishers and to establish workflows that allow us to purchase the eBooks for students and distribute them to their devices. We have managed to narrow down the number of eBook readers to just three (Kindle, iBooks and VitalSource), and students have received training and support in the use of these readers. Next year we hope to use only two eReader platforms. There have been a couple of students who have resisted the use of eBooks, but we have stayed strong to our commitment to the paperless learning environment, and have provided additional support to assist them with this transition. We have been able to work with one of our students, who has a visual impairment, to use the accessibility features of the iPad to help him to overcome this hurdle. By the end of the third year of the digital learning strategy, we expect to have completely moved across to eBooks for all 24 units in the programme.

10.5 Self-Publishing

In the second year we further explored the possibilities for self-publishing with our student handbook (EMBA Survival Guide), International Tour Workbook and student learning guides in an interactive PDF format. We had great success with this, and the students have responded very positively to our ability to leverage the functionality of GoodReader, an app they are very familiar with, to make highlights and notes, hyperlink to solutions, include interactive quizzes and create a stylish, visually appealing eBook with clear diagrams, images and colour. This has certainly made a difference in the quality of the materials we produce for student learning.

From our perspective, these interactive PDF eBooks have been a great solution, as they are simple and relatively quick to create and do not require specialist design skills or a steep learning curve. Importantly, it allows us to create documents in a format that can be read on any device, including phone, Android, PC or Mac.

10.6 Electronic Forms

In our quest to become a paperless learning environment, we have started trialling the use of forms that are electronically distributed to students. The form is completed on the iPad, and by tapping on the embedded submit button an email is automatically generated with the completed form attached and emailed to the academic. Initially this was used for student peer feedback forms and it is now being trialled with criterion-reference assessment sheets (rubrics for grading student assessment).

10.7 Apple TV

For a number of academics the Apple TV has been the WIFM factor. They are now unchained from the lectern and can move freely around the classroom whilst displaying the content of their iPad remotely via the data projector to the class. Apple TV is a simple technology that allows academics to work in a new way. They are also finding Apple TV to be a useful tool for students to showcase their group work from their iPads to the class, from their chair.

10.8 Web Conferencing

In expanding the capabilities of the iPad we have been testing a range of web conferencing tools for the iPad. The chosen tool is Fuzebox. This is a full functioning web-conferencing tool, and, unlike many other iPad web-conferencing tools, allows you to host a meeting or webinar directly from the iPad, wherever you have Internet access. All other web conferencing apps only allowed you to participate in meetings from the iPad. The version of Fuzebox that we have purchased allows us to have ten people in videoconferences and up to 100 participants on audio in a meeting. We are also looking at using Fuzebox for webinars and student group consultations with academic staff, as well as a teaching tool for units relating to the management of virtual teams and virtual team negotiations.

10.9 Recording Learning and Content Creation on the iPad

Students this year have been using their iPads to record their learning electronically through note taking, recording their reflections and with video and photographs. Some students have recorded their class presentations using the iPad, to allow them to playback and review the presentation for extending their learning. Students are also taking photos of whiteboard notes that can be shared with peers.

A couple of academics have changed their assessment tasks to include more creative, content creation tasks such as digital stories or videos using the iMovie or Explain Everything apps instead of, or as a supplement to, a traditional academic paper.

10.10 Evaluation of the Second Year of Implementation

An evaluation of the second year of the iPad programme has just been conducted using a student survey that was sent to all 25 students who commenced their EMBA program in January 2013. The survey was designed to find out how students are using the iPad as a personal learning device and whether the iPad could replace a laptop in the classroom.

The 14 students who completed the survey indicated that, overall, they had a very positive experience using the iPad as a personal learning device. The ease of use, flexibility and portability of the iPad were identified as the greatest benefits for students. One student commented "It is portable and lightweight when travelling. I can take it anywhere and it is more convenient than carrying a bag full of textbooks".

The majority of students are taking what they have learned about the iPad and are applying it to their work and/or personal lives. Students are predominantly using the device for accessing information and research purposes followed by management of their learning. At this stage, students are not strong users of the iPad for content creation, which is an area that we will focus on in the next phase of the project.

The majority of students indicated that they felt there was still a need for a laptop in the classroom, which supports our observations that the majority of students are using both the laptop and iPad in the classroom.

11. Phase 4: iPads in the Classroom and Mobile Learning

We have already been experimenting and exploring with some faculty how the iPad can be used in teaching. However, 2014, our third year of implementation, will be the year of iPads in the classroom. We intend to investigate ways that the iPad can be used to actively engage students in learning and the more effective use of the iPad as a content creation and collaboration device.

We are also looking at extending our work with self-publishing and the creation of learning materials through video and screen capture apps as well as exploring mobile learning development tools, which will enable us to deliver more interactive and engaging learning experiences for postgraduate students.

11.1 Challenges Faced

The implementation of iPads within the EMBA programme has not been without its challenges. There have been many obstacles that we have had to overcome including:

11.1.1 IT Infrastructure

The QUT Wi-Fi network already had the capacity to cope with traffic from students' use of laptops and iPads, as we were only dealing with small numbers of part-time students. Where we did have issues was in arranging access and the security required by some of the apps we wanted to use, such as Blackboard Mobile, Idea Flight, Keynote Remote and Apple TV. IT Services blocked the use of these apps on the QUT Network due to security reasons or incompatibility issues with QUT systems.

Twelve months later most of these issues were resolved by accident rather than good planning. The Graduate School of Business was renovated, which included the installation of a separate Wi-Fi network to provide corporate clients attending short courses or conferences with Internet access. This separate network meant that we could use Apple TV and other apps previously blocked by IT Services. The one app that we are still not able to use is Blackboard Mobile, but we are continuing to work on getting this resolved.

11.1.2 IT Help Desk Support

Although we did notify the IT Services and IT Help Desk of the iPad launch, in hindsight we did not work as closely with the technical support teams as we should have in the first year. The IT Help Desk tried to assist students with issues relating to their iPads, but the technology at the time was very new and technicians were not familiar with the iPad and the problems students would face. This resulted in the Graduate School of Business having to be the de-facto iPad Help Desk, which significantly added to our workload, especially in the first couple of months of the implementation.

11.1.3 iCloud Calendar Issues

Just prior to student orientation, we discovered issues with the QUT web-based Microsoft Outlook email client that prevented students on their PCs from being able to subscribe to the iCloud calendar. Although the calendar integrated seamlessly into the calendar app on the iPad, it was important for us to demonstrate to students how the iCloud calendar would also sync with their other devices. This was eventually resolved with the help of the IT Services team.

11.1.4 QUT Email

QUT by default uses a web version of Microsoft Outlook for student email. The process for setting up this email on the iPad is not simple and involved numerous steps, requiring students to switch between their Settings and Safari apps. Although we managed this effectively in the pre-implementation trial when working with only six students, we underestimated the challenges in trying to assist 30+ students all at once. It was chaotic. Email is such a critical app to set up, as without email on the device students are not able to get an Apple ID, purchase apps or set up Dropbox.

In the first year of implementation we found the QUT web-based Outlook client to be problematic. In the second year we resolved this issue by ensuring students set up a Gmail account and redirected their QUT email to this account. The selection of a Gmail account over other free email accounts was made on the basis that if we required students to upload videos to YouTube they would already have a login and would not be required to create yet another account. The adoption of a Gmail account made the whole process of setting up iPads much smoother, and removed the issues we had experienced earlier with the iCloud calendar.

11.1.5 The Challenges of a BYOD Policy

The adoption of a BYOD policy meant that the purchase of an iPad was only a recommendation and not a requirement. This decision raised two issues. Prensky (2012) highlights that pressure to use the devices, once schools have invested in them, is extremely high. We found that the pressure is significantly more if students are purchasing the devices themselves. We had not been clear in setting expectations at the beginning of the year. Students were purchasing the iPad; they had a much higher expectation that the faculty would use the iPad in the classroom. It was also expected that we would roll out apps at a much quicker pace, but we were constrained by the guidelines we had set

The second issue relating to the BYOD policy was that some students decided to purchase an Android device. This added an extra layer of complexity when trying to assist students to set up their devices during orientation and had flow-on effects when selecting apps for students.

11.1.6 eBooks

Initially publishers were only willing to provide us with eBooks that had a 12-month licence, after which the eBook would be disabled and the notes and annotations would be lost. We provide students with textbooks as part of their course fees, and when we provide a print book the students are able to use and refer to it for life, and are able to sell their book if they no longer want it. We could not understand why an eBook, which was only slightly cheaper and in some cases the same price as a print book, could only be used for 12 months, especially as our EMBA programme was a 22 month programme and some of our units used the same textbook. It would be possible for us to have to purchase the same textbook twice for each student. This impasse had the potential to restrict our ability to implement eBooks using only Kindle or Google eBooks, as these did not expire.

We managed to resolve this by negotiating with a publisher for a lifetime eBook licence. This then allowed us to negotiate with other publishers, and in 2014 all of our textbooks will be available as lifetime eBooks.

12. Recommendations for Implementing iPads

1. **Have a clear plan**: What is the purpose of your iPad implementation? What is it that you want to achieve? What is your 1-3 year plan for this implementation? How will you evaluate whether you have been successful? Will you have a BYOD policy or provide iPads to students? Ensure that you clearly communicate your goals to both staff and students to ensure that expectations are managed.
2. **Get a support group**: Find some like-minded passionate people with whom to collaborate, and explore the potential that iPads offer for learning.
3. **Work with the IT services and IT help desk staff**: Ensure that the infrastructure of the university is able to handle the increased volume of connected devices. Work with the IT Services team to identify blockages such as network security, restrictions on Apple products etc., and develop workarounds to these issues in advance.
4. **Thoroughly test the apps**: There are over one million apps available for the iPad and this can be quite overwhelming for students. It can also be expensive to purchase apps that do not live up to their promise. Identify those that best suit your learning environment and thoroughly test and evaluate the functionality of these apps. Our testing of apps against set criteria has enabled us to identify some outstanding apps, with many being able to be integrated with other apps.
5. **Get faculty on board**: Faculty are the key to the successful implementation of iPads into the classroom. For a number of them, iPads represent a significant change and challenge to their current classroom practices. Staff need to be supported to incorporate iPads into the classroom. Although we have conducted a number of workshops for staff, by far the most effective way has been to provide 1:1 support to faculty.

6. **Do not underestimate the WIFM (What's in it for me?) factor**: Understand your students and staff; identify the killer apps that will make them see the value of this device for learning and start with them first. What is it that the device can do that will make their life easier?
7. **Allocate sufficient time in orientation to support students**: As reported by Woodcock, Middleton and Northcliffe (2013) in their study of the use of smartphones, many students will use their iPad for email, searching the web, playing games and social media, but few are using them for learning. Even those who are already using apps such as GoodReader, in my experience, are not exploiting the full potential of the app, and are surprised when introduced to the full functionality supported.
8. **Provide JIT support for students and staff**: Throughout the students' programme, schedule follow-up work in the use of specific apps that will be used in the classroom, e.g. the use of iMovie just prior to the students needing to create a digital story for a leadership unit, or the use of Simple Mind+ just prior to their problem solving class, or the use of the VitalSource Bookshelf reader prior to students being issued with an eBook using this platform. The provision of self-access resources to support students and staff in their use of iPads cannot be underestimated.
9. **Evaluate! Evaluate! Evaluate!** It is critical to regularly evaluate the use of iPads to allow you to see if you are meeting the needs of students and are able to use the feedback provided to further refine the implementation.
10. **Go hard and just do it**.

13. Conclusion

The iPad in our context has become the Swiss army knife of learning, a mobile, lightweight, quick to set up and use, multi-functional device. Its introduction will have allowed us, over a three-year period, to transition from a learning environment reliant on paper to one that is entirely paperless. The portability and flexibility of the iPad and our desire to better meet the needs of our executive students has been our impetus and catalyst for change.

Whilst we accept that our approach to implementing iPads may seem quite slow and measured compared to other implementations (Cavanaugh et. al., 2012), our approach has been specifically designed to change behaviour, reduce the learning curve and to find the most efficient ways to use the device for mature, mobile, busy executives who are studying a postgraduate programme. We believe that we have been successful in meeting the goals of our iPad implementation.

Although the implementation is ongoing, our initial conclusions are that the iPad can be effectively used as a personal learning device. Mature-aged students need support to learn new workflows and how to maximise the potential of the device, eBooks and apps. Although the iPad is a powerful device and its functionality has greatly improved since the introduction of the iPad 1, at this stage it is still not a replacement for a laptop, but the iPad certainly increases mobility and the flexibility to work anywhere, at any time, on any device. Students have become multi-device learners.

Planning is currently underway for Phase 4 of the implementation in 2014 to explore the use of the iPad in the classroom and opportunities to engage students in using the iPad as a content/knowledge creation device as well as exploring more sophisticated approaches to interactive eBook learning guides, including learning analytics and the development of custom mobile learning apps to support Executive MBA students.

Evaluation of iPads in the EMBA programme is continuing. A new cohort of EMBA students commencing in 2014 will provide us with the opportunity to apply and extend our new learnings for further improvement. It is planned to undertake a formal evaluation of the entire programme at the end of 2014 once our current cohort of students has completed their programme. This will evaluate the extent to which the goals of the digital learning strategy have been achieved and whether this is a sustainable model for extending the implementation into other areas of the Business School or other faculties within QUT.

References

Alyahya, S., & Gall, J.E. (2012). iPads in education: A qualitative study of students' attitudes and experiences. In T. Amiel & B. Wilson (Eds.), Proceedings of *World Conference on Educational Multimedia, Hypermedia and Telecommunications 2012* (pp. 1266-1271). Chesapeake, VA: AACE. Retrieved December 29, 2014 from http://www. editlib.org/p/40913

Bower, J. L., & Christensen, C. M. (1995). Disruptive technologies: Catching the wave. *Harvard Business Review*, *73*(1), 43-53.

Bradshaw, D. (2011, February 14). MBA students start taking the tablets. *Financial Times*. Retrieved December 29, 2014 from: http://goo.gl/qLYwgI

Cavanaugh, C. Hargins, J. Munns, S., & Kamali, T. (2012). iCelebrate teaching and Learning: Sharing the iPad experience. *Journal of Teaching and Learning with Technology*, *1*(2) 21-12.

Chester, T. M. (2010, May 5). CIO predicament: What to do about the iPad. Campus Technology. Retrieved December 29, 2014 from: http://goo.gl/yD9kyT

Christensen, C. M., & Overdorf, M. (2000). Meeting the challenge of disruptive change. *Harvard Business Review*, *78*(2), 66-76.

Fischer, N., Smolnik, S., & Galletta, D. (2013). Examining the potential for tablet use in a higher education context. In R. Alt and B. Franczyk (Eds.), *Proceedings of the 11th International Conference on Wirtschaftsinfomatik, 2013, Leipzig, Germany*. Retrieved: 29 December, 2014 from: http://goo.gl/fWECHF

Fuch, D. (2010, May 6). 3 questions to answer before a wide-scale adoption of the iPad. *Academic Impressions*. Retrieved December 29, 2014 from: http://goo.gl/7r8WX5

—. (2011, January 27). Piloting the iPad. *Academic Impressions*. Retrieved December 29, 2014 from: http://goo.gl/oMQyw5

Hubbard, L. A., & Ottoson, J. M. (1997). When a bottom-up innovation meets itself as a top-down policy. The AVID untracking program. *Science Communication*, *19*(1), 41-55.

Herrick, C. (2011, October, 14). iPads have reduced costs, improved communication for Uni of Adelaide. Computerworld. Retrieved December 29, 2014 from: http://goo.gl/uA4rsu

Jennings, G., Anderson, T., Dorset, M., & Mitchell, J. (2011). Report on the step forward iPad pilot project. Trinity College, University of Melbourne. Retrieved December 29, 2014 from: http://goo.gl/LmbL6t

Manuguerra, M., & Petcoz, P. Promoting student engagement by integrating new technology into tertiary education: The Role of the iPad. *Asian Social Science*, *7*(11), 61-65.

Melhuish, K., & Falloon, G. (2010). Looking to the future: M learning with the iPad. *Computers in New Zealand Schools*, *22*(3), 1-16.

Murphy, G. D. (2011). Post-PC devices: a summary of early iPad technology adoption in tertiary environments. *E-Journal of Business Education & Scholarship of Teaching*, *5*(1), 18-32,

Pegrum, M., Howitt, C., & Striepe, M. (2013). Learning to take the tablet: How pre-service teachers use iPads to facilitate their learning. *Australasian Journal of Educational Technology*, *29*(3), 464-479.

Prensky, M. (2001). Digital natives, digital immigrants. Part 1. *On the Horizon*, *9*(5), 1-6.

—. (2012). Before bringing in new tools, you must bring in new thinking. *Amplify*. Retrieved December 29, 2014 from: http://goo.gl/b1ULBg

Rice, A. (2011, October 18). Colleges take varied approaches to iPad experiments, with mixed results. *Chronicle of Higher Education*. Retrieved December 29, 2014 from: http://goo.gl/1qRFv

Roblyer, M. D. (2005). Educational technology research that makes a difference: Series introduction. *Contemporary Issues in Technology and Teacher Education*, *5*(2), 192-201.

Rogers, E. (2003). *Diffusion of innovations* (5th ed.). New York: Free Press.

Shepherd, I. J., & Reeves, B. (2011, March). iPad or iFad – The reality of the paperless classroom. Paper presented at *Abilene Christian University - Mobility Conference*. Retrieved December 29, 2014 from: http://goo.gl/fa2Qc

Traxler, J. (2010). Will student devices deliver innovation, inclusion and transformation? *Journal of the Research Centre for Educational Technologies*, *6*(1), 3-15.

Woodcock, B., Middleton, A., & Northcliffe, A. (2012) Considering the smartphone learner: an investigation into student interest in the use of personal technology to enhance their learning. *Student Engagement and Experience Journal*, *1*(1). Retrieved December 29, 2014 from: http://goo.gl/pivLLo

Adoption and Knowledge Continuum in the iPad-enhanced Classroom: A Working Note

Oliver Young[1] and Richard Tresidder[2]

Abstract

This paper explores the relation between iPad use in educational settings and the various levels of engagement by users within a Technology-Enhanced Learning (TEL) environment. The research undertaken for this paper demonstrates that existing assumptions of student engagement are inappropriate and do not recognise the complexity of the individual's interaction with the iPad. This interaction is determined and influenced by their levels of knowledge and philosophical relationship with technology in general. It can be argued that it is the need to understand not just the relationship with technology, but also the ongoing transition in the learning environment through the utilisation of mobile technology that enables mobile learning. This paper proposes a model that enables the exploration of the complex learning environment.

1. Introduction

The introduction of the first iPad in 2010 (Smith & Evans, 2010) can be seen as an important marker in the evolution of mobile learning. It provided a simple and interactive platform for learners to engage and interact collaboratively outside of the traditional learning environment, and this defines contemporary "asynchronous" learning. The benefits of mobile technology in supporting academic endeavours are well charted (Gawelek, Spataro & Komarny, 2011; Getting & Swainey, 2012; Geist, 2011) and well supported by learning orientated institutions, who are

[1] Sheffield Hallam University, United Kingdom. Email: oliver.young@shu.ac.uk
[2] Sheffield Hallam University, United Kingdom. Email: R.Tresidder@shu.ac.uk

increasingly utilising technology as a part of their teaching and learning strategies.

Mobile technologies such as 2nd generation mobile phones (2G), notebooks, Palm PDAs and other handheld computers have been in existence for some time, and many of these early examples adopted primitive web-based platforms. Whilst these primitive systems were innovative and pioneering they were also time-consuming and a drain on resources. Despite much advancement, these devices were stifled due to a number physical parameters such as size, weight, battery life, real-time interaction and, most importantly, processing power. The iPad with its touch screen, multi gesture and video / audio capacity to capture and create data in real time has revolutionised the learning environment. Thus the ability to adopt this type of modern mobile technology within the contemporary learning environment has become significantly easier.

Much of the research undertaken into the use of iPads has provided very positive data in terms of supporting dyslexic students (Shah, 2011; Reid, Strnadová & Cumming, 2013), use within science education (Robinson, 2011) and increasing the level of engagement and achievement amongst students from all areas of the education sector (Murray & Olcese, 2011; Sinelnikov, 2012). Although this data is useful, success of the iPad within an educational perspective still relies upon the adoption and interaction with the technology by both the student and teacher. Thus this paper explores the relationship between students, teacher and technology in the learning environment.

During the academic year 2012-13 a pilot study undertaken with undergraduate final year students studying Conference and Meetings Management attempted to explore their interaction with mobile technologies, their approach to usage and the impact on their learning and productivity. Two cohorts of students were analysed in a quasi-experimental approach. Data was collected in the form of a longitudinal questionnaire that assessed their current usage and expectation for technology in the classroom. The questionnaire was administered at the beginning of the module. Students were then provided with iPads to complete their academic work. Additionally, the questionnaire was administered at the mid-point and at module conclusion. At the end of the module the students completed module evaluation questionnaires that assessed how they perceived the module and identified areas of good practice. Their performance was also monitored, and findings were compared with a control group who did not have access to iPads. Additionally, comparisons were made with previous cohorts studying the module, who were not provided with iPads.

From this initial study, observations highlighted that not all students were operating at a similar level. Their knowledge and understanding of a range of applications varied amongst the cohort. General assumptions that current students undertaking Higher Education (HE) courses are the Net or Digital generation and generation Y may also be challenged by these findings. Prensky (2001, p. 1) refers to the Net, Digital and generation Y as "Digital Natives" who are the "…native speakers of the digital language of computers, video games and the Internet…" This pilot demonstrated that existing models of interaction are inappropriate and do not recognise the complexity of individual and collective interaction with the iPad within a technology-enhanced learning environment.

2. Defining the Ideal Learning and Teaching Environment

This paper puts forward the idea that by understanding the effective exchange of knowledge the constructive transmission of knowledge within the contemporary learning environment can be replicated. This is determined by understanding that there is a point of synchronicity where information flows freely and effectively, as such creating an idealised learning zone in which knowledge is communicated. Adapting the work of Durkheim (1995) and Turner (1969) it is possible to think of the most effective or "ideal" interaction between the student, the teacher and mobile learning technology as a form of communitas. In this instance there is perfect clarity, and barriers and boundaries are removed to create an enhanced learning "space" where communication is optimised. In order to replicate this idealised space, an understanding of the knowledge and interaction levels of users and how technological advancement continually alters this relationship needs to be understood.

Understanding the relationship between students, teacher, mobile technologies in the learning environment and their effective use becomes increasingly complicated. This complication is due to the ongoing technological development of both hardware (e.g. smart technologies; phones, tablets, watches, etc.) and software (e.g. social media, web based collaborative tools, cloud and web 2.0 / 3.0 technologies, etc.). Consequently, although we can locate an individual based on their individual perspectives, consideration for the dynamic nature of the users' relationship with technology and their individual learning or teaching style also needs recognition. Hence the position of the user needs to be re-evaluated upon the introduction of any new technological intervention, and this is demonstrated in the model below (Figure 1).

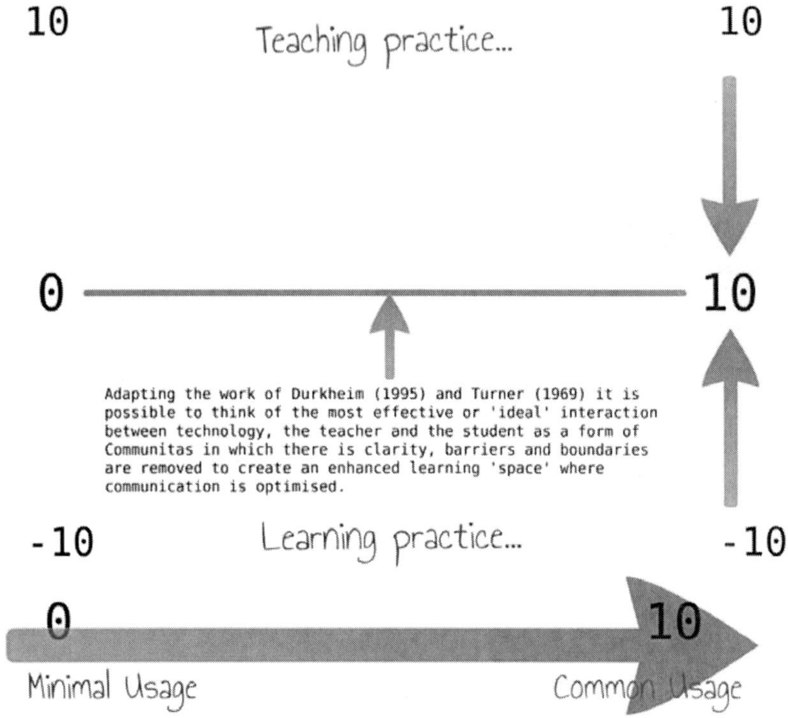

Figure 1. Adoption and knowledge continuum model

Ensuring the continued success in the use of mobile technologies within the educational environment requires establishing an understanding of both the individual's position within the Adoption and Knowledge Continuum (Figure 1) presented above. Both student and teacher can be represented on the model and this will identify the idealised learning space in which communitas of learning takes place. Furthermore, plotting the student and teacher on the Adoption and Knowledge model not only allows for the identification of the idealised learning space, but can also highlight areas of digital distance. This idea is based upon the fact that failure to establish communitas would result in "Digital Distance", i.e. the opposite of communitas. Figures 2 and 3 below provide a graphical representation of an example of the digital distance concept.

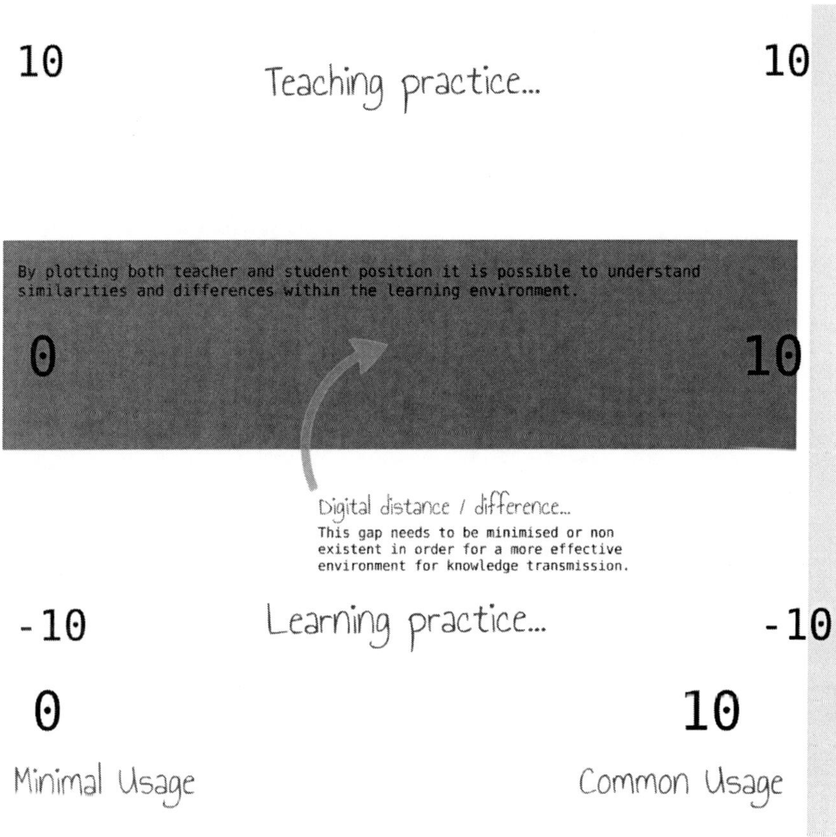
10
Teaching practice...
10
By plotting both teacher and student position it is possible to understand similarities and differences within the learning environment.
0
10
Digital distance / difference...
This gap needs to be minimised or non existent in order for a more effective environment for knowledge transmission.
-10
Learning practice...
-10
0
10
Minimal Usage
Common Usage

Figure 2

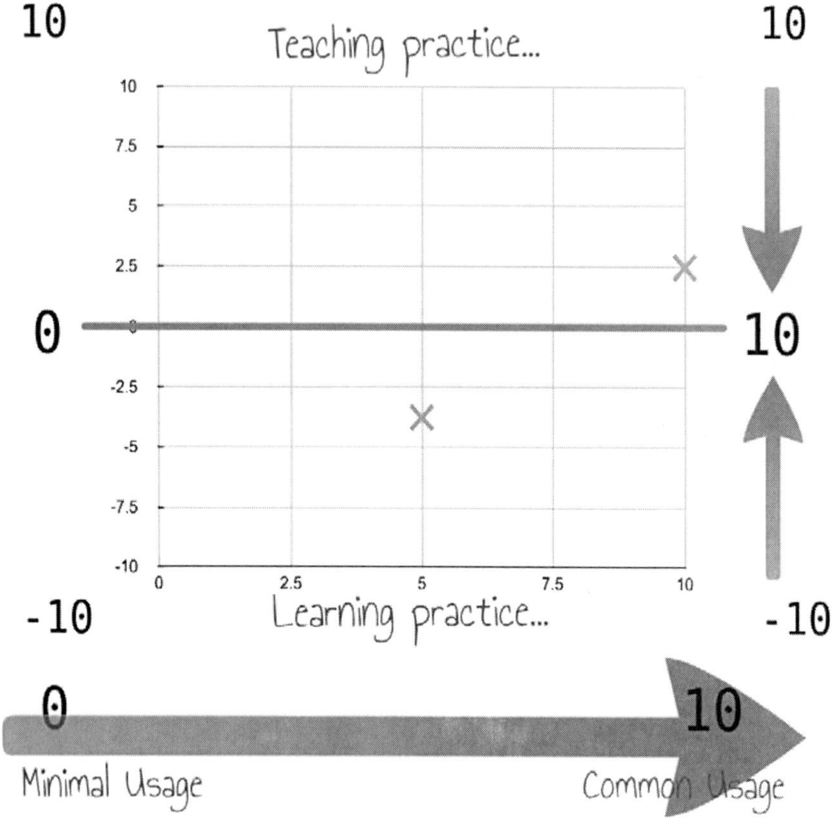

Figure 3. Digital distance concept

Note that in Figure 3 the teacher is highlighted in green and an example of a student is highlighted in blue. Here it is clear to see that both teacher and student are not operating on the same level; as such communitas has not been reached, and this is therefore an example of digital distance.

In order to generate this graphical representation the data collected from the participants can be converted into quantitative data that will then allow the relationship or digital distance to be identified between two parties (student to student, student to teacher or teacher to teacher) and also on a community or collective basis. This has been plotted in Figure 4.

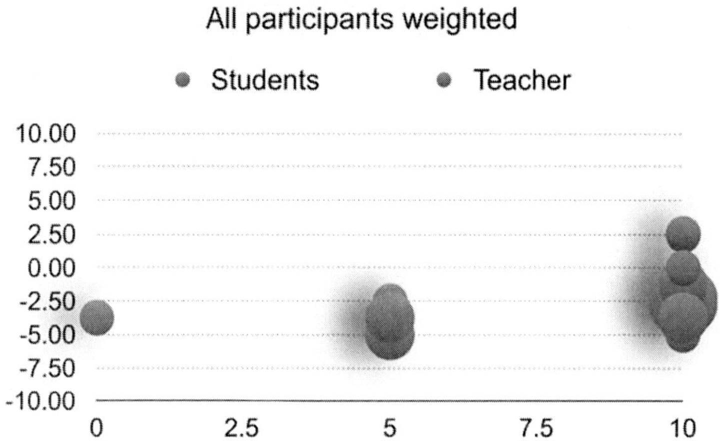

Figure 4. Distance between two parties

3. Methodology

The rationale behind the 2013-14 study was to explore the nature of student perspectives on the use of technology within their education. This study utilised a qualitative thematic approach to develop themes to explore the data collected within this study. Data collection was carried out through individual questionnaires administered to the participants. As questionnaires are empirical information gathering tools, it is the ideal method to explore student perspectives (Tymms, 2012). The questionnaire served two primary functions. To enable the exploration of the topic area and to understand the nature of the population being studied, this preliminary exploration was conducted on a smaller sample set selected form a wider population. This also enabled the proposed model to be tested.

The questionnaire comprised two main sections comprised of three subsections. The first section focused on obtaining demographic data about the participants. This was achieved through closed questions. The second section focused on the perspectives of the participants who responded to open-ended questions. The first subsection focused on the aforementioned demographic data. The second established an understanding of the respondents' technology ownership and usage. The third sought to understand the participants' perspectives on technology use in their education.

The responses were analysed, and in order to check for accuracy and consistency an attempt to triangulate the results was undertaken. This identified whether the results from the questionnaires are in line with the views of the individual participants. The triangulation process was undertaken in the form of a focus group selected front the questionnaire participants as discussed by Gibbs (2012). In this instance conducting the focus group allowed the exploration of the collective views of the sample based on their individual responses.

The focus group consisted of six participants from the sample set. Progressing this study was achieved through using a larger sample set, and this resulted in reasonable assumptions about the participant responses on the topic area. There are strengths in using a focus group to discover the collective perspectives of the sample set. A key strength is that the core concepts identified within the data can be further explored. Using this opportunity to question the perspectives of the respondents may help strengthen or dismiss these themes.

As mentioned previously, this preliminary study aimed to explore the relationship between technology use and student perspectives in education. In order to achieve accurate data collection, the decision to use a module that is technology-neutral in context enabled the relationship to be explored and the proposed model to be tested, therefore meaning that the module should not be overly exposed to, or restricted from the use of technology in the day-to-day delivery of the module. Finally, the module itself did not bias or influence the data collected on the participant perspectives. Thus, the module delivery team needed to be neutral as well.

The sample set of participants studied had to be representative of the module population and degree programme.

4. The Participants

The sample set was selected from a mixture of students from the department of Service Sector Management (SSM). These courses are delivered within a Higher Education Institution (HEI) in Northern England. There is a mixture of modules within the SSM portfolio of courses. The department these students are selected from is divided into four subject areas, and the module selected was chosen from one of these subject teams.

Second-year undergraduate students were selected as they have already completed a year of their studies within the institution. As such, these students had ample time to settle in to the university's method of working. They also have plenty of experiences to reflect on in providing responses to the questionnaires. Previously mentioned is the need to pick a technology-neutral module to explore student perceptions. The module selected is not on a technology, media and arts or digital production-oriented degree programme. Therefore any technology used was in the context of delivering the student learning experience.

Currently studying on the SSM second-year programme there are 350 students. This group is made up of a mixture of male, female, local, European Union and international students. It must also be noted that there are a handful of mature students studying on these degree courses as well. The sample set for the study will be taken from a second year module consisting of 43 students. The module has the following make-up: 12 males, 31 females; of these there are 11 international and 32 Home EU students. From this group the sample set consists of three males and 13 females, with 10 of them being home EU students and the remainder being international (all from China). Lastly, the age range for the sample set is from 19 to 22 years old. These students were selected on their arrival times. The first sixteen to walk into a predetermined lecture, this activity was not disclosed to the participants prior to it taking place. This should therefore keep the process blind and random.

5. Analysis of Results

Responses were analysed with NVivo analysis software. This program allows the relationships between the participants' perspectives and technologies used to be identified. Although not an exhaustive study, the idea here is to see if there are identifiable themes emerging from the data collected from the participants and if these relate to their plotting on the proposed model.

After the analysis the following observations were made: The age range of the participants was 19 to 22 years old [19yrs (5), 20yrs (4), 21yrs (6) and 22 yrs (1)]. Based on this information the sample set would be classified as Generation Y, digital generation or digital natives. Of the 16 participants, 11 recorded they had previous work experience. However, only one participant responded to say they had never used technology within an employment capacity. Based on five stating they had never worked, it would be reasonable to assume that there should be at least five stating they had never used technology within an employment capacity. This may be due to confusion on the participants part, but will require further exploration.

The analysis of the technology usage scenario:

Scenario	Never	Occasionally	Frequently	Total
Gaming	4	10	2	16
Social	0	1	15	16
Education	1	5	10	16
Employment	1	10	5	16

Table 1. Technology usage scenario

There is clear evidence above that the participants frequently used technology in a social capacity. This was strongly followed by the use of technology in an educational context. These characteristics again are typical of digital natives. Furthermore, technology usage for gaming and in employment also scored highly in the occasional categories. An interesting observation is that of gaming; it is widely recognised as another characteristic of digital natives. This however scored lower than expected, mainly due to the low levels of males within the population and sample set. There is evidence within the literature that gaming is a trait commonly displayed by male digital natives. Looking at the responses to using technology in an educational context, the frequency and the participants' confidence levels in using technology were compared. Although displaying characteristics typical of digital natives, i.e. technologically immersed, this comparison paints an interesting picture.

Of the sample set, those that used educational technology were evenly spread. A third stated their confidence levels in using educational technology were either neither confident nor unconfident, unconfident or very unconfident. Two stated they were very confident and the remainder (nine) claimed to be confident. Another key observation is that of those who used technology frequently three stated that they were neither and unconfident. So despite using technology frequently their confidence in using them seems to be low. Similarly, one participant stated that technology was never used in their studies, and equally their self-confidence in using educational technology as very unconfident.

Participant identifier	Gender	Age	Home or international	Level of usage	Confidence response
Hd20	Male	20	International	Frequently	Very confident
Oc19	Male	19	UK	Frequently	Very confident
As20	Female	20	UK	Frequently	Confident
Az21	Female	21	International	Frequently	Confident
Am19	Female	19	UK	Occasionally	Confident
Am22	Male	22	UK	Occasionally	Confident
Eh19	Female	19	UK	Frequently	Confident
Jl21	Female	21	International	Occasionally	Confident
Mh19	Female	19	UK	Frequently	Confident
Rc21	Female	21	International	Frequently	Confident
Tg20	Female	20	UK	Occasionally	Confident
Aw21	Female	21	International	Frequently	Neither
Sc20	Female	20	UK	Frequently	Neither
Rh19	Female	19	UK	Frequently	Unconfident
Wl21	Female	21	International	Occasionally	Unconfident
Sb21	Female	21	UK	Never	Very unconfident

Table 2. Educational confidence and usage comparison

Of all the applications the participants responded to using or owning seven (7) key groups emerged. These key groups are social sharing, news, communication, social learning, banking or finance management, dating and employment. Facebook, Twitter, Whatsapp, Youtube, Instagram and Snapchat ranked as the most popular. This seems to suggest a strong use of social-oriented applications. All of the participants had an iPhone, furthermore, five of the participants had a smartphone, tablet and a laptop. Subsection three, which focused on the participants' perceptions of their educational technology interactions also highlighted significant issues. Additionally, questions were asked to ascertain the student perspectives of technology usage within an educational context. These questions are explored below.

5.1 What are Your Expectations of Technology Within Your University Education?

Expectations that the basics actually work and are up-to-date, and considerations should be made for developing apps in house to aid the student learning in relation to the task they have to undertake, seem to be commonplace. Respondents also mentioned that there should be increased technology and app usage within timetabled sessions. Improving access to the resources available was another key issue raised. It was also felt that where possible resources should be provided to allow for increased Instant Messenger (IM) apps to enhance communication with one another and also teaching staff. It was also felt that technology had a big part to play in making research and module tasks easier and more convenient to complete. Key negative issues identified under this section related to the age of the equipment and restricted access to some of the resources. There were calls for more equipment to be made available in sessions as well. Additionally, functionality of one of the main apps used needed addressing as sometimes it failed to work. However, many were content with the online Virtual Learning Environment (VLE) and a range of other provisions provided by the institution.

5.2 What are Your Views on the Impact of Educational Technology on Your Creativity?

The respondents provided an overwhelmingly positive response to the ability of technology to improve opportunities to be more creative, particularly in class based scenarios. Participants reported that they felt technology increased creativity, and improves their ability to conduct research, especially in class-based situations. One key issue highlighted here was the range and accessibility to sources of information through the use of devices. The respondents also felt that technology enhances effectiveness of study activities and also saves time on researching activities. Furthermore, technology has the potential to improve the sharing of information.

5.3 What are Your Views on the Educational Technology You Used Within Your Education?

Issues identified under this section related to the age of the equipment and restricted access to some of the resources. There were calls for more equipment to be made available in sessions as well. Additionally, functionality of one of the main apps used needed addressing as sometimes it failed to work. However, many were content with the online VLE and a range of other provisions provided by the institution. These views seem to mirror those raised in previous questions. However, there were some respondents who felt that technology also increases the potential for plagiarism. In fact, these respondents also mentioned that they felt technology could also limit creativity, as there could be a reliance on external sources rather than engaging in creative processes. In summing up, it was felt that technology increases the ease and enjoyment of learning, improves the quality of the materials produced for learning, but may not have a great effect on creativity.

As mentioned above, the participant data can be collected and converted into quantitative data to allow the digital distance to be measured on the Adoption and Knowledge Continuum Model above (Figure 1). A graphical representation of the table below has been plotted on Figure 4 and this highlights the variation within the sample set who participated within this preliminary study. Figure 5 demonstrates the digital variance within that community.

Participant identifier	Gender	Age	x	Y
Hd20	Male	20	10	-7.5
Oc19	Male	19	10	-8.75
As20	Female	20	10	-7.5
Az21	Female	21	10	-5
Am19	Female	19	5	-5
Am22	Male	22	5	-7.5
Eh19	Female	19	10	-7.5
Jl21	Female	21	5	-5
Mh19	Female	19	10	-6.26
Rc21	Female	21	10	-7.5
Tg20	Female	20	5	-6.25
Aw21	Female	21	10	-6.25
Sc20	Female	20	10	-8.75
Rh19	Female	19	10	0
Wl21	Female	21	5	-6.25
Sb21	Female	21	0	-6.25
Teacher	Male	36	10	2.5

Figure 5. Digital variance within within the community

6. Discussion and Further Research

All the participants demonstrated characteristics typical of Digital Natives as described by Prensky (2001). This has been further evidenced through the participants' usage of technology socially and the broad range of social applications listed. Although there was a good representation of participants using technology in education, it seemed to be weaker than would be expected for a technologically immersed generation. Additionally, there is no evidence to suggest what technology the participants would like to use within their education or how they would use it. Considering the analysis of the responses to confidence and technology usage, four of the participants responded in a way not expected from digital natives. Further exploration around the use of educational technology and confidence levels needs to be undertaken to establish a better understanding of this situation. Although this may have been the result of confusion a more in-depth study should clarify this situation.

All the applications listed by the participants could be used within an educational setting, although there was no evidence to suggest this was the case. There needs to be further clarification on how the participants actually use their devices and applications within social and educational settings. Lastly, any future research on this topic should select a module with a balanced population and sample. Although the technology neutrality was observed, it is felt that having a balanced population and sample would strengthen the study.

7. Conclusion

This paper presented an overview of the initial conclusions from the 2012-13 pilot study, and a second adapted cycle of research being undertaken during 2013-14. The initial findings identified a number of important issues, the most significant of these was the recognition that we cannot adopt a single generic approach to understanding the relationship between technology and the users, but rather there is a continuum in which a direct link between the individual's relationship with technology coupled with their existing knowledge.

That said, there is an ideal space in which the notion of communitas and mutual collaboration during the educational journey can become synchronous in nature within the traditional learning environment. Moreover, it may be argued that mobile technologies also encourage asynchronous learning outside the traditional learning environment. Yet the relationship between learning and technology is a dynamic one, as such the continuum needs to be continually re-evaluated as the synchronicity between the user and technology will be continually changing.

The implication of this research is to generate knowledge and understanding that allows us to effectively embed mobile learning technologies such as iPads in a mutually beneficial manner that explores the notion of communitas within the learning and teaching environment.

References

Belk, R., Wallendorf, M., & Sherry, J., (1989). The sacred and the profane in consumer behaviour: Theodicy on the Odyssey. *Journal of Consumer Research*, *16*(1), 1-38.

Betts-Lacroix, J., (2010). Gartner hype cycle and Geoffrey Moore's technology adoption life cycle. Retrieved December 29, 2014 from http://goo.gl/r7ZWGO

Culén, A. L., & Gasparini, A., (2011). iPad: a new classroom technology? A report from two pilot studies. In C. Billnness, A. Hemera, V. Meteljan, M. Banek Zorica, H. Stancic & S. Seljan (Eds.), *Information sciences and e-society* (pp. 199-208). Zagreb :Department of Information Sciences, University of Zagreb

Durkheim. E., (1995) *The elementary forms of religious life*. George Allen and Unwin, London.

Gawelek, M. A., Spataro, M., & Komarny, P., (2011). Mobile perspectives: On iPads-why mobile? *Educause Review*, *46*(2), 28-30

Geist, E., (2011). The game changer: Using iPads in college teacher education classes. *College Student Journal*, *45*(4), 758-768.

Getting, S., & Swainey, K., (2012). First graders with iPads? *Learning and Leading with Technology*, *40*(1), 24.

Gibbs, A. (2012). Focus groups and group interviews. In Arthur, J., Waring, M., Coe, R., & Hedges, L., (Eds.), *Research methods & methodologies in education* (pp. 186-192). London, England: Sage.

Iwabuchi, M., Takahashi, M., Nakamura, K., & Draffan, E. A., (2012, March). Mainstream but specialized: Mobile technology for cognitive support in education. In *Wireless, mobile and ubiquitous technology in education (WMUTE), 2012 IEEE seventh international conference on* (pp. 117-121).

Linden, A., & Fenn, J. (2003). Understanding Gartner's hype cycles. Retrieved December 29, 2014 from: http://goo.gl/r7ZWGO

Murray, O. T., & Olcese, N. R., (2011). Teaching and learning with iPads, ready or not? *TechTrends*, *55*(6), 42-48.

Prensky, M. (2001). Digital natives, digital immigrants part 1. *On the Horizon*, *9*(5), 1-6.

Robinson, S., (2011). Promote active learning with iPads. *Radiologic Technology*, *83*(2) 204-207.

Reid, G., Strnadová, I., & Cumming, T., (2013). Expanding horizons for students with dyslexia in the 21st century: Universal design and mobile technology. *Journal of Research in Special Educational Needs*, 13(3), 175-181.

Shah, N. (2011). Special education pupils find learning tool in iPad applications. *Education Week*, *30*(22), 1-16.

Sinelnikov, O. A. (2012). Using the iPad in a sport education season. *Journal of Physical Education, Recreation & Dance*, *83*(1), 39-45.

Smith, C., & Evans, B. (2010). Apple Press Info. In *Apple launches iPad.* Retrieved November 25, 2013, from: www.apple.com

Turner. V. (1969). *The ritual process*. Harmondsworth: Penguin.

Tymms, P. (2012). Questionnaires. In Arthur, J., Waring, M., Coe, R., & Hedges, L., (Eds.), *Research methods & methodologies in education* (pp. 231-240). London: Sage.

iPADS, COFFEE AND CAKE: BECOMING EXPERTS TOGETHER - INFORMAL LEARNING WITH iPADS AT THE UNIVERSITY OF SOUTHAMPTON

FIONA HARVEY[1] AND TAMSYN SMITH[2]

Abstract

The iPad (and Alternative Devices) Coffee Club has successfully brought together an informal support structure for individuals who are interested in using iPads within their academic and professional working lives at the University of Southampton. This paper specifically looks at the informal environment for the adoption of this technology, and refers to how, despite the university not specifically having an implementation policy, the iPad has become the most popular tablet used by academics and professional service staff. A mixed methods approach was undertaken to identify the impact that these events were having on staff and students' professional and personal lives. Information we obtained allowed us to gather feedback to make changes to the existing structure. The monthly sessions are based around social, informal learning, and this paper provides details on how they have been organised and developed, discussing additional support, and concludes that the informal network could be developed nationally to provide a network of Coffee Clubs to enable staff and students to become experts together.

1. Introduction

The Centre for Innovation in Technologies and Education (CITE) at the University of Southampton is a relatively new unit created in 2011 to support the development and enhancement of educational technology and

[1] University of Southampton, United Kingdom. Email: Fiona.Harvey@soton.ac.uk
[2] University of Southampton, United Kingdom. Email: fg@soton.ac.uk

innovation across the University. CITE is led by Professor Hugh Davis, and its staff supports academics across the University to engage with technology to enhance the student education experience.

One of the themes of the Centre is digital literacies, as defined by JISC (Joint Information Systems Committee) in the report *Learning literacies for the digital age* (Beetham, McGill & Littlejohn, 2009): "Digital literacy defines those capabilities which fit an individual for living, learning and working in a digital society."

In order to support the development of digital literacies, CITE has created a series of initiatives that allow staff and students to be supported in their digital literacies development. One of these initiatives is the iPad & Alternative Devices (iPAD) Coffee Club.

2. Context

The idea for a Coffee Club was in part related to a visit that Fiona Harvey (Education Development Manager, CITE) had made to the International Office team, who had requested support for their iPads as they were issued with them and needed to use their devices effectively when travelling abroad. When offering them advice and support it became apparent that they were benefiting more from discussions between themselves, rather than by watching a demonstration.

The International Office was not alone. Across the university departments and academic units were purchasing devices to be used for academic and administration services. There is no policy at the university for supporting any one device, but the use of iPads has become, by far, the most popular device on campuses. Since 2010, over 840 iPads have been purchased centrally for faculties and professional services. As all IT equipment must be purchased centrally through the iSolutions (IT Support) Department, establishing an accurate figure has been relatively easy. The data available does not include purchases made via funds within faculties through "services rendered funds".

With such diverse and widespread use of iPads across the University it was clear that there needed to be a level of engagement with this growing community to share good practice and to develop this enthusiasm for digital technology in a supported and informed way, and in turn furthering the digital literacies skills of the University. The aim was to bring together the expertise of the "early adopters" with the "late majority" (Geoghegan, 1994) those who had devices and felt that they were underutilising them. It was also hoped that by offering an informal social space (Straub, 2009), it would ease the successful adoption of iPads by those who had been given them as part of their practice.

3. Informal Learning

There have been numerous projects on the use of iPads in Higher Education, many of them focusing on the efficacy of iPads for education, in terms of ease of use, accessibility, cost and application (Gawelek, Spataro & Komarny, 2011; Wagoner, Hoover & Ernst, 2011; Murphy, 2011). These factors are clearly one of the key reasons for such widespread take-up amongst the education community. The first iPad was released in April 2010, and since then the use of iPads in education gathered momentum, so that by October 2010 it could be argued that the iPad was at the peak of Gartner's hype cycle (Gartner, 2013). Initial consumer expectations were that people would be able to replace their computer or laptop with an iPad, which led to the "trough of disillusionment" as purchasers realised that their iPad did not have all of the functionality of their desktop PC.

However, we have now moved onto "enlightenment" as users have realised that iPads are not designed to replace computers, but are a useful supplementary tool with additional functionality that makes them good for specific tasks in relation to their portability, the inclusion of a camera and the range of apps available. This is now leading towards a plateau of productivity for many users as they work out which tasks are better suited to their device and which are better performed on a computer (Macography, 2013). Initial training has revealed that many people find the devices are relatively simple to use, but they need a change of mindset to be able to use them effectively, instead of seeing them as a replacement for a computer.

In order to enable this change of mindset it is important to create the right conditions for any technology to become adopted by the mainstream. Educational technology has notoriously been affected by a general discomfort in its use and also by a lack of confidence (Geoghegan, 1994). iPads have been able to address this by allowing early adopters to become familiarised with them in a personalised space, allowing the freedom for development by the users and thus creating the right conditions for experimentation in a more professional environment (Andzenge & North, 2013). This has allowed the adoption through diffusion, and over time (since 2010) it has meant that these devices have become part of many people's social framework (Straub, 2009).

A natural step towards supporting the use of m-Learning (Crompton, 2013) is by Informal Learning. The latest New Media Horizons Report notes that the skills gained via Informal Learning are valued more than the skills acquired through universities (New Media Consortium and Educause, 2013). Informal Learning is not new and has been part of lifelong learning research, in particular, "learning beyond the classroom" (Bentley, 1998) amongst many others. Learning in this way is not independent of community, and social learning has played a significant part in the past over choosing which technologies to use and how to use them (Ellison & Fudenburg, 1993).

4. Research Design

The process for setting up the Coffee Club is very simple. The Coffee Clubs are deliberately located in relaxed social areas at the University. The Coffee Clubs will be operating on all campuses by January 2014 and to a very similar pattern. Using the catering facilities available, participants at the Coffee Clubs meet at the designated time, and sitting together they use the time to chat about the devices that they own and how they have been using apps for a variety of tasks, including their own productivity, teaching and research. Refreshments are available via the locations of the Coffee Clubs (usually either a café or bar) with the cost subsidised by CITE.

There is deliberately no set pattern for the discussions. The clubs meet once a month for 90 minutes and members are invited to "drop in" as they are able. Members of CITE come along to the Coffee Clubs, and ensure that they are available within the groups that form. By not having a set "lecture" or "workshop" the forum is open for all levels and all abilities to sit and listen, or actively ask questions about issues or ideas that they have relating to teaching with devices, researching or questions around their own administrative tasks.

5. Methodology and Results

For this paper we have reviewed data collected on attendees between October 2012 and June 2013, and used a mixed methods design to identify areas of success and to ascertain areas for development. Between October 2012 and June 2013, nearly 100 visits (N=97; Female 56%; Male 43) were made to the Coffee Clubs at the main campus. Attendees at the sessions were a range of academic and support staff, from Senior Academics (Professorial level and above) to junior staff. Students who attended were mainly PhD level with two undergraduates. This is fairly representative of the education community at the University. The Coffee Club is completely open for any member of staff, students or the local community. The Coffee Clubs have been requested in all the university campuses and so new Coffee Clubs have been organised for our oceanfront campus, the National Oceanography Centre Southampton (NOCS), Winchester School of Art (WSA), Southampton General Hospital (SGH) and Avenue Campus.

We used the data that we have collected through the registration system Eventbrite (http://www.eventbrite.com) for attendance at the Coffee Clubs to establish details about our attendees (n=67, male=28, female= 41). We have also gathered anonymous feedback from those who have attended via our internal survey system, iSurvey (n=19, gender not included). This online questionnaire comprised six open-ended questions, giving us a rich selection of ideas and improvements for future Coffee Clubs. Other data was gathered via the evaluations of the training sessions. Using thematic analysis, this data provided us with a clear indication that the use of informal learning methods was having a positive impact on productivity and the professional lives of those who attended. Again, this feedback has influenced the format and locations of the Coffee Clubs.

Feedback from the attendees of the Coffee Clubs has been very positive. The attendees of a recent Coffee Club (over 86%) indicated that it had a positive impact on their professional life and that they would like to see similar kinds of initiatives across the university.

Examples of participants' comments:

> "It has raised awareness of how devices might be used with groups of students. It has increased my efficiency and effectiveness at using my own device for academic purposes. It has allowed me to network with people from different faculties so is spreading best practice on using technology for academic purposes." (Anonymous participant, academic staff)
> "Colleagues have helped me make a better use of my iPad for productivity by highlighting useful apps and tips for interacting with the device (hand gestures etc). (Anonymous participant, academic support staff)
> "I learnt so much about how to use my iPad for work particularly setting it up to connect to the M drive!" (Anonymous participant, academic support staff)

The result of this kind of environment has allowed the community to work in partnership and become experts together, each identifying ideas and apps that they have knowledge about and sharing them between each other.

6. Discussion

The concept of social learning is nothing new and places an emphasis on observational learning (Bandura, 1971). The iPad Coffee Clubs have been based around the ideas of social, informal learning. They have aimed to develop the competencies and digital literacies skills of them for their own productivity and practice, which has resulted in a steady increase in the amount of iPads in use at the University. This enthusiasm for iPads could be attributed to the suggestion that “adoption is innately social, influenced by peers, change agents, organisational pressure and societal norms” (Rogers cited in Straub, 2009). All of these factors are present, certainly socialisation, change agents, in the guise of CITE staff and colleagues enthusing over their own use of the technology.

They were not deliberately designed to be just for iPads, but this has been the focus of discussions around apps and usage. The iPad has proved to be easy to use, and requires very little training in terms of demonstrations of functional usage. The set-up is very easy, and they continue to evolve to be extremely reliable, user-friendly and through the Apple community, offer high quality support for education. In this context it is easy to see why the iPads have been so popular, and continue to be popular with the education community (Teach Thought, 2012).

The Coffee Club has created a vibrant community across the university of enthusiastic users of technology. Staff have been encouraged by each other’s activities with their iPads and have become creative, using apps with their cohorts.

In October 2013, our newly created “Life Lab”, an outreach centre at our Southampton General Hospital Campus (http://www.southampton.ac.uk/medicine/outreach/index.page), operated between the Faculty of Medicine and the Education School, has been furnished with thirty-two (32) iPads for use with local schoolchildren. This was a direct result of the support offered through the Coffee Clubs as the team was able to evaluate the usefulness of the iPads against their own skills using the devices.

The range of staff and students that have attended the Coffee Clubs has been diverse, and included faculty from the Natural and Earth Sciences, Social and Human Sciences, Physical Sciences and Engineering and Engineering and the Environment.

Members of iSolutions (our IT support service) have come along to the Coffee Club and offered their advice around accessing University systems. This has been particularly advantageous for them as they have been able to break free from the usual weighty bureaucratic process that is in place for formal support. By attending these Coffee Clubs they have been able to demonstrate the "human face" of IT support, and it has been greatly appreciated by members of the Coffee Club.

7. Further Support

Through the Coffee Club there has been additional "formalised support". This has evolved out of the ideas and discussions during the Coffee Clubs. Sessions have been arranged on the main campus (Highfield) for workshop-type sessions where colleagues are able to view how a few specific apps can be used. The apps that are discussed are those that were introduced to members of the Coffee Clubs. These could be anything that the members have found useful and wanted to share. These occur two weeks after the Coffee Club for one hour and are led by CITE staff, although it is our intention that any member of the Coffee Club can demonstrate their favourite or most useful app. This addition to our Coffee Club offer is in the very early stages and will be adapted and developed as we continue to evaluate.

In terms of additional support for iPads and as a direct result of our Coffee Club we have been able to offer a three-day workshop for all academic staff via Apple Distinguished Instructor, Joe Moretti. This was arranged by our area Higher Education lead for Apple, Lawrence Stephenson. It was an important workshop for us, as it allowed staff to be guided through the use of a range of apps for teaching.

Staff were not only able to develop their skills, but they were also inspired and enthused. Over 50 academic staff attended the sessions over three days, including the Pro-Vice Chancellor for Education and other senior academics. 73% of those who attended had been to one or more Coffee Clubs, and 80% said that they would use the ideas that they had been shown in their professional work at the University. CITE staff ensured that this enthusiasm was carried through to the next Coffee Club, so that staff unable to attend were able to benefit from the experiences of those who were able to attend.

8. Future Plans

CITE have already increased their Coffee Clubs to start at all campuses from January 2014. Coffee Clubs have been organised for:

- Winchester School of Art;
- National Oceanography Centre Southampton (NOCS);
- Southampton General Hospital (SGH), and;
- Avenue Campus.

Much of the success of the Coffee Clubs has been due to the attendance by CITE staff to initiate discussion as knowledgeable "enthusiasts", and so it is important for the other Coffee Clubs to be facilitated in the same way. CITE has identified champions in each of the campuses to be the point of contact and to ensure that the experiences from the Highfield Campus are mirrored for these campuses. This has worked with some success already at the Avenue Campus. Initially the Avenue Campus Coffee Club was led by an academic, who specifically looked at apps with a humanities bias. The academic is now on sabbatical and so a new champion has been identified thus ensuring continuity. Members of CITE staff will also attend these Coffee Clubs to provide a link between each of the events.

As part of the Higher Education Academy (HEA) Changing the Learning Landscape series of events, the Coffee Clubs were presented along with other digital literacies initiatives from the University of Southampton at a workshop in London. As a result of this it is hoped that other universities will adopt this model and offer similar informal sessions at their institutions. To date, start-up funding has been offered to University of Huddersfield, and Olaojo Aiyegbayo visited the University of Southampton Coffee Club in November 2013. Likewise, an informal discussion with learning technologists in Library & Learning Support at Bournemouth University has resulted in the creation of "Tablet Talk" - informal lunchtime "get-togethers" where staff can share their discussions and good practice on the use of mobile devices. It is hoped that we can work together and form a community, sharing experiences, research and guidance on best practice.

Future research should involve the impact that the Coffee Clubs have had on the use of technology for education across campuses, and we should be able to compare this with other institutions that adopt the Coffee Club model.

In conclusion, informality is the key to the development and enhancement of skills for using iPads within both academic and administrative capacity. By having the right environment for support, attendees at the Coffee Club have commented that they feel they have been able to experiment without feeling that they would be intimidated by others there, unlike in formal "training" settings where structured activities have meant that varying levels of ability have either slowed down or gone too fast for some individuals. The Coffee Club has become a vibrant and active community of learners, and in addition a by-product of the informal setting has been that further links have been created for other projects within the university, cementing networks and raising the profile of CITE to academics and services who may have been unaware of the support and services that are available.

References

Andzenge, S. T., & North, S. F. (2013). Experiences of a faculty-driven iPad integration initiative in teacher education. In J. Herrington (Ed.), *Proceedings of the World Conference on Educational Multi-Media, Hypermedia & Telecommunications* (pp. 1616-1622). Chesapeake: AACE.

Bandura, A. (1971). *Social learning theory.* New York: General Learning Press.

Beetham, H., McGill, L., & Littlejohn, A. (2009). *Thriving in the 21st century: Learning literacies for the digital age.* JISC.

Bentley, T. (1998). *Learning beyond the classroom: Education in a changing world.* London: Routledge.

Crompton, H. (2013). A historical overview of mobile learning: towards learner-centred education. In Z. L. Berg, & L. Muilenburg, *Handbook of mobile learning* (pp. 3-14). Florence, KY: Routledge.

Ellison, G., & Fudenburg, D. (1993). Rules of thumb for social learning. *Journal of Political Economy*, *101*(4), 612-643.

Gawelek, M., Spataro, M. P., & Komarny, P. (2011). Mobile perspectives. *Educause Review*, *46*(2), 28-32.

Geoghegan, W. (1994). Whatever happened to instructional technology? Paper presented at *22nd Annual Conference of the International Business Schools Computing Association*, Baltimore, Maryland.

Macography (2013, September 13). The hype cycle and the iPad. Retrieved December 30, 2014, from Macography: http://macography.net/2013/09/hype-cycle-ipad/

Murphy, G. (2011). Post-PC devices: A summary of early iPad technology in tertiary environments. e-*Journal of Business Education and Scholarship of Teaching*, 5(1), 18-32.

New Media Consortium and Educause (2013). *NMC Horizons Report*. New Media Consortium and Educause.

Straub, E. (2009). Understanding technology adoption: Theory and future directions for informal learning. *Review of Educational Research*, *79*(2), 625-649.

Teach Thought (2012, September 21). 9 ways universities are using the iPad in & out of the classroom. *Teach Thought*. Retrieved December 30, 2014, from http://www.Teach thought.com/ipad-2/9-ways-universities-are-using-the-ipad/

Wagoner, T., Hoover, S., & Ernst, D. (2011). *CEHD iPad initiative*. University of Minnesota, College of Education and Human Development.

USING IPADS TO ENABLE CULTURAL CHANGE IN TECHNOLOGY-ENHANCED LEARNING: A CASE STUDY

STEVEN FURNELL[1]

Abstract

The iPad has significant potential to have a transformative effect upon teaching and learning practices in a higher education context. As evidence of this claim, this paper presents a case study that examines the approach and resulting benefits experienced when introducing the devices within the School of Computing and Mathematics at Plymouth University. The approach taken was a phased introduction of the devices, firstly amongst academic staff, then a subset of first-year undergraduate students, leading to adoption across the whole School based upon the success of the earlier stages (with success in this case being judged on the basis of both user engagement, e.g. staff production, and student use of materials and positive user feedback). iPads have been provided to both staff and students, with a range of positive impacts upon the teaching and learning practices that can now be regarded as standard within the School (including podcasting, use of eBooks, and interactive services). The iPad has been key to supporting and integrating the various applications, and has delivered a significant uplift in the technology-enhanced learning practices of the staff, each delivering associated benefits in the resulting student experience.

1. Introduction

Since their launch in early 2010, iPads have been responsible for instigating a step change in our use and interaction with IT across many contexts. Even within their first year of sale they were heralded as marking

[1] Plymouth University, United Kingdom. Email: steven.furnell@plymouth.ac.uk

a paradigm shift in our use of technology, and had witnessed a faster rate of adoption than prior electronics products (Foresman, 2010). Their ability to support educational activities can be considered a key example of this, with the devices offering an excellent basis from which to both engage students and encourage staff participation. Indeed, even in the relatively short time that iPads have been available, prior research and reports have already documented their successful use in educational contexts at all levels (Wainwright, 2013).

This paper presents a case study example, reflecting upon the positive experience within the authors' school at Plymouth University in terms of building an iPad-centric approach to Technology-Enhanced Learning (TEL). A key point to note is that although there had been pockets of prior activity, it would be fair to say that activities such as podcasting and lecture capture were not part of an established culture at Plymouth University. As such, the introduction of the technology offered by the iPad (and the things that could be integrated around it) was seen as an opportunity to change the standard practice, and uplift the student experience as a result.

The paper begins by presenting the background to the iPad initiative within the case study environment, and the explicit desire to engage staff and students in the process. The discussion then proceeds to examine each of the specific activities for which the iPad has acted as an enabler, from lecture podcasting through to in-class voting and feedback. Finally, conclusions are drawn regarding the success of the case study, and the implications for the future.

2. Provision of iPads For Staff and Students

In order to ensure that the iPad could fulfil its perceived potential as an enabler for technology-enhanced learning, it was recognised early on that it needed to be directly in the hands of the staff and students whose culture we wished to advance. As such, a key decision within the School of Computing and Mathematics has been to invest in the technology, taking us to the current point where iPads are provided to all staff and students by default.

3. Background

The School-level initiative began in the summer of 2011, when staff were offered an iPad 2 (which was newly released at the time) as a means of incentivising their engagement with the TEL agenda. The basic idea was that iPads were purchased for all academic staff, and the qualifying criteria to obtain them was that staff needed to commit to engaging with either podcasting or electronic assessment feedback (e.g. annotation of PDFs or audio feedback). The baseline podcasting requirement was simply to provide audio recordings for distribution to students via the virtual learning environment, with associated options being to record lectures or to produce supplementary supporting materials. While a basic audio recording of the lecture would clearly represent only a very minimal level of podcasting, even this was considered to represent a useful contribution for students, as academics would regularly find students wishing to make their own recordings (with some placing recording devices near the front of the lecture room, and others very likely doing it surreptitiously from within the audience). Thus, getting the academics themselves to record and upload the session would save the effort for students, as well as to ensure that everyone would get access to a good quality recording taken at source, rather than a potentially noisy recording taken some distance away from the lecturer.

It should be noted that staff were not required to use the iPad itself as the means of creating the content, and they were free to use any means that they were comfortable with in order to do so. However, they were equally advised that the iPad could be useful in this context and made aware of apps that could be used to support their activities. Moreover, once the iPads had been issued (with all but two staff members out of around 70 electing to take the opportunity based upon the aforementioned "conditions of use"), it quickly became apparent that staff were also discovering and sharing practice amongst themselves, such that other useful apps were also highlighted for possible adoption.

The provision of iPads to students was a later part of our approach, requiring a more significant level of investment given the numbers involved. When considering our strategy in this context, our interest was particularly raised by the prospect of the iPad mini, insofar as the device would not only be potentially more affordable (as it indeed proved to be), but would also offer a more convenient form factor given that we could ultimately be expecting students to carry the device everywhere with them in order to support their learning activities on and off campus. Moreover, the decision to invest in devices for students did not occur until we were sure that the staff initiative had been successful. Once this was established over the course of the subsequent academic year, we could be confident that students would actually benefit from the device in relation to things that we would be producing and providing for them.

4. Approach

A pilot of the student initiative was conducted in the spring term of the 2012-2013 academic year, with the decision to purchase devices for all of the students across the first year of our programmes. In order for this to occur, we (as a school) required confirmation of buy-in and support from each of the topic areas that wished to participate (noting that the school offers programmes under three key topic areas: computing; electronics and robotics; and mathematics and statistics). As it turned out, all topics elected to come on board, thus further underlying the need for their commitment in terms of actually providing content for students to use on them.

An initial batch of devices was then issued on this basis, noting that the students had received no prior indication that they were to expect to receive them.

In addition to ensuring that the students had no real basis to be anything other than happy to receive them (other than those that would for some reason have preferred an Android or Windows device in preference to iOS), this allowed an opportunity for staff to adjust to the fact of students now having iPads as standard rather than needing to hit the ground running from the outset of the year. Following on from the success of the pilot, the context has changed in the subsequent deployment insofar as the provision of iPads was announced to students in advance as part of the marketing of the programmes (Figure 1), and so they now enter with an expectation of receiving the device soon after arrival.

The approach has been relatively light-touch in terms of attempting to control the students' use of the technology. Although related solutions are available to support it, there has been no explicit attempt at device management in order to preconfigure the iPads or push content to them. Students have needed to sign up to a series of basic ground rules for use (including clauses stating that they will not jailbreak the devices, and to ensure that they leave sufficient capacity to enable them to store the educational content that we may need them to download), but other than this they are being encouraged to regard them as personal devices. Other than capacity of the devices themselves, there is no restriction on their ability to use them for storing music, video and non-educational apps, and they will be regarded the same as any other student devices in terms of their need to comply with the terms and conditions of acceptable use on the university network.

Figure 1. iPad minis provided to all students

At the time of writing, we have purchased over 1,200 iPad minis, with the consequence that every student from stage one undergraduates through to taught Masters students has been provided with one in order to support their learning. With this in mind, the next section examines the uses to which they have actually been put, and the related activities that staff have needed to engage with.

5. Findings

The provision of the iPads for students has provided an enabling platform on which a number of distinct TEL-related activities being pursued within the School have been able to be integrated. These are listed and described in the paragraphs that follow. While none of the activities specifically requires an iPad, and almost all had been conducted in some form prior to their deployment, the fact that the iPad allows easy and convenient access to all aspects from a single device has meant that the activities as a whole can now be more easily seen as part of a coherent overall approach.

Lecture podcasts: As a result of the "iPads for staff" initiative, the practice of creating lecture podcasts and/or supplementary materials became a much greater part of the standard culture for our traditional taught modules. Many modules now have a full set of accompanying podcasts on the VLE, alongside the traditional slide and handout materials that module staff have long provided as standard. In many cases staff have tended to go beyond the baseline of providing audio-only recordings, and have created video-based screen capture of their slide shows as well, or created enhanced podcasts with the slides embedded alongside the audio.

The provision of the podcasts has proven very popular with students, particularly in the cases where the full lectures have been recorded and made available in some form. The key benefit, unsurprisingly, has related to flexible delivery, with students having access to a catch-up resource if they happened to miss all or part of the session, and a recap resource if they want to go over something again. As an aside, although concern was initially expressed that the provision of lecture podcasts would undermine students' attendance at the actual sessions, this has not proven to be a substantial problem in practice (as indeed earlier research, such as that documented by Ovadia (2007) in relation to the experiences of Duke University and University of Washington, had already suggested to be the case). In reality, students are likely to have missed sessions that would have always proven problematic anyway (e.g. those timetabled in undesirable slots), and so from that perspective the provision of podcasts is actually providing a safety net in terms of allowing students the option to engage with the session at some point rather than missing it altogether.

In addition to the flexibility for students, a notable side benefit for the academics is that it has allowed them to evolve the content of their lecture series without having to lose coverage of older topics. For example, in addition to providing students with the recording of the session from the current year, they may also be provided with a recording of an earlier version of the same lecture, which may include different material and examples. Alternatively, some topics may be dropped from the face-to-face delivery altogether, allowing students to access that material via podcast while the lecture slot is then available for covering something completely different. In short, the use of podcasting has opened up a significant degree of flexibility for both students and staff, and the iPad provides a very appropriate device from which to access and view the materials.

iTunes U: In addition to the provision of podcasts for our own internal students, staff have also been encouraged to engage with creating content for dissemination via iTunes U, which Plymouth University first joined in November 2010 (as part of an initiative supported directly at Vice-Chancellor level). As an institution, Plymouth reached a million downloads within around 18 months, and has established a number of popular podcast collections (with the School of Computing and Mathematics proving to be a particularly key contributor in this regard, thanks to the strong base of content and podcasting practice established through the prior activities) (Furnell, 2013). In some cases staff are using elements of material captured from their normal lecture sessions and making them more widely available, but in other cases they have produced additional materials specifically for wider dissemination (but which can, of course, be accessed via our own students via their iPads as standard). An illustrative example of a resulting collection – one of several based upon content from the authors' School – is shown in Figure 2.

In addition to producing their own materials, academics are also able to encourage students to seek relevant iTunes U content from other institutions, or indeed to recommend specific resources (Bird, 2011). A good example of how this might be used is to provide students with an opportunity to hear alternative or additional views on a topic that has been covered within their lecture series at Plymouth. By providing the iPad minis to the students, we have ensured that the academics are in a position to make such recommendations safe in the knowledge that all students have the necessary technology to support the task.

Figure 2. Plymouth University iTunes U content as viewed on an iPad

Ebooks: Following on from award-winning practice already established in our School of Psychology, first-year students across all of the computing and mathematics and statistics courses have been provided with eBook versions of the key textbooks to support their modules. The eBooks in this particular case are readable using Vitalsource Bookshelf (www.vitalsource.com), via the associated app, which can then be used on the iPads (noting that an associated reader is also available for Windows, Mac, and Android, thus also enabling use on students' other devices as well). In addition to providing the students with their core texts without additional charge, this enables lecturers and students to annotate texts and share their notes and views online. As mentioned, this work was initiated in our School of Psychology, and was the winner of the "Teaching Excellence" category in the Guardian University Awards 2013 (BBC, 2013).

Student attendance monitoring: Another feature that has been used for the last couple of academic years has been electronic attendance monitoring, with data logged and uploaded as one of the many features of a locally developed student support system (S3). The collection of this data was originally achieved via paper-based sign-in sheets and then manually uploaded by academics after the sessions. However, this quickly evolved into the issuance and use of barcode scanners, which academics could then pass around the room to allow students to scan their university ID cards. The availability of the iPads offers yet another route here, with the ability for students to self-register attendance via their device (with the option for each session to be time and password-protected and IP address locked in order to prevent students from being able to register after the event, or without actually being physically present).

The attendance monitoring is another factor that has proven to engage the interests of academic staff, as it dramatically improves the potential to track overall student engagement with modules, as well as to check the status of individual candidates' attendance across the breadth of modules that they are studying (which is in turn useful for supporting activities such as personal tutoring and student retention).

Assessment: Especially in the computing part of the school, students typically submit their work for assessment electronically rather than on paper. Staff have been able to use their iPads to access and mark submissions using apps such as iAnnotate (www.branchfire.com), which enables annotations using text and audio comments to be embedded in PDF reports. The ease with which this can be achieved together with the portability of the iPad mini (marking can be done anywhere) has resulted in a faster turnaround of marked work and an increase in both the quantity and quality of student feedback.

In-class voting and feedback: The one activity in the list that was specifically initiated after it was known that students would all be provided with an iPad was the in-house development of an app to support Wi-Fi based interactive voting and student response. Figure 3 illustrates the use of the app in multiple-choice question mode, but it is also supports a free-text response mode as well.

As mentioned earlier, in all but the last case, the provision of iPads to students was not the *cause* of these activities. It was actually one of the later steps of the strategy, serving as a point of integration once other key components were already established. As such, investment in the devices was considered to be a relatively safe investment, insofar as we were largely guaranteed that students would see the provision of the devices as useful, relevant and embedded in their learning experience, rather than a gimmick merely intended as part of the recruitment activity.

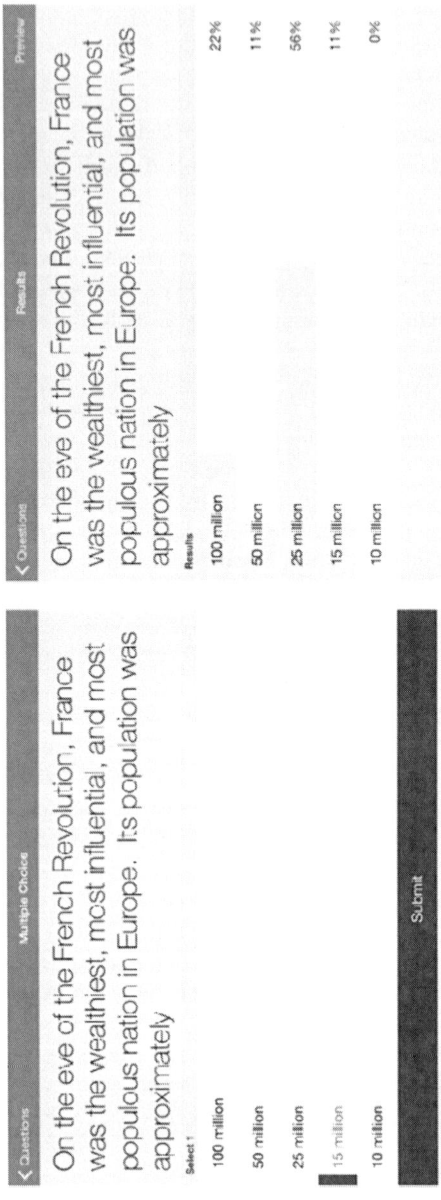

Figure 3. Example question and results interfaces from the iPad voting app

6. Conclusion

From our experience across both the staff and student populations, the iPad can play a very useful role in the HE context, and can act as a significant catalyst in terms of developing and evolving teaching and learning practices. One of the key issues from the cultural perspective is the recognition that if students have been provided with a device then it creates an expectation of usage, and it only takes a few staff to engage positively before it builds a sense of wider expectation that others should do likewise. There is, of course, a potential risk factor here if insufficient staff are not willing to follow the desired approach, as this could actually cause student resentment on the basis that the preferred practice does not become widespread. However, this has not been the case within our experience.

Looking at the case study experience as a pilot for wider advocacy, one unfortunate but (for us) unavoidable downside was that the change took place within the School of Computing and Mathematics. When relaying the experience to others, this often seems to lead to a general assumption that it was a somehow natural move, because the computing staff were bound to find it easy because it involved using technology. In actual fact, there is little basis for this assumption, as the types of tasks and applications involved are typically more creative and artistic than IT-centric (e.g. video and audio editing tools).

The experience gained through this case study has served to highlight the various ways in which iPads can support and enable a variety of TEL-oriented initiatives. Although they are far from the only devices that could be used in each of the cases, they have proven to provide a very effective means of integrating the access to activities from a single device in an effective manner. As such, we see them making a very effective ongoing contribution to the TEL practices within our School and ideally the wider institution.

References

BBC (2013, February 28). Plymouth University wins teaching excellence award. Retrieved December 30, 2014 from: http://www.bbc.co.uk/news/uk-england-devon-21619678

Bird, T. (2011). iTunes U: a successful model of open educational resource distribution? Retrieved December 30, 2014 from: http://www.slideshare.net/tbirdcymru/i-tunesu-successfuloer11

Foresman, C. (2010, October 5). iPad adoption rate fastest in electronics product history. CNN. Retrieved December 30, 2014 from: http://goo.gl/FuwAOV

Furnell, S.M. (2013). International OERs with iTunes U. In *Proceedings of OER13*. Nottingham, UK, 26-27 March 2013.

Ovadia, M. (2007). PoducateMe: Practical solutions for podcasting in education. Retrieved December 30, 2013 from: http://poducateme.com/guide/index15.php

Wainwright, A. (2013, February 18). 8 studies show iPads in the classroom improve education. Retrieved December 30, 2014 from: http://goo.gl/U6aJRd

Comparing Student and Faculty Perceptions on the Instructional Value of iPads in Art and Design Education

NICOS SOULELES[1], STEFANIA SAVVA[2],
HILARY WATTERS[3] AND ANGELA ANNESLEY[4]

Abstract

This paper compares the perceptions of art and design students and faculty of the instructional value of iPads. More specifically, this paper draws from the main conclusions of two previous studies to compare the views of the two stakeholders, using as a framework of comparison the Rieber and Welliver (1995) five-step hierarchical model of technology adoption. Briefly, in the two previous studies both students and faculty were given the freedom to use iPads for teaching and learning, but without a specific task to guide their use. This bottom-up approach was deliberate, and together with the characteristics of art and design education and in particular the dominant modes of teaching and learning, provide the delimitations of the earlier studies. When comparing - in this paper - the outcomes of the previous two studies we noted that the adoption pattern was restricted mostly to the first two stages of the Rieber and Welliver (1995) model, familiarisation and utilisation, with some effort from faculty to integrate iPads in curricula. We argue that integration, reorientation and evolution – the latter stages of the model – require change that can only be achieved if all stakeholders share in the process.

[1] Cyprus University of Technology, Cyprus. Email: nicos.souleles@cut.ac.cy
[2] Cyprus University of Technology, Cyprus. Email: st3phania@hotmail.com
[3] Falmouth University, United Kingdom. Email: Hilary@falmouth.ac.uk
[4] Falmouth University, United Kingdom. Email: Angela.Annesley@falmouth.ac.uk

1. Introduction

In 2012, the authors of this paper, representing the research lab "Art + Design: elearning lab" at Cyprus University of Technology, and academic colleagues from Falmouth University, embarked on a long-term empirical study on the use of iPads in art and design Higher Education (HE). During the first stage of this task the authors investigated the perceptions of and experiences of undergraduate art and design students with regards to the instructional potential of the iPad (Souleles, Savva, Watters, Bull & Annesley, 2014). During the second stage they examined the attitude of art and design faculty towards this tablet computer. The purpose of this paper is to provide a comparison with the perceptions and outcomes from the two previous stages, based on the Rieber and Welliver 1995) model of technology adoption.

The authors referred to readings about the models of implementing instructional technology in educational institutions and organisations in general. The latter is examined as a starting point for this paper. This is followed by a description of the main characteristics of teaching and learning in art and design, because the pedagogical context inevitably and largely underpins and informs the attitudes of all stakeholders. Then follows a description of outcomes from the first and second stages (students and faculty) of the original study. The concluding part of this paper provides a comparison and synthesis of the perceptions of students and faculty of the instructional value of iPads in art and design.

2. Models of Technology Adoption

There is a lack of empirical studies on how to adopt instructional technologies in HE that combine the views of different stakeholders, for example academics and learners. The same applies on how to embed new technologies in art and design education. Even though this indicates potential lacunae, it is acknowledged that it is difficult to develop a formula on how to combine the different and often conflicting perspectives of all stakeholders. Context-specific challenges make such scenarios ideal for participatory action research (Grundy, 1982). There is, however, some literature that compares the views of stakeholders on instructional technologies to highlight areas of potential difference or to compare views (See for example: Hsu & Chang, 2009; Li, 2007). These are mostly case studies that allow for little or no transferability of outcomes and lessons learnt.

Al-Senaidi, Lin and Poirot (2009, pp. 576-577) provide a useful summary of the three most influential and prominent theoretical models for the adoption of Information and Communication Technologies (ICTs). Firstly, the authors present the Technology Acceptance Model (TAM) that explains the behavioural intention of a user's computer usage. This model considers subjective factors such as beliefs, attitudes, perceived usefulness and perceived ease of use. Secondly, the authors elaborate on Rogers' diffusion theory, which suggests that the diffusion of an innovation is a process driven by early innovators, followed by the early adopters, the early majority, the late majority, and lastly the laggards. Briefly, this theory argues that the rate of technology adoption is relative to the speed with which people adopt an innovation over time. According to Al-Senaidi et al. (2009) the third most influential model is that developed by Rieber and Welliver (1995), who propose a five-step process for technology adoption at post-secondary level (Table 1).

Evolution	
Reorientation	
Integration	
Utilisation	
Familiarisation	

Table 1. The Rieber and Welliver (1995) five-step hierarchical model of technology adoption

The first step of this model covers familiarization and entails a baseline exposure to new technology. At this level teachers may consider the relevance of the technology for teaching and learning, but often the technology is rejected. The next stage of the same model consists of utilisation, and this involves the teachers using the technology once or twice. Teachers may have some ideas about the usefulness of the technology and can perceive some relevance for teaching and learning, but if the technology malfunctions, they tend to abandon it. Alternatively, they may use the technology for minor tasks, such as record-keeping, but do not attempt to integrate it into the curricula. Utilisation is followed by integration, i.e. the start of use of the technology for instruction. At this stage, teachers make a choice about the appropriate way that the technology can be used for teaching and learning. Should the technology be removed, teachers would have difficulties in reworking their lessons to accommodate alternative options.

The stage of integration marks the beginning of appropriate uses in delivering and developing instruction. Teachers at this level do not use the technology for the sake of using it, but rather have made a choice about instructional delivery that is most appropriately handled by the technology. Should the latter be taken away at this point, teachers at the integration phase would have a hard time reworking their lessons to accommodate an alternative option. In the reorientation stage, the teacher uses the technology as a tool to facilitate the reconsideration of the purpose and function of teaching and learning. Finally, at the evolution stage, teachers are able to continually modify instruction to include evolving learning theory, and lessons learned from the teaching and learning experience.

In conclusion, the TAM approach elaborates on attitudes that inform individual technology use. Rogers' diffusion theory focuses mainly on the relative speed with which members of an organisation adopt an innovation (Al-Senaidi et. al, 2009, p. 576). For this paper we selected the Rieber and Welliver (1995) model as a framework for the synthesis of student and faculty perceptions about the instructional value of the iPad, because it provides a framework developed specifically for post-secondary education, and the different stages it entails allow for the mapping and comparison of the views of the two groups of stakeholders (students and faculty).

3. The Art and Design Context

Art and design education encompasses a number of overlapping disciplines with increasingly blurred boundaries (Kennedy & Welch, 2008). It is characteristic of these disciplines that they are considered to be of low paradigmatic development. In other words, there is little agreement among the members of the related disciplines about theory, methods and techniques. In contrast, disciplines such as biology, chemistry, physics and the sciences represent disciplines of high paradigmatic development (Braxton, Olsen & Simmons, 1999, p. 301). Due to the open-ended nature of most art and design outcomes, the curriculum tends to be fluid (Shreeve, Sims & Trowler, 2010, p.135). Subsequently, teaching and learning practices emphasise the development of a broad set of intellectual skills and competencies, which the Art and Design Subject Benchmark Statement lists as "…intellectual maturity, curiosity, personal innovation, risk-taking, independent enquiry, and effective management and planning skills" (Kennedy et. al, 2008, p. 9).

Another characteristic is that the instructional approaches that take place in art and design disciplines often entail the setting of a conceptual problem, regular lectures, informal presentations of student work under development, and a series of critiques of student outcomes also known as "crits". It is common practice that a group of academics undertakes the final assessment of completed student outcomes (Ellmers, 2005, p. 2; Cennamo, Brandt, Scott, Douglas, McGrath, Reimer & Vernon, 2011, p. 14). The teaching and learning practices in art and design tend to be student-focused rather than teacher-centred. The focus of overall instruction is project-based learning, whose instructional aim is to replicate as much as possible contextualised design problems in real life settings (Ellmers, 2005, p. 5).

Lastly, learning in art and design has a visible dimension. Outcomes manifest as artefacts that are open to debate and examination. Learners increasingly learn to incorporate critical feedback and to work with a decreasing amount of support and feedback. In addition, learning is primarily social, that is teaching and learning practices are visible and discussed often in an informal manner and in the presence of peers. Process and development are of significance, because they support the ongoing exploration and refinement of outputs. Therefore, assessment focuses on process as well as the finished artefact.

4. Research Methodology and Design for Stages One and Two

For the first two stages of the research task, the authors pursued a phenomenographic approach. Despite the critiques of qualitative approaches in relation to the objectivity of the researcher, the reliability and transferability of outcomes, and the lack of predictive power, all of which are inevitable consequences of the anti-positivist paradigm, phenomenography provided the opportunity to investigate attitudes towards the iPad from a broad perspective (Souleles, 2012). This research approach was considered suitable to capture the variation of perspectives and views among all stakeholders. Some phenomenographic studies (Pang, 2003) focus not only on what the different ways are of experiencing a phenomenon, but also on what is a way of experiencing a phenomenon. The former is referred to as the "referential" aspect (what) of the variations of perception, and the latter as the "structural" (how).

The fundamental assumption of phenomenography is the existence of a finite number of qualitatively different ways of perceiving a particular phenomenon, in our case to illuminate the variations in ways which students and faculty consider the instructional potential of iPads in undergraduate art and design disciplines. All the answers from students and faculty were mapped on the Rieber and Welliver (1995) five-step model of technology adoption. Although this model was developed to gauge the attitude of teachers towards adoption, we used it to also map the student perceptions of the instructional value of iPads.

For the first stage of the study, participating students came from both institutions, but first- and final-year students were excluded. In the case of the former, it was considered that they did not have sufficient time to adapt to the teaching and learning culture of the related disciplines. Equally, students undertaking their final year of study were also excluded, because it was considered that they may not have sufficient time to engage in a meaningful manner with the research project. Thus the population comprised a non-probability, purposive sample, and this implies a potential risk of bias in comparison to probability sampling.

Each student was handed an iPad and a stylus, with a number of pre-installed free applications (apps). These comprised four categories: utilities, social networking, productivity and creativity, and were selected by the authors of this paper based on their perceived value. The students were not provided with instructions on how to use the tablet. This was deliberate, because the focus of the investigation was to capture – through open-ended interviews - a bottom-up appraisal of the value of iPads from the perspective of undergraduate students in studio-based disciplines.

During the second stage of the project thirty-two faculty members from both institutions participated. These faculty members teach in various undergraduate programmes in art and design and in different years of study. Some of the subjects they teach involve more practical (hands-on) teaching and learning tasks, for example Fine Arts, Printmaking and Drawing, while others such as Semiotic Theory and Creative Writing are of a theoretical nature. There was an effort to balance the sex of participating faculty (17 male, 15 female), although this was not possible due to the voluntary nature of the project. Thus, the gender of participating faculty comprises a sample of convenience. It needs to be noted that although the literature on how female users engage with tablets is not extensive, studies indicate some differences. Male users tend to be early adopters and use tablets for a wider range of activities (Snyder Bulik, 2011, p. 12).

Each participating faculty member was handed an iPad and a stylus, with the pre-installed software (apps) limited to the default factory settings. However, faculty members were allowed to download their own apps without restriction. Lastly, participants were not provided with instructions on how to use their iPad; this was deliberate, because the focus of the investigation was to capture their unhindered perceptions of the value of iPads for teaching and learning based on the use of the tablets over a period of one academic semester. Data were gathered through open-ended questions that were developed to elicit answers about effort expectancy, performance expectancy, social influence, and facilitating conditions.

5. Mapping on the Rieber and Welliver (1995) Model

In stage one the following questions were asked of participating students: a) Based on your experience in using the iPad for one semester, how did you find it for your studies? b) In your opinion, in what kind of situations do you think the iPad can be useful for learning? c) In terms of usability, how did you find the iPad? d) In your opinion, how does the iPad compare with a laptop? e) What is your opinion about the apps that were installed on the iPad? The replies to these questions, depending on where they fit in terms of the answers given during the interviews, were mapped on the Rieber and Welliver (1995) five-step hierarchical model (Table 2). The right fit of statements vis-à-vis where they fit exactly in the model, is not always obvious, and the authors judged the category allocated on the Rieber and Welliver (1995) model from the overall impression and general meaning developed from reading each individual interview transcript.

Questions	Familiarisation	Utilisation
Based on your experience in using the iPad for one semester, how did you find it for your studies?	Preference for tactile learning experiences (as opposed to using an iPad)	Varied ways to support learning Focus on uses and limitations
In your opinion, in what kind of situations do you think the iPad can be useful for learning?	Unable to describe any learning use	Described more than three uses Described more than two uses
In terms of usability, how did you find the iPad?	Perceived as difficult to use	Perceived as easy to use

In your opinion, how does the iPad compare with a laptop?	Identified uses and limitations for each device Perceived superiority of the laptop based on processing power	Emphasis on speed of access and interface of the iPad Combined use of both iPad and laptop Described different uses for each device
What is your opinion about the apps that were installed on the iPad?	Some apps useful and some not Not easy to learn apps and not enough time to explore Apps were not useful	Range of apps useful for different tasks Selective choice of apps for learning Many apps share similar features

Table 2. Mapping student perceptions on the Rieber and Welliver (1995) model of technology adoption

In stage two the following questions were asked of participating faculty: a) Do you think that the iPad can influence the academic performance of students? b) How easy do you consider it is to use the iPad for teaching and learning? c) Would influence from peers and/or students affect your decision to use the iPad for teaching and learning? d) Do you consider that you have access to the right institutional infrastructure to support your use of the iPad for teaching and learning? The replies to these questions, depending where they fit in terms of the answers given during the interviews, were mapped on the Rieber and Welliver (1995) five-step hierarchical model (Table 3). As with Table 2 (above), the right fit of statements is not always obvious, and the authors judged the category allocated on the Rieber and Welliver (1995) model from the overall impression and general meaning developed from reading each individual interview transcript.

Questions	Familiarisation	Utilisation	Integration
Do you think that the iPad can influence the academic performance of students?	Expressed doubts whether the iPad can influence teaching and learning	Emphasised the significance of good instruction versus distracting potential	Identified practical ways to facilitate learning
How easy do you consider it is to use the iPad for teaching and learning?		Effortless completion of certain instructional tasks Some tasks require more effort than others Time-consuming to properly complete task	
Would influence from peers and/or students affect your decision to use the iPad for teaching and learning?		Peer and student views matter Preference for own experience with the technology	
Do you consider that you have access to the right institutional infrastructure to support your use of the iPad for teaching and learning?		Emphasis on good IT support and wireless Internet Lack of sufficient technological infrastructure	

Table 3. Mapping faculty perceptions on the Rieber and Welliver (1995) model of technology adoption

6. Analysis and Conclusion

The characteristics of the art and design teaching and learning milieu, as described above, underlines and informs to a large extent the approach of the two stakeholders (students and faculty) towards the instructional potential of iPads. These characteristics need to be considered as the delimitations of the two previous studies (stages one and two) that inform this paper, and in particular the fact that in both stages participants deliberately were not given specific learning tasks to accomplish. There was no clearly defined instructional context to use the iPads.

When comparing the two tables above (Tables 2 and 3) that map student and faculty perceptions on the Rieber and Welliver (1995) model of technology adoption, we note that the majority of perceptions held by both stakeholders on the instructional value of iPads fall within the categories of familiarization and utilisation. More specifically, at the level of familiarization both students and faculty considered the relevance of iPads for teaching and learning. When rejecting the tablet, they used arguments in support of tactile (non-digital) learning experiences, they were unable to describe any potential use of teaching and learning, they perceived the tablet as difficult to use, they identified limitations, and in some cases considered that a laptop is more useful.

At the level of utilisation there were some attempts to incorporate the iPads in teaching and learning (capturing data, presenting work and developing visual draft ideas and concepts), and some usefulness was identified for certain apps. However, only at the level of the faculty was there an attempt to integrate in a more systemic way the use of iPads in teaching and learning. This is to be expected, as faculty are the ones that determine how curricula are delivered, and, although students may identify some uses, in the end the former are responsible for curricula.

In conclusion, when comparing student and faculty perceptions of the instructional value of iPads in art and design education, and within the delimitations of the research completed, we note that the next stages of the Rieber and Welliver (1995) five-step hierarchical model of technology adoption require a more complex technology adoption stance and possibly a campus-wide approach. The effective integration of iPads in the curricula, the reorientation and reconsideration of the purpose and function of teaching and learning due to the opportunities provided by iPads, and finally the evolution stage that implies continuous action research to learn from the related teaching and learning experiences, all these require change that can only be achieved if all stakeholders share in the process (See for example the paper in these proceedings: iPads at the University of

Western Sydney (UWS): Initiating institutional transformation, by Lynnae Rankine, Dennis Macnamara). Otherwise, the adoption level of the different stakeholders will remain out of sync and piecemeal.

References

Al-Senaidi, S., Lin, L., & Poirot, J. (2009). Barriers to adopting technology for teaching and learning in Oman. *Computers & Education, 53*(3), 575–590.

Braxton, J., Olsen, D., & Simmons, A. (1999). Affinity disciplines and the use of principles of good practice for undergraduate education. *Research in Higher Education, 39*(3), 299-318.

Cennamo, K., Brandt, C., Scott, B., Douglas, S., McGrath, M., Reimer, Y., & Vernon, M. (2011). Managing the complexity of design problems through studio-based learning. *The Interdisciplinary Journal of Problem-Based Learning, 5*(2), 12-36.

Grundy, S. (1982). Three modes of action research. *Curriculum Perspectives, 2*(3), 23-34.

Ellmers, G. (2005). A re-examination of graphic design pedagogy, and its application at the University of Wollongong: Towards a PhD study in design education. *Proceedings of the Annual ACUADS 2005 Conference: artists, designers and creative communities*. Perth, Western Australia: Edith Cowan University.

Hsu, C. M., & Chang I. H. (2009). Design faculty and students' perspectives and attitudes toward web-based instruction and platform design. *Asian Journal of Health and Information Sciences, 4*, (2-3), 124-142.

Li, Q. (2007). Student and teacher views about technology: A tale of two cities? *Journal of Research on Technology in Education, 39*(4), 377-397.

Kennedy, G., & Welch, E. (2008). *Subject benchmark statement, art and design*. Gloucester: The Quality Assurance Agency for Higher Education.

Pang, M. (2003). Two faces of variation: On continuity in the phenomenographic movement. *Scandinavian Journal of Educational Research, 47*(2), 145-156.

Rieber, L. P., & Welliver, P. W. (1989). Infusing educational technology into mainstream educational computing. *International Journal of Instructional Media, 16*(1), 21-32.

Shreeve, A., Sims, E., & Trowler, P. (2010). 'A kind of exchange': Learning from art and design teaching. *Higher Education Research and Development, 29*(2), 125-138.

Snyder Bulik, B. (2011). Always on women: A survey on how women are using technology today. New York: Ad Age Insights. Retrieved December 30, 2014, from http://goo.gl/EC1oSC

Souleles, N., Savva, S., Watters, H., Bull, B., & Annesley, A. (2014). A phenomenographic investigation on the use of iPads among undergraduate art and design students. *British Journal of Educational Research*. Retrieved December 30, 2014 from http://goo.gl/A6E5Ya

Souleles, N. (2012). Phenomenography and elearning in art and design. *Proceedings of the 8th International Conference on Networked Learning* (pp. 466-473). Maastricht School of Management, Maastricht, The Netherlands.

Venkatesh, V., Morris, M., Davis, G., & Davis, F. (2003). User acceptance of information technology: Toward a unified view. *MIS Quarterly, 27*(3), 425-478.

DESIGNING MOBILE LEARNING ACTIVITIES FOR OUTDOOR LEARNING

HAGIT MEISHAR TAL[1], YAEL SNEH[2] AND ARNON MEDZINI[3]

Abstract

In recent years, there has been a significant increase in the adoption and the use of mobile technologies by students, especially smartphones and tablets. Students use them mostly for personal needs and not for learning purposes. However, these devices, which allow access to the Internet anytime and anywhere and equipped with a camera, voice recorder and GPS, have enormous potential to be used for teaching and learning, particularly in contexts of outdoor learning. This study reports a preliminary study demonstrating an attempt to use mobile technologies in an outdoor context, namely an educational trip. The study is an evaluation study of a pilot course named "Mobile Technologies in out of the classroom learning" that took place at Oranim College in Israel. This course had two main purposes: the first is exposing the students to the potential of smartphones and tablets by using them as a supporting tool for learning outside the classroom. The second is teaching the students how to design learning activities while integrating smartphones and iPads in a way that reaps the benefits that these devices can offer without impairing the outdoor experience. The paper presents a theoretical framework that links the outdoor learning pedagogy and mobile learning. The paper also presents the findings from a survey of the students' attitudes towards their learning experience and an analysis of the learning activities that the students have designed. The findings show high levels of satisfaction and high level of performance.

[1] Oranim College and The Open University of Israel. Email: hagitmt@gmail.com

[2] Oranim College and The Open University of Israel. Email: yaelsneh@walla.com

[3] Oranim College and The Open University of Israel. Email: arnon_m@oranim.ac.il

1. Introduction

The dissemination and use of tablets and smartphones has grown impressively in recent years. Their high mobility, low weight, Internet access, and ability to serve as a platform for diverse applications have made them ideal candidates as aids in outdoor study as takes place, for example, in school outings.

Smartphones and tablets that have SIM cards for online communication are multipurpose instruments for field study. They give access to information anywhere and at any time; various applications (e.g., distance measurement) make them measurement tools, their cameras and recording devices allow users to document information in the field, and their combination of built-in GPS and map applications makes them navigation tools.

In a course at Oranim College of Education on mobile technologies in outdoor learning, students of teaching geography encounter mobile communication technologies (smartphones and iPads) in order to test their use as aids for outdoor learning. The students are exposed to the vast potential of these instruments, and learn how to develop lesson plans that integrate mobile technology. Students who took the course prepared and conducted a school outing in geography that included stopovers for technology-supported activity.

This study's purpose was evaluating the viability and utility of integrating smartphones and iPads into learning and students' ability to develop outdoor learning activities that put technology to intelligent use. In the beginning of the paper, a theoretical framework that links the outdoor learning pedagogy and mobile learning is presented. Afterwards, we present the findings from a survey of the students' attitudes towards their learning experience and an analysis of the learning activities that the students have designed.

2. Theoretical Background

2.1 Out-of-Classroom Learning

We usually think of learning as something done in a classroom, where a teacher manages learning and students acquire knowledge by reception and practice.

A classroom environment is a safe and protected learning venue; leaving it is sometimes perceived as a risk or a leisure activity. In many contexts, however, outdoor activity has a major advantage over classroom learning. For one thing, it introduces students to phenomena and concepts via direct interaction with the object studied (Orion, 2003). Importantly, direct interaction is attainable in the classroom as well, e.g., in laboratory studies. In certain cases, however — mainly in geography-related topics of study — an outing has a large advantage over classroom study.

By heading into the field, students may experience an encounter free of go-betweens and means of substantiation. They experience the learning as a holistic process of discovery and adaptation to the world (Burridge et al., 2008). Outdoor learning is experiential; it allows students to understand phenomena and processes that might not be understood without being tested in the field (Adkins & Simmons, 2002).

A school outing per se does not automatically ensure learning. To make a field activity effective, a teacher must be knowledgeable in the area studied and must design learning activities at specific locations that are suited to the study of specific phenomena. The choice of locations and nature of the activity to be conducted there are keys to successful outdoor learning (Orion, 2003). Effective outdoor activity must engage students in investigation and experiential learning (Lewis & Williams, 1994; Luckner & Nadler, 1997; Kolb, 2005; Wilson, 2006). In such activities, the teacher serves not as a fount of knowledge, but as a facilitator who moves among groups of students that perform experiential activities in the field; s/he helps them solve problems and guides them commensurate with their needs.

2.2 Mobile Learning

Smartphones and tablets have immense teaching and learning potential (Prensky, 2005). Since students increasingly use them for their own purposes, teachers may, instead of banning their use in school, exploit their availability to create an interactive and interesting learning experience. By utilising their special characteristics, teachers may design a new and fascinating learning experience in class, and thereby enhance students' learning motivation (Jones et al., 2006).

The main potential contribution of smartphones to learning, however, is outside the classroom. In educational school outings and museum visits, smartphones may enrich learning by providing conditions for authentic and contextual study (Sharples et al., 2009). M-learning, as learning with mobile instruments is known, may create new learning opportunities and situations by eliminating the dissociation between the field and the sources of information.

There have been successful attempts to put mobile technologies (palm computers, first-generation cellphones, mobile computers, etc.) to learning use (Traxler, 2005; Lai et al., 2007). None of these vanguard attempts, however, were able to scale from project to widespread use, evidently because the old instruments lacked the flexibility and the wide dissemination of today's smartphones (Kukulska-Holmes et al., 2011; Chen et al., 2008). Smartphones and tablets are multipurpose tools—useful in daily life and also in educational contexts that range from gathering location-based content to creating knowledge in, and disseminating it directly from, the field.

Smartphones and tablets that have SIM cards allowing online communication are multipurpose tools for study of the outdoor environment. They can transform any student into a field correspondent, navigator, investigator, photographer, and broadcasting station. One may identify five possible uses of these devices in outdoor learning (Figure 1):

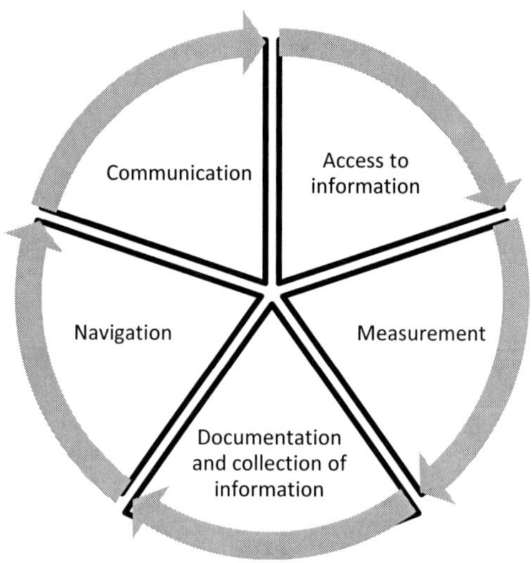

Figure 1. Five possible uses of smartphones and tablets in learning

a. **Accessing information** - these instruments give students access to information anywhere and at any time. This information may support outdoor research processes, e.g., identifying flora encountered in the field. By using the phones, students may easily and conveniently access online plant glossaries that will help them perform the assignment. Information in support of outdoor learning may also be obtained by means of a QR (Quick Response) code reader. QR is a two-dimensional barcode of sorts that encrypts information in a visual graphic format. Camera-equipped smartphones and tablets can use the QR Reader application to obtain learning-supportive information. When the camera scans the code, the appropriate online content appears on the screen. This is a very convenient and efficient way of presenting online information; it avoids the complication of having to input complex addresses, which cannot be done in the field. By preparing virtual stops at the activity sites on the route of the outing, teachers may guide students toward activities or useful information that will support their activity in the field (De Pietro & Frontera, 2012). A more advanced possibility of providing location-dependent information (LDI) is the use of augmented-reality applications. The equipping of smartphones and tablets with GPS has created a new class of services — location-dependent information services (LDIS) that these instruments can deliver in the field and are enormously important in learning. Such applications allow users in a specific location to obtain information about the location and its surroundings via the instrument. A person on an outing who is unfamiliar with nearby sites, for example, may bring up an application that maps nearby locations and generates a list of recommendations. Augmented-reality applications are similarly usable for scholastic purposes.

b. **Measurement** - the wealth of applications available on the web includes a variety of measurement tools that can be installed on these devices and used in the field. A distance meter, an altimeter, a compass, and a noise meter are only a few examples. Once installed on the mobile device, they provide abundant opportunities for the measurement of phenomena observed in field research.

c. **Documentation and collection of information** - since these instruments are equipped with cameras, recording devices, and text-processing options, one can use them to document information in the field (Clough, 2007). Once stored, the information reaches the classroom for ongoing study after the outdoor activity is over. One may, for example, record birdcalls or take pictures of natural phenomena, land uses, and landscapes, and present them in class. In another possibility, students immediately document information in the classroom environment by establishing direct access from the field to a virtual classroom site, an online class forum, or another indirect environment that serves as a virtual classroom learning space. The integration of mobile device capabilities with learning management systems such as Moodle, personal and cooperative learning environments such as Google Docs, and other websites can help teachers to administer shared and constructivist learning processes that create continuity between field learning and classroom learning (Cochrane, 2010; Cochrane & Bateman, 2010).

d. **Navigation tools** - these instruments, equipped with built-in GPS and maps, may serve as excellent outdoor navigation tools and location-aware activities (Prensky, 2005; Clough at al. 2008). Like printed maps, they let students try their hand at navigation and map-reading. Unlike ordinary maps, however, they generate exact location data and prevent navigation errors and loss of way.

e. **Communication** - smartphones and tablets are, of course, communication devices that allow vocal and textual reportage. This is very important in the field, from the early stage of organising and managing students in the field up to learning contexts, in which the devices let groups of students in different locations outside the classroom to communicate with each other.

3. Principles for the Design of Mobile Outdoor Learning

One of the main concerns about the integration of technologies into outdoor learning is that the integration will have an adverse effect on the outdoor learning, i.e., students will get information from their smartphones instead of learning from their experiences in the field (Lai et al., 2007). Busy with their phones and iPads, they will be distracted from the field experience itself, defeating the purpose of the educational outing.

The challenge in using mobile technologies in outdoor learning is to defeat this distraction while making intelligent use of the instruments to broaden learners' abilities and abet active experiential study instead of substituting for it. In other words, the technology should serve as an instrumentality not only for the study of the outdoors environment, but also for its investigation.

To combine the purpose of outdoor study with the technical capabilities of smartphones and tablets, outdoor learning activities that integrate mobile technologies should be based on four main design principles:

a. **Location dependency** - The activity must be doable only in the field. It must turn the learner's gaze to the field, help him/her orient him/herself there, and point out sites of interest there.

b. **Inclusion of accessing information in the activity** - Learners should use the mobile devices' potential in accessing information to enhance their knowledge of findings and phenomena that they encounter in the field.
c. **Use of research and measurement tools** - Learners should use applications for the research, measurement, and documentation of phenomena in the field in order to construct knowledge on their own.
d. **Self-learning** - Outdoor learning aided by mobile technologies should be self-learning and active learning by the learner or a group of learners, without a teacher's mediation.

4. Research Questions

This article describes an attempt at Oranim College to train students for outdoor teaching aided by mobile technologies. Its purpose is to evaluate the process and the products of the course in reference to three main aspects:

1. The viability of integrating mobile technologies (smartphones and iPads) into outdoor learning, with reference to organisational requirements, suitability of the instruments, operating difficulties, etc.;
2. Geography students' attitudes toward the use of mobile technologies in outdoor teaching in terms of the learning experience, learning motivation, and contribution to learning;
3. The ability of geography teaching students to put the technology to pedagogical use in developing outdoor teaching activities.

Accordingly, the following research questions are asked:

1. Is integration of mobile technologies into outdoor learning possible? What does it entail in organisational terms? What equipment does it require? What difficulties did the learners encounter? Did they overcome them and, if so, how?
2. How do the students perceive the use of these technologies in outdoor teaching?
3. What technology-integrated activities did the students produce, and how well did they put the resources available to them to appropriate use?

5. Research Methods

The study had three components:

1. A questionnaire administered at the beginning of the course, composed of open-ended items that yielded a profile of the students' initial attitudes toward the use of mobile technologies in learning and the extent of their exposure to the topic;
2. A summarising questionnaire at the end of the course, with closed- and open-ended questions that revealed students' attitudes toward the activities in which they took part during the course, the contribution of mobile technologies to learning, and difficulties that they encountered as they learned;
3. A qualitative analysis of the mobile-supported activities that the students produced.

6. Description of the Course

The course titled "Mobile Technologies in Outdoor Learning" was given at Oranim College in February 2013. The participants were ten teaching students — two men and eight women from various degree programmes (Geography, Community Social Education, Communications, Hebrew Language, Civics, Literature, Special Education). Their average age was twenty-six. The college made five SIM-equipped iPads that allowed cellular serving in the field available to them.

The course took place over four intensive days. On the first day, the participants were exposed to the theme of mobile technology and outdoor learning. They gained acquaintance with principles for the pedagogical design of a geographic school outing in which mobile technologies are integrated. The second day was devoted to a practical experiential activity in which the students learned how to use measurement and research applications such as GPS-aided maps, a compass, a plant glossary, a camera, and a video clip producer; then they demonstrated the use of these tools as they circulated around the college. On the third day, the students broke into couples and headed out to learn the places where they would have to develop cellphone-aided learning activities - the area between the vicinity of Beit Shearim and the Kishon River at Tivon. Each couple was assigned a location, visited it, studied it, and established five places at the site where students would stop for activity. Then the participants returned to class to produce the activities and generate a QR code for each. On the fourth day they returned to the field, distributed the instructions for the field activities by QR code, and performed each other's learning activities. Once the activities were over, they were asked to evaluate them and provide peer feedback.

7. Findings

7.1 Preliminary Questionnaire

The preliminary questionnaire investigated students' expectations of learning aided by smartphones and iPads, and their experience in using these technologies for scholastic purposes. The questionnaire results indicate that most participants (nine out of ten) owned personal mobile devices (smartphones or iPads). Most had no experience in using mobile technologies in learning. Most had positive expectations about the use of iPads and smartphones in outdoor activity. The following examples bear this out: "Look, all kids are attached to their smartphones anyway, so let them do something useful with them. There must be plant glossaries in applications or somesuch that you can use when you're out in the field." Another: "iPads, smartphones, and various applications can be used to enrich an experience gained in an outdoor educational outing or activity, such as photography, documentation, recording, and responding to tasks in the field that are given online."

7.2 Concluding Questionnaire

The concluding questionnaire asked the participants about their learning experience in the course and what the course contributed to learning. Participants were also asked to evaluate the extent of the contribution of the cellphone to learning as manifested in the course.

In response to the question "To what extent did the course contribute to me in the following respects.?" arrayed on a five-level scale, the following responses were given:

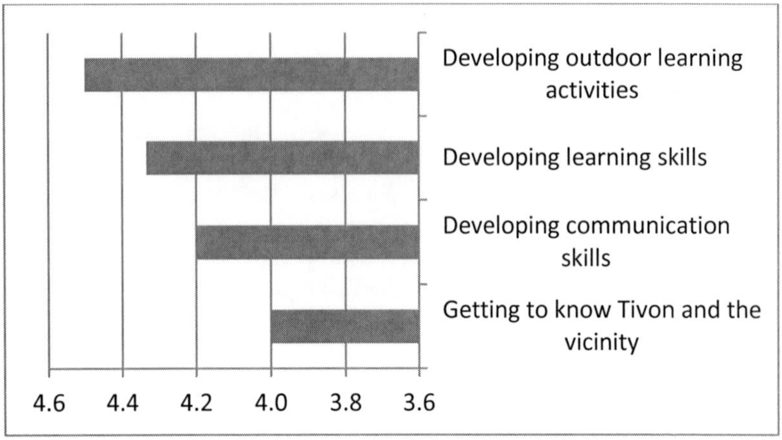

Figure 1. Contribution of the course

Figure 1 shows that the participants perceived a strong contribution in each of the indicators. Due to small sample size, statistical procedures to measure the variance of the results could not be performed.

The participants were also asked to explain and specify the nature of the contribution in each indicator. In explaining the "getting to know Tivon" indicator, for example, the following answer was given: "Getting to know new places and more about existing ones." One participant noted that because he already knew the area very well, the activity in this regard contributed nothing to him. Explaining the indicators of developing skills and designing a outdoor learning activity, the following responses appeared: "It also forced me to answer questions about my attention and concentration problems," and, "Experiencing investigative learning." Explaining the indicator of skills in designing a learning activity, the following was offered: "It made me try to think about identifying the activity that would be the most enjoyable while making the most of the learning space." Explaining the communication skills indicator, participants mentioned "getting to know applications" and "getting to know QR code—using it and creating things with it."

In response to the question about the contribution of mobile technologies to outdoor study, the following responses were obtained across the five-level scale:

The list of contributions fell into three groups:

1. Indicators of the use of tools that the telephone provides: measuring phenomena, navigation and orientation, documentation;

2. Indicators of the use of the telephone to obtain information: accessing instructions and useful information;
3. Indicators of a contribution at the level of learning management: learning motivation, order and organisation, continuity in the connection between outdoors and classroom learning.

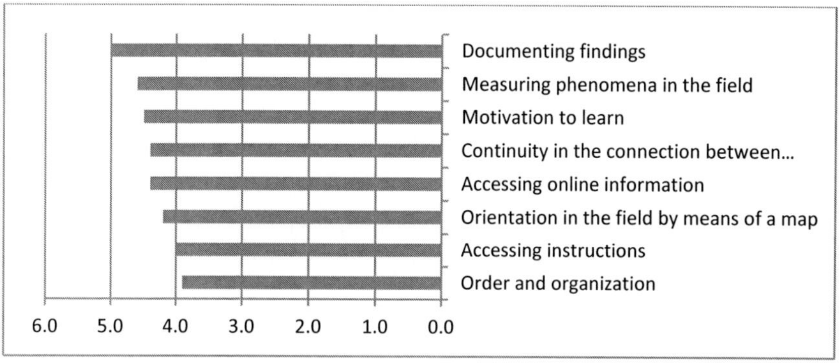

Figure 2. Contribution of mobile technologies to outdoor learning

As figure 2 suggests, the mobile devices are perceived as making a large/very large contribution in all respects. Again, measurements of variance among the responses could not be performed due to small sample size.

When asked to note difficulties encountered in the integration of mobile technologies into learning, the participants' responses addressed the technical and pedagogical aspects. On the technical side, participants mentioned signal problems, the need for an instrument equipped with a SIM card and a surfing package, the need to recharge the battery and difficulties caused by malfunctioning applications. On the pedagogical side, they noted problems originating in the need to know how to use the applications and - as teaching students - they expressed concerns about their ability to implement these activities with their future students. Their main apprehension concerned loss of control over students and distraction among students once they are allowed to use these devices in the learning process.

The participants were also asked what device they preferred for outdoor learning, a cellphone, a SIM-equipped iPad, or a combination of both. Eighty percent preferred an iPad to a cellphone and the rest preferred a combination of the two. The reasons that they gave for preferring the iPad were (1) a larger screen, allowing more convenient display and input of information; (2) iPads cannot be used as telephones and, therefore, do not encourage distracting text messages and phone calls during the activities.

7.3 Evaluation of the Results (Participants' Activities)

To combine the purpose of outdoor study with the technical capabilities of smartphones and iPads, outdoor learning activities that integrate mobile technologies should be based on four main design principles:

a. **Location dependency** - The activity must be doable only in the field. It must turn the learner's gaze to the field, help him/her orient him/herself there, and point out sites of interest there.

b. **Inclusion of accessing information in the activity** - Learners should use the mobile devices' potential in accessing information to enhance their knowledge of findings and phenomena that they encounter in the field.

c. **Use of research and measurement tools** - Learners should use applications for the research, measurement, and documentation of phenomena in the field in order to construct knowledge on their own.

d. **Self-learning** - Outdoor learning aided by mobile technologies should be self-learning and active learning by the learner or a group of learners, without a teacher's mediation.

The participants produced sixteen activities that were evaluated for the design of a mobile-technology-aided task:

1. Is the activity location-dependent?
2. Does the activity include accessing of online information?
3. Does the activity use research and measurement tools? Which?
4. Can the activity be performed independently and without mediation?

Table 1 presents an analysis of the activities that the students designed due to the four criteria (Location dependent, access to online information, use of applications for measurement and documentation and self-study):

Activity	Location-dependent	Access to on-line information	Use of applications for measurement and resaerch	Self-study
1.	✓		Measuring distance on a map, screen capture, publishing on course forum	✓
2.	✓	✓	Compass, producing a video clip	✓
3.	✓		Shared plant glossary, camera, course forum	✓
4.	✓	✓	Reading a topographic map, camera, publication on course forum	✓
5.	✓	✓	Google Docs form, compass, pedometer, publication on course forum	✓
6.	✓	✓	Camera, publication on course forum	✓
7.	✓	✓	Video clip	✓
8.	✓		Camera, collaborative map	✓
9.	✓	✓	Video clip	✓
10.	✓		Collaborative topographic topographic map, pedometer	✓
11.	✓	✓	Shared plant glossary, publication on course forum	✓
12.	✓	✓	Collaborative topographic map, camera	✓
13.	✓	✓	Camera	✓
14.	✓		Collaborative topographic map, compass	✓
15.	✓		Video clip	✓
16.	✓		Plant glossary, compass	✓

Table 1. Analysis of iPad- and smartphone-aided activities

The table shows that all activities were designed to be location-dependent and for self-study. Nine activities used online information. All used documentation, research, and measurement tools. Most activities satisfied all principles of the design of mobile-technology-aided study as we defined them.

Here is an example of an activity that combines the use of online information and the creation of the information by means of photo applications, a topographic map, and publishing on an online forum:

Point on a Map—Nir Kahane's Memorial

"Read the memorial text for Sgt. Nir Kahane. What song did he like to listen to? Search for the song on YouTube and play it. What mountain does it talk about? Identify it in the field.

"Use the collaborative topographic map application to find the highest elevation of the mountain and use the map to identify localities on the mountain. Take a picture of the mountain and upload it, along with information that you have found, to the course website."

The next figure summarises the frequencies of use of various measurement and research applications in the student's activities:

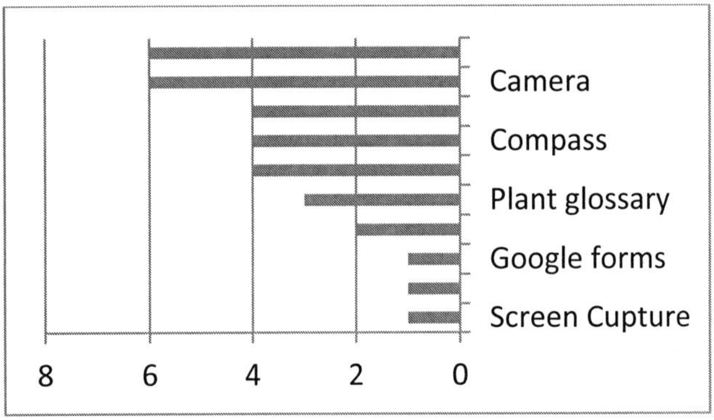

Figure 3. Use of measurement and research applications

The figure shows that the most frequently used tools were the camera and the forum; less use was made of screen capture, measuring distance on a map, and Google Docs forms. The reason for the variance may be the extent of complexity and students' familiarity with these tools. The more familiar the tool, and the less it required new experimentation, the more preferred it was. This led to the conclusion that in order to diversify the use of applications in activities, it may be necessary to intensify the stage of acquiring skills in the use of new applications.

8. Conclusion

This pioneering experiment in the use of iPads and smartphones phones in learning proves that such activities are very viable, and that the technology is mature enough to enhance learning in the field. The students expressed a high level of satisfaction from the course and reported high levels of perceived learning in all four aspects (learning skills, ICT skills, learning activity design and content knowledge of the school outing). Presumably, the participants' favourable opinion of the activity has to do with the compliance of their learning outputs with the principles behind the design of outdoor mobile activity. The activities were not only interesting and diverse; they also exploited mobile technologies meaningfully. Therefore, they were perceived as aids that can contribute much to a school outing.

The study elicited many conclusions about how the iPads and smartphones may be integrated into outdoor learning. What remains is to continue the experiment and perform further research to determine the best practices in this mission.

References

Adkins, C., & Simmons, B. (2002). Outdoor, experiential, and environmental education: Converging or diverging approaches? *ERIC Digest*.

Burridge, P., Carpenter, C., & Cherednichenko, B. (2008). Outdoor experiential learning: Building exemplary practice. In *11th International Conference on Experiential Learning: Challenges for Experiential Learning*. University of Technology - Sydney, Sydney.

Chen, F. C., Lai, C. H., Yang, J. C., San Liang, J., & Chan, T. W. (2008, March). Evaluating the effects of mobile technology on an outdoor experiential learning. In *Wireless, mobile, and ubiquitous technology in education, 2008. WMUTE 2008. Fifth IEEE international conference* (pp. 107-114).

Clough, G., Jones, A. C., McAndrew, P., & Scanlon, E. (2008) Informal learning with PDAs and smartphones. *Journal of Computer Assisted Learning*, *24*(5), 359-371.

Cochrane, T.D. (2010). Exploring mobile learning success factors. *Research in Learning Technology*, *18*(2), 133-148.

Cochrane, T., & Bateman, R. (2010). Smartphones give you wings: Pedagogical affordances of mobile Web 2.0. *Australasian Journal of Educational Technology*, *26*(1), 1-14.

De Pietro, O., & Frontera, G. (2012). Mobile tutoring for situated learning and collaborative learning in AIML application using QR-code. In *Complex, intelligent and software intensive systems (CISIS), 2012 sixth international conference* (pp. 799-805).

Jones, A., Issroff, K., Scanlon, E., Clough, G. and McAndrew, P. (2006). Using mobile devices for learning in informal settings: Is it motivating? *Proceedings of IADIS international conference mobile learning Dublin*. Barcelona, Spain: IADIS Press.

Kukulska-Hulme, A., Sharples, M., Milrad, M., Arnedillo-Sanchez, I., & Vavoula, G. (2011). The genesis and development of mobile learning in Europe. In D. Parsons (Ed.) *Combining Elearning and M-Learning: New applications of blended educational resources* (pp. 151-177). Hershey, PA: Information Science Reference.

Lai, C. H., Yang, J. C., Chen, F. C., Ho, C. W., & Chan, T. W. (2007). Affordances of mobile technologies for experiential learning: The interplay of technology and pedagogical practices. *Journal of Computer Assisted Learning, 23*(4), 326-337.

Lewis, L. H., & Williams, C. J. (1994). Experiential learning: Past and present. *New Directions for Adult and Continuing Education*, (62), 5-16.

Luckner, J. L., & Nadler, R. S. (1997). *Processing the experience: Strategies to enhance and generalize learning*. Dubuque, IA: Kendall/Hunt Publishing Company.

Orion, N. (2003), The outdoor learning environment: Why and how. *Eureka 17* (Hebrew). Retrieved December 30, 2014, from http://goo.gl/Kjcmp6

Prensky, M. (2005). What can you learn from a cell phone? Almost anything! *Innovate 1*(5).

Sharples, M., M. Milrad, I.A. Sanchez, & G. Vavoula. (2009). Mobile learning: Small devices, big issues. In N. Balacheff, S. Ludvigsen, T. de Jong, A. Lazonder, S. Barnes & L. Montandon (Eds.) *Technology enhanced learning: Principles and products* (pp. 233-249). Berlin: Springer.

Sharples M., Taylor J., & Vavoula G. (2005). Towards a theory of mobile learning. In *Proceedings of Mlearn 2005 conference* [CD-ROM]. Johannesburg, South Africa: Qualimark Printing.

Traxler, J. (2005). Defining mobile learning. In *Proceedings IADIS international conference mobile learning 2005*, Malta, 261-266.

Wilson, J. J. P. (2006). *Experiential learning: A best practice handbook for educators and trainers*. London: Kogan Page.

A Case Study on Using iPads to Encourage Collaborative Learning in an Undergraduate Web Development Class

AEKATERINI MAVRI[1], FERNANDO LOIZIDES[2] AND NICOS SOULELES[3]

Abstract

Since its release in 2010 the iPad has become the leading computer tablet in the market. Due to its popularity, the iPad is widely used in different higher education (HE) institutions around the world. However, the research on the use of this tablet in HE remains limited. This paper describes how the iPad was used in an undergraduate web development class to encourage collaboration through participatory exercises. Firstly, the students were provided with the tablet in order to contribute to the class exercise, and then the iPad display was streamed real-time to a projector. The device was passed from student to student, thus bypassing the need for them to individually walk up to the lecturer's computer. This instructional approach also eliminated the use of laptops or workstations, and encouraged collaborative and active learning. Data was gathered through surveys and interviews with participating students, and a mixed methods approach was applied to the analysis. This paper reports on the user experience and the perceived learning outcomes, as well as the advantages and disadvantages of using this instructional approach for the specific lesson.

---

[1] Cyprus University of Technology, Cyprus. Email: aekaterini.mavri@cut.ac.cy
[2] Cyprus University of Technology, Cyprus. Email: fernando.loizides@gmail.com
[3] Cyprus University of Technology, Cyprus. Email: nicos.souleles@cut.ac.cy

1. Introduction

General pedagogy and educational psychology research shows that active learning can facilitate knowledge assimilation more effectively than traditional lecture-based teaching approaches (Felder, Stice & Rugarcia, 2000). Furthermore, active collaboration is an effective component for student engagement (Kuh, Cruce, Kinzie & Gonyea, 2008) associated with positive learning outcomes (Diemer, Fernandez & Streepey, 2012). Active learning implies that students are "actively engaged in the learning process" (Prince, 2004). In short, it involves students in "learning through doing" while "thinking about what they are doing in a classroom" (Bonwell & Eison, 1991), as opposed to passively listening. It implies moving away from teaching transmission towards knowledge assimilation through participatory activity, and aims to enhance student motivation through "higher order thinking" (analysis, synthesis and evaluation) (Prince, 2004).

Amongst the various methods that make use of the active learning model is mobile learning. Current studies show that mobile computing is found to increase student motivation and engagement in the learning activity (Swan, Kratcoski & Unger, 2005). They also highlight the collaborative potential of mobile devices, especially when producing or editing work (Traxler, 2005). Although the practice of mobile learning looks at the use of handheld devices, both inside and outside the classroom, this study focuses on a particular tablet device, the iPad, as the means for incorporating an active learning method into the classroom. The reasons behind this choice lie, mostly, in the fact that most design education institutions run on Apple Mac technology (Souleles, Savva, Watters, Bull & Annesley, 2014). Similarly, the Department of Multimedia and Graphic Arts at the Cyprus University of Technology provides a wide range of Apple Mac computers and peripherals for use by the students in its labs. As a result students are well acquainted with the Mac OS environment and user interface as well as other native or related software.

The researchers were interested in investigating the potential of learning using the affordances of a portable device (in this case the iPad) in a four-week-long undergraduate web development unit. The study was implemented in collaboration between the Cyprus Interaction lab and the Art and Design: elearning lab in the same department. Its aims were to elicit information and report on the student experience in using the iPad as part of a collaborative active learning approach as well as the perceived impact of this method on their learning outcomes. Data were collected by means of empirical assessment (survey and focus groups) and peer observation and analysed using a mixed methods approach.

Results indicate that the active learning method generated excitement, participation and productive collaborative activity during class. It was also perceived to enhance motivation and lead to better comprehension of theoretical concepts. Usage of the device also received mixed responses due to its lightweight and convenient use both in and out of the classroom. Nonetheless, serious problems were reported in producing code through its touchscreen interface and the process was thought to be more effectively facilitated through any other device with a keyboard and a mouse, i.e. a laptop.

The following sections report on the work that has been produced to date (Related Work) and provide a detailed description of the experiment, the data collection as well as the analysis methods (Study Design). Both quantitative and qualitative results are presented and analysed (Results and Discussion), and finally the main outcomes are outlined (Conclusion).

2. Related Work

A wide number of studies denote that an active learning approach is deemed as beneficial to teaching in K-12 education (Felder et al., 2000). Active learning differs to the active "lecture-and-practice-through-assignments" method in that it takes place predominantly in the classroom. It also places an emphasis on transforming students from "passive recipients" to active learners, a condition that is usually induced by traditional lecture-led classes (Jenkins, 1998). This method of learning forms a constant "dialogic process" between instructor and students, whereby the latter are encouraged to discover and experience principles by themselves through the constructive process of learning-by-doing (Bruner, 1966). Additionally, it is known to encourage a deep rather than a surface approach to learning, one that is adequate for all educational disciplines, but crucial in practical modules such as programming (Jenkins, 1998).

Programming is difficult due to the fact that it deals with understanding a lot of abstract concepts. Another major issue is also the fact that novice learners "are very local in their comprehension of programs" (Wiedenbeck & Ramalingam, 1999). In other words they often know the syntax and semantics of the code line by line, however, they do not know how to combine these together in order to produce more compound code structures (Winslow, 1996). Combined with limited personal assistance in larger groups, as a result it is hard for students to cope and they frequently fail the class (Lahtinen, Ala-Mutka & Järvinen,

2005). This problem is further exacerbated in design education, where students are reluctant to accept that programming skills are necessary for their academic and professional careers.

There are many studies that attempted to investigate the reasons behind this and provide solutions to these issues. For example, Jenkins (Jenkins, 2001) argues that the traditional lecture-led method is the wrong environment setting for programming. Other studies (Krieckhaus & Eriksen, 1960) highlight that learners are bound to engage more and remember what they have learned, when they care about and understand the subject. Kukulska (Kukulska-Hulme & Shield, 2008) proposes that a technology-supported learning approach through mobile devices in the classroom can promote a more situated, contextualised and experiential way of learning. Evidently, sophisticated multi-touch mobile devices that work with intuitive gesture-based interactions can "garner a lot of excitement" (Johnson, Adams & Cummins, 2012); combined with a challenge-based approach, they provide the kind of genuine student interest and necessary mental involvement that educators have long strived for in programming modules. To date there have been a few studies that examine the use of mobile devices and particularly the iPad (Cavanaugh, Hargis, Munns & Kamali, 2013; Diemer et al., 2012; Kinash, Brand, Mathew & Kordyban, 2011a; Manuguerra & Petocz, 2011; Souleles et al., 2014) both horizontally and vertically in academia.

Universities, schools and even kindergartens are following iPad-related initiatives for a number of reasons, a few of which are portability, multi-modality, cost savings and sustainability (replacement of textbooks) (Diemer et al., 2012). Additionally, one of the major advantages of the iPad as an instructional tool may lie in the ability to promote collaboration (Parker, Bianchi & Cheah, 2008), which is known to promote active learning involvement (Diemer et al., 2012). Results from other studies, however, indicate that the device has little to do with the positive impact, if any, on the learning process; they argue that mobility does not necessarily "equate learning" (Kinash et al., 2011a). Additional evaluations attribute this to the fact that iPads are largely focused on media consumption rather than media creation and re-use (Norman, Nielsen & Group, 2010). However, there still is a noticeable shortage of research looking at the use of the iPad within the context of dedicated programmes in HE (Souleles et al., 2013), such as programming or web development.

This study hypothesises that introducing the iPad as a platform for active, challenge-based learning and student collaboration in a web development module can aid in better comprehension of code and therefore lead to a deeper learning outcomes. It aims to investigate the students' perceptions in using the tablet to "learn-by-doing" and it observes in-class behavioural phenomena deriving from the active collaborative learning approach.

3. Study Design

This section describes the design of a four-week-long study that incorporates the iPad in order to introduce an active collaborative learning approach in a web development course. Specifically, "Web design and development 2" is a 13-week, three-hour-long elective class and requires successful completion of "Web design and development 1". (For the purposes of this paper, these will be referred to as Web 1 and 2). Both courses' objectives mainly concentrate on the major components of front-end web technologies, such as HTML, XML, CSS and Javascript. Web 2 additionally introduces server-side technologies, such as PHP and MySQL. Although combining design, technical and user-centered knowledge is the primary evaluation criterion, Web 2 focuses more on code development. The course consists of three distinct units: a) Javascript and XML, b) PHP and MySQL, c) HTML5, CSS3 and content management systems (CMS).

The study spanned the first unit of the course. The participants of the study, ten fourth-year multimedia students, six females and four males, had also attended Web 1 in the previous semester. It is important to provide a brief insight into the teaching style used in Web 1 in order to understand the students' experience in this type of modules.

4. Web 1

Web 1 is also a 13-week, three-hour-long lesson divided into two sessions. a) Lecture presentation session that aims to introduce theory, concepts and coding structures as well as to provide application paradigms, and b) Lab-based practical session during which students have to complete practical exercises – with help from the tutor, if needed. This process often requires longer than the remaining lesson time. Students therefore have to finish their assignments at home, based on assistance from the lecture notes and other online resources.

5. Web 2

Web 2 follows a student-centred learning approach, in that the lecture is clustered into several theoretical units coupled with problem-solving exercises. In contrast to Web 1, coding applications are to be gradually constructed by students, as opposed to readily appearing on the whiteboard. These applications also require additional information that can either be retrieved by collective group suggestions or from online documentation resources. In this study, the lesson plan in Web 2 was as follows:

a) First, an informal communication setting was encouraged and students were assured that their performance on the iPads would not affect their marks.
b) The instructor ensured that both the problem and required solution were fully understood by the students.
c) Through constructive dialogue students identified the steps needed and how these were translated from natural to programming lingo.
d) Students performed the steps.

As explained in previous sections (see "Introduction"), this model was based on both single and team exercises, described below.

6. Single-Input Exercises

The single-input exercises were carried out by a volunteer, who was handed the iPad that had the exercise (in set-up mode) already loaded. This bypassed logistics such as the creation of a new file, initialisation and storage, and focused on the important tasks at hand. The user's input was projected on the whiteboard in real time by means of a remote desktop protocol (RDP)[4] client, Doceri™, which was connected to the instructor's workstation. The rest of the group was encouraged to provide verbal assistance in order to help their fellow student solve the coding exercise. If the student was unable to continue or wished to stop, the iPad was passed onto the next volunteer.

7. Groups-of-Two Exercises

Unlike the single-input, team exercises were compulsory for students in the class, who were asked to form teams of two and were given an iPad per team to complete an exercise. These were also pre-loaded on the iPads,

---

[4] Remote Desktop Protocol (RDP) is a proprietary protocol developed by Microsoft, which provides a user with a graphical interface to connect to another computer over a network connection.

but this time in separate web-based IDE[5] accounts (per team); the teams worked independently from one another, and there was no real time projection. There was also a time constraint, after which the solution of the first team to finish was displayed on the whiteboard through the instructor's computer. Since the instructor was the administrator of the accounts, there was fast access to the coding documents.

8. Technical Details

8.1 Doceri™

In the single-input exercises, the coding process was projected on the board in real time through RDP to the instructor's personal computer. Doceri™, an interactive whiteboard, screencast recorder and RDP tool was used for this. This step-by-step simulation (similar to Google Documents) to the level of basic input activity such as "select", "copy/paste", "delete" and cursor insertion point was important in that it illustrated precisely the cognitive processes that took place at the time. That was also the reason why an RDP client rather than an IDE was used. An IDE would undoubtedly provide a faster and better interface solution minus the poor visual screen reproduction. However, at the time of the study there were no adequate IDE tools on the iPad that facilitated the anticipated level of real-time projection needed. Installation of the Doceri™ application on both the instructor's computer and the iPad was required - the Doceri™ desktop and the Doceri™ app respectively.

Doceri™ has a built-in interface keyboard that enables users, who are remotely logged in to a desktop computer, to type as if they were actually working on the actual computer. Additionally the screen area could be moved up-down and left-right by using two fingers to pan, and scaled by pinching and spreading two fingers again.

8.2 JS Bin

While there are a number of IDEs that support Javascript, HTML and CSS (i.e. Stypi, Floobits, Cloud9) most of these failed to fulfil the requirements of this study; these were a WIDE (web integrated development environment) tool providing concurrent views of code and

[5] An integrated development environment (IDE) or interactive development environment is a software application that provides comprehensive facilities to computer programmers for software development.

output windows and supporting JavaScript, HTML and CSS development. It needed to also provide "Save" and version control features. For this reason, JS bin was used in this study.

9. Post-Study Analysis

Individual information and participant bias prior, as well as empirical evidence following the study, was collected from students, who participated both as users and viewers. The information was elicited through two surveys (pre and post-study) and two focus groups (first and last class), and the resulting data was analysed using a mixed methods approach:

a. Quantitative analysis and reporting on the close-ended questions:
   All close-ended answers were imported through Excel sheets as separate datasets into nVivo 10 (qualitative data analysis software), and were ordered as "classification nodes". As a result all pre-defined options were automatically classified as "attributes" and the individual answers (choices) as respective "values".
b. Qualitative analysis:
   Results from open-ended questions in surveys as well as focus group transcriptions were imported in nVivo and clustered into codes by means of thematic coding. Following an iterative coding approach and the resulting code saturation, a total of 46 thematic codes were identified. These were also classified by attitude type as "positive", "negative" and "neutral" in order to examine generic trends. Following coding iterations, a fourth attribute was identified and added later on: "prerequisite" since participants had made a lot of conditional expressions such as "if the iPad had this…" or "if that was like this…" and so on. Aside from survey and focus group data, observational information from the four-week classes was recorded and analysed by the researchers.

10. Results and Discussion

10.1 Quantitative Results (Close-Ended Questions), Pre-Study

Question	Totally disagree	Disagree	Undecided	Agree	Totally agree
I believe that I can learn quickly how to use the iPad	-	-	10%	60%	30%
I believe that is easy and pleasant to use the iPad	-	-	20%	50%	30%
I believe that the use of iPads during the teaching part of a class can enhance the learning process	-	-	60%	40%	-
I believe that the use of iPads during the teaching part of a coding/ programming class can enhance the learning process		10%	50%	30%	10%
Question	female	male			
Gender	60%	40%			
Question	none	minimal	average	above average	excellent
Previous iPad experience	-	10%	30%	30%	30%

Table 1. Pre-study survey close-ended questions

10.2 Post-Study

Question	Totally disagree	Disagree	Undecided	Agree	Totally agree
The area and size of the iPad screen was sufficient for writing, editing and displaying the code.	8%	38%	31%	23%	-
It was easy to write code using a touchscreen device	-	46%	46%	8%	-
It was easy to write code using the iPad's native keyboard	15%	39%	15%	23%	8%
The iPad was easy to use in terms of shape and weight	-	8%	-	54%	38%
I was able to understand and solve a coding exercise through the single projected approach, with possible help from others in class, better than solving it on my own	8%	15%	-	54%	23%
I prefer the active learning approach through the use of the iPad, than the traditional method used before in this type of lesson	-	8%	-	54%	38%
I prefer the single-projected exercise (with active contribution from the rest of the class) compared to the exercise in groups of two people	8%	8%	53%	23%	8%

The active learning approach could work equally well through the use of any other device	-	-	46%	23%	31%
Question	horizontal	vertical			
I used the iPad in the following orientation:	100%	-			
Question	very long	long	moderate	brief	very brief
The period of time required for learning to use the iPad interface for writing and editing code was:	15%	8%	31%	38%	8%

Table 2. Post-study survey close-ended questions

10.3 Qualitative Results

The following sections focus on the overall user experience and perceived learning outcomes elicited from the participants in the study. We report on the themes that have surfaced from the results of the follow-up surveys and focus groups analysis next.

10.4 Active Learning

The quantitative and qualitative results indicate a strong consensus towards a "learning by doing" method. Students have based this on the fact that they were enrolled in a "practice-based" course, and have so far become accustomed to "digesting" knowledge better through application. More specifically, they explained that while coding statements appeared simple and comprehensible in traditional lectures, it was hard for them to reflect on the tutor's instructions and "how-tos" when working on assignments from home later on. Additionally, it is worth noting that there usually are multiple concepts (e.g. variables, arrays and loops) included in a single lecture. Students commented that previously, while each unit "made sense on its own", it was more difficult to put it into practice later on, after learning about the rest of the units. In agreement with Winslow (1996), they were also at a loss when combining these units to create more compound coding structures.

In order to address these issues each iPad exercise required students to use knowledge from previous exercises as well as performing additional research on the topic (Lim, 1998) to find a solution. This provided the kind of specific focus needed as well as an incremental knowledge build-up (scaffolding). The benefits from simultaneously "applying-while learning" were evident in remarks such as "we were better learning through practising with the code at the same time…", "it helped more with understanding…while practising at the time of teaching and also making mistakes".

Regardless of the obvious advantages of the active learning approach, students confirmed that some degree of initial instruction was needed prior to the application stage: "it will be impossible to start solving an exercise from scratch without being taught about it first or… how it must be syntaxed", " …we need a little theory and a lot of practice", "we just need the basic important things like functions and what each one does before we proceed…". Existing literature also agrees that proper "programming ability must rest" amongst others on ideally "theory and formal methods" (Robins, Rountree & Rountree, 2003).

10.5 Problem-Solving and Collaboration

Students deemed mistakes as important for their coding performance. Without exception, all responses with a "positive attitude" attribute, classified under the "active learning" and "collaboration" thematic categories, pointed to the trial-and-error process.

In particular, students reported that during the projected method, observation of mistakes and attempts to solve a coding problem helped both participant and viewers arrive at a more "effective understanding of programming methods" than by "being served with the solution right away". Research also denotes that "people progress to the next level by solving problems" (Winslow, 1996). Perkins, Hancock, Hobbs, Martin, and Simmons (1986) highlight that the students' attitude to problems is essential when it comes to programming, and proceed to classify novice learners into "stoppers" and "movers". As the words indicate, "stoppers" are those who are bound to give up easily when they face a problem they cannot solve, and "movers" are those who keep "modifying their code" until they reach a solution.

As expected, the Web 2 group, like any other class, consists of both types. However, the instructor observed persistent successive verbal contributions from the entire group towards resolving a task during the single-input exercises. Similar to previous work (Ioannou & Artino Jr, 2010), this study also shows that students were better able to understand through the group discussions on problem-solving. As a result, the vast majority was eager to have this method incorporated into the module, with or without the use of iPads, either in an open setting or in smaller groups. They commented that it was extremely helpful to "solve the exercises collectively" and that "the process helped them answer their own questions by actively participating in the resolution process".

Undoubtedly this collective approach may have thrown in a safety net for "stoppers", but all the same - based on the outcome - it is possible that the "crowd" method has exposed that arriving to a solution through iterations between "wrong and right" is the correct way to address a programming problem; it also illustrated that such tasks require patience, persistence and repetition. Schön (1987) focuses on the advantages of this method, and states that only in this way can programming novices become "reflective practitioners basing learning on reflection of experience". Likewise, students mentioned that they found it easier to remember the knowledge acquired from the lesson afterwards: "it helps more in comprehension. Instead of seeing only theory during the class and being a "zombie" during class… and then go home and remember nothing".

A student has emphasised that active learning, especially through the projected method, provided a degree of "equal comprehension amongst everyone". Although the terms "equality", "similarity" and even "unity" were not explicitly phrased by others, there was significant feedback in regards to "setting off from common grounds of knowledge" or "seeing what I had in mind, others did too as it appeared on the projector" and "it was nice for all of us to be on the same level".

10.6 Single-Input Projected Exercises

One of the major problems instructors face is students' "unwillingness to expose their own ignorance" (Jenkins, 2001) in front of their peers or tutor. This can have a considerable effect in the active learning progress, especially when this requires student involvement in an open setting. Likewise, although participants in the study favoured the "projected" approach, very few of them volunteered to work with the iPad themselves.

Although results from the close-ended questions place the "projected" approach higher than the "groups-of-twos", the disadvantages of this approach surfaced during the focus groups. Issues drew upon uncovering personal limitations such as learning disabilities i.e. dyslexia, the use of English as not the first language, gaps in knowledge or delays during public task-solving. Surprisingly, such attitudes are to be expected in larger groups where students are reportedly "feeling rather lonely" (Race, 2001), and are unwilling to partake in the learning process. One would assume that this would not apply to smaller, more familiar groups;

students in Web 2 are going through the fourth year together; they are well acquainted and also participate in common social activities. This was also the second consecutive module taught by the same tutor; thus a good relationship had already been established between the two parties, whereby students were referred to on a first-name basis.

Observation showed that while viewers would enthusiastically step in and help the "operator" during a task, they were unwilling to take the part themselves. A student commented, "it is as awkward for the person with the iPad as it is for a student watching a fellow student struggling to cope…" Additionally he argued, "help is good and will help solve the exercise in the end, but the person who's handling the iPad might feel useless in the meantime". Likewise, other students added that although they might know how to go about solving an exercise, they "can get confused and fail" by being aware of the "public or time pressure". The possible reward of publically accomplishing a task successfully was under-rated by students, compared with being "criticised" by their peers. Gibbs (1992) suggest that the reasons for this are based on fear of being considered "stupid, attention seekers or creeps". Results of the study prove that this fear is dominant, in that it transcends the feelings of familiarity and intimacy and finds its way even in smaller, friendlier groups.

10.7 Groups of Two

As explained this method followed a different approach; there was a time constraint, by which the solution of the first team to finish was displayed on the whiteboard through the instructor's computer. The rest of the groups would then have to stop working and the class proceeded to the next unit. The downside to this was that the remaining groups were readily offered the completed exercise.

Conversely, one can argue that this may pose an incentive for groups to focus on the instructions in order to complete the tasks faster. Previous work with computer science students supports this by stating that a friendly competitive programming method was found to "increase student motivation" (Lawrence, 2004). By comparing code against that of their peers, students were encouraged to put "more effort in its development". Competition is known to promote interaction and involve students with different learning styles (Felder et al., 2000). However, female students repeatedly stressed that collaboration was crucial for their understanding of programming. "Peer-tutoring" (Topping, 1996) was also found to be "rewarding", as female students were keen to "fill in the gaps" about something that they themselves felt confident about. This result came as no surprise since women are known to value teamwork over competition (Lawrence, 2004). On the contrary, many of the male students felt that heterogeneity in personal coding styles can be an obstacle in teamwork.

10.8 Virtual Keyboard

The perceptual outcome of the collaborative active learning method was compromised, based on the users' experience with the iPad keyboard. Previous studies concerned with usability in both education and industry domains indicate that users dislike typing on touch devices; they find it "uncomfortable and error-prone" (Kinash, Brand, Mathew & Kordyban, 2011b; Norman et al., 2010). This study offers similar evidence. Two of the major issues recorded were a) the inability of the keyboard to cater for specific coding needs and b) the obscured screen view issue after keyboard activation; the native keyboard spans the entirety of the screen width and a good deal of the screen height. The same occurs in the Doceri™ interface. The keyboard-screen asymmetry - adopted from Nielsen's (Budiu & Nielsen, 2011) read-tap asymmetry - seemed to frustrate the students while trying to type code: "basically the biggest problem is the keyboard because it covers up half of the screen and we cannot see or do anything with the code…". Programmers typically need to have simultaneous overview of the entire code as well as large-enough font sizes to work with specific code chunks. A clear view is of utmost importance when something as trivial as an extra dot or a comma may cause havoc in the output window. On the iPad, magnification offers detail at the expense of overview. Subsequently, one finds oneself constantly "pinching and spreading" (zooming in and out), swiping fingers left and right (panning) and expanding - collapsing the virtual keyboard.

Likewise, students found that they had to go through "too many movements" in order to achieve something that was literally effortless on a device with a "tangible" keyboard; the problematic keyboard situation was, in fact, detrimental to students' overall perception of coding with the iPad. The instructor offered to lend the iPads out to students for practising their code exercises at home, in order to get used to them. The offer was immediately rejected by the claim that "there was no time to waste". Some students suggested that pairing the iPads with a wireless keyboard might solve the issue, an idea that generated reactions: that would defeat the point of using a tablet after all.

An additional context-specific issue was the absence of certain characters and symbols required from the keyboard. The native keyboard does not accept a customised selection of characters. At the time of the experiment, the only keyboard apps (such as a five-row keyboard tool) that allowed this required jailbreaking[6] the device; this was not an option. In order to access symbols such as < > {} = + ( ) " for javascript, students needed to tap once on the "numbers" key to access a few, then once again on the "symbols" key to display the rest. Unarguably, remembering when and how many times to tap combined with the complex mechanisms of reflecting the code syntax can significantly increase mental overhead, something that novice programming learners are better off without. Other problems reported, especially by male participants, were the small size of keys compared to fingertip size (read-to-tap asymmetry) (Budiu & Nielsen, 2011), which resulted in repeated mistakes and caused considerable time delays.

10.9 Point to (Click)

A much needed and second-most criticised feature was the "point-to-click" functionality. This is equivalent to a mouse click on a normal computer; on a touch device it is subject to the fingertip diameter. As mentioned, programmers can spend hours on debugging, only to find that the error was a capital-cased character, a zero instead of an o, or even an extra space. Copy-paste is also an important function when programming because it guarantees exactness and re-usability; that is, the correct match of multiple instances of elements (such as functions, variables and objects) throughout the code. Selecting is an integral part of the copy/paste action. Smooth mobility and pointing precision are therefore vital. One of the biggest drawbacks experienced while using the iPad to code was pointing to a specific location in text so as to make such selects and edits. Students complained repeatedly and mentioned that they resorted to deleting and re-writing the whole line instead as it was "easier to control and less time-consuming" than editing existing code; it was "too hard to point to the exact spot", "what was infuriating was that I wanted to take my mouse to a specific letter of a word but couldn't!"

Evidently, students were aware of the built-in lens feature, from their previous experience with the iPad. Using it within this context though helped them to quickly reach a common verdict: "confusing and misleading" in that it appeared above the actual position of the finger, as if corresponding to "some other indivisible pointing device". The ambiguity

---

[6] iOS jailbreaking is the process of removing the limitations on Apple Inc. devices running the iOS operating system through the use of software and hardware exploits.

in actual versus virtual position is intensified in light of two important context-specific factors:

a. In text-heavy environments such as programming documents, where the default line-height is quite dense, this can trick users into thinking they are editing the line above: "The touch or gesture is a little bit off". Users intend to touch somewhere but end up touching something else instead since proximity is so dense between items due to the small screen size.
b. When experienced by expert users in graphic/animation/image editing software; combined with a mouse, these offer extremely high precision levels. Hence, the distinction between the two (touchscreen and mouse) is intensified in this case.

10.10 Code Editing Interface

Modern development editors and IDE interfaces allow for side-by-side coding and preview windows. These behave like two separate entities in that the preview pane is unaffected from changes that occur in the source code pane such as select, scrolling and sometimes magnification. Through the use of Doceri™, students could view both panes in the software; however, this feature was compromised, primarily during magnification, which affected the whole interface rather than just the coding panel.

On another note, scrollbars were too small and thin to handle, unless the screen was magnified, in which case the "edges" of the code lines were cut off from the screen while the outline view was lost in the meantime. Students who were used to this standard functionality found it hard to code through Doceri™, whereas they commented that the IDE environment "was slightly better": it offered isolated manipulation of the code on the left and the results in a stable pane on the right.

It nevertheless lacked two important features: code hinting and auto-completion; these are important for programmers; they can increase productivity by decreasing development time in avoiding common "spelling and logic errors", eliminating unnecessary keystrokes and averting from browsing in documentation sources for code syntax (Omar, Yoon, LaToza & Myers, 2012). A few students enquired whether Adobe Dreamweaver could be installed on the iPads to facilitate a familiar, code-oriented environment. Even if there were an iOS-compatible app for Adobe Dreamweaver, this would not match the criterion of real-time edit simulation required for the purposes of this experiment.

11. Discussion

Evidence from this study agrees with the key concept in that "all genuine education comes about through experience" (Dewey, 2007). In the case of practice-based courses such as programming or web/code development, it is necessary for educators to comply with the nature of the course and substitute ineffective one-way lecturing with interactive student-oriented self-derived learning through active participation and collaboration. However, one outcome is explicit: theory should not be entirely precluded in favour of practice; both are essential. Teachers and learners need iterative interaction on both levels (Laurillard, 2009). The responsibility lies with instructors; they need to carefully make the right decisions about what and how much content goes where as well as the order and treatment of that content in relation to its practical counterpart.

Similarly, this study finds that the participants' requirements on this level were clear: a better refined delivery of basic concepts and ideas: "we just need the basics like functions and syntax in order to continue on our own". Jenkins (2001) contrasts this to the common obsession of faculties to push as much content as possible into a single session, and states that this is nothing short of "tyrannical". The emphasis should be shifted instead towards encouraging deep learning and reflection (Robins et al., 2003), through shorter and more interesting theory-and-practice sessions. In doing so educators need to overcome the instilled tendency for controlled and organised lecture-led approaches that possibly derive from their own HE educational backgrounds (Jenkins, 2001). On a more practical level, this study also shows that the iterative "theory-then-practice" approach can sometimes promote a form of disorder, generated by individual technical issues, large number of questions, delays and chatting; essentially, a state where learner attention and focus diminishes rapidly. This usually requires resources beyond a single instructor to help provide support and ensure that the lesson maintains a controlled rhythm and flow.

In this study the active learning process induced collaboration and through collaboration, especially in problem-solving, students admitted to better comprehension of coding problems and related theory, as opposed to performing exercises on their own. Interestingly, the help and support between students during exercises promoted an overall heightened sense of "equality" that favoured sharing a "synchronised" level of assimilated knowledge with peers. Prince (2004) states that such evidence may challenge the traditional assumptions that individual work and competition best promote achievement. Based on current results, we find that it is beneficial to maintain a balance; we quote Prince again, in that "the entire course need not be team-based… nor must individual responsibility be absent".

This study suggests that a total lack of individual responsibility is not likely to occur in such settings; being a small group, students felt accountable towards their teams, the class and themselves. Receiving help and support to successfully complete a task in front of the entire group led to the realisation that this was not a personal achievement; this had both positive (i.e. effort for further improvement) and negative effects (i.e. embarrassment, low self-esteem). However, a comparison between the outcomes of collaborative learning against competitive or individualistic effort is quite ambitious and not the focus of this paper.

This work denotes that through active, real-time collective "problem-solving" students perceived to have accomplished a higher level of comprehension and recall of coding concepts and structures. However, there is no evidence indicating that the use of the iPad was central in this process. Similar to other work, positive outcomes evidently are based upon two key factors: technology-supported student learning and the educational decisions made by the instructor (Kinash et al., 2011). The author states that "…the authentic independent variable is the collection of pedagogical decisions that the educator puts into play".

Technology can indisputably facilitate a constructive learning-by-doing framework, something received with interest and keenness in this study; in fact, learners were so keen that they went the extra mile to contribute suggestions to ensure that the method would be effectively adopted into the lesson; none of these included the use of iPads; in reality, they all excluded the device in exchange for normal laptops or any other "equipment" that offered a "keyboard and a mouse". The requirements were clear; they were rooted in a series of usability issues encountered in attempting to produce code on the device: lack of control and feedback in the gestural interface, accidental error-prone activation, keyboard-to-screen and read-to-tap asymmetry (Budiu & Nielsen, 2011), problematic typing on the touchscreen and inability to point and select with precision. In some cases these were not perceived as irrecoverable; the response was "forgiving"; a number of students felt that these problems might have occurred due to lack of experience with the device. Regardless of the perceived causes, results show that the potential of the technology in learning code development is hindered by, unsurprisingly, bad usability. Evidence from this study agrees with Traxler's (2005) outcomes, that although the ability to "synthesise data in real-time" is exciting since it restructures the learning dynamic, yet in most cases equipment problems "constrain the use of mobile technology in education".

12. Conclusion

Similarly to Kinash's (2011) work, this study shows that the device had little to do with the positive attitude towards the active-mobile-learning approach. Unarguably, the iPad was favoured in that it was small, lightweight and portable and could conveniently rotate amongst the group of students. The process was found to be pleasant and entertaining, partially based on the iPad's intuitive and "cool" interface, the gestures employed, and partially due to the "inexperienced" manner in which participants strived to complete coding tasks in front of an audience. Students were keen on using the iPads, but only as a means to diverge from a traditionally-led lecture-based class. Projection of the simulated coding activity on the board was favoured. However there was an explicit preference to do so through a different device, one that offered a normal keyboard and a mouse instead, i.e. a laptop. Collaboration between peers and equal levels of knowledge amongst the entire group were highly valued; the latter was preferred rather than smaller group exercises.

The disadvantages of the projected approach draw upon considerations in exposing weaknesses and gaps in knowledge, failure to complete a task, embarrassment, pressure of time and stress even in small and friendly teams. Although the mobile-active-learning method was perceived to increase knowledge assimilation and memorability through a collective problem-solving practice, there is no strong evidence that there was a significant positive learning impact relating to the use of iPads.

Acknowledgments

Special thanks to Zacharias Mavris, Antigoni Parmaxi, Dr Andri Ioannou, Web Design and Development 2 class 2013.

References

Bonwell, C. C., & Eison, J. A. (1991). *Active Learning: Creating Excitement in the Classroom. 1991 ASHE-ERIC Higher Education Reports*. ERIC Clearinghouse on Higher Education, The George Washington University, One Dupont Circle, Suite 630, Washington, DC 20036-1183.

Bruner, J. S. (1966). *Towards a theory of instruction*. Cambridge, MA: Harvard University Press.

Budiu, R., & Nielsen, J. (2011). *Usability of iPad apps and websites*. Nielsen Norman Group, 2nd edition.

Cavanaugh, C., Hargis, J., Munns, S., & Kamali, T. (2013). iCelebrate teaching and learning: Sharing the iPad experience. *Journal of Teaching and Learning with Technology, 1*(2), 1–12.

Dewey, J. (2007). *Experience and education*. New York: Simon and Schuster.

Diemer, T. T., Fernandez, E., & Streepey, J. W. (2012). Student perceptions of classroom engagement and learning using iPads. *Journal of Teaching and Learning with Technology, 1*(2), 13-25.

Felder, R. M., Stice, J. E., & Rugarcia, A. (2000). The future of engineering education II. Teaching methods that work. *Chem. Engr. Education, 34*(1), 26–39.

Gibbs, G. (1995). *Improving the quality of student learning*. Bristol, UK: Technical & Educational Services Ltd.

Ioannou, A., & Artino Jr, A. R. (2010). Learn more, stress less: Exploring the benefits of collaborative assessment. *College Student Journal, 44*(1), 189–199.

Jenkins, T. (2001). Teaching programming - A journey from teacher to motivator. In *Proceedings of the 2nd Annual Conference of the LSTN Center for Information and Computer Science*. University of North London.

Johnson, L., Adams, S., & Cummins, M. (2012). *NMC horizon report: 2012 Higher Education edition*. Retrieved December 30, 2013 from http://www.editlib.org/p/48964/

Kinash, S., Brand, J., Mathew, T., & Kordyban, R. (2011). Uncoupling mobility and learning: When one does not guarantee the other. In R. Kwan (Ed.), *Enhancing Learning Through Technology*. Education Unplugged: Mobile Technologies and Web 2.0. Communications in Computer and Information Science, (pp. 342-350). Berlin: Springer.

Krieckhaus, E. E., & Eriksen, C. W. (1960). A study of awareness and its effects on learning and generalization. *Journal of Personality, 28*(4), 503–517.

Kuh, G. D., Cruce, T. M., Kinzie, J., & Gonyea, R. M. (2008). Unmasking the effects of student engagement on first-year college grades and persistence. *The Journal of Higher Education, 79*(5), 540–563.

Kukulska-Hulme, A., & Shield, L. (2008). An overview of mobile assisted language learning: From content delivery to supported collaboration and interaction. *ReCALL, 20*(3), 271-289.

Lahtinen, E., Ala-Mutka, K., & Järvinen, H. M. (2005). A study of the difficulties of novice programmers. In *Proceedings of the 10th annual SIGCSE conference on Innovation and technology in computer science education - ITiCSE '05*.

Laurillard, D. (2009). The pedagogical challenges to collaborative technologies. *International Journal of Computer-Supported Collaborative Learning, 4*(1), 5–20.

Lawrence, R. (2004). Teaching data structures using competitive games. *Education, IEEE Transactions, 47*(4), 459–466.

Lim, B. B. L. (1998). Teaching web deyelopment technologies in CS / IS curricula. *ACM SIGCSE Bulletin, 30*(1), 107-111.

Manuguerra, M., & Petocz, P. (2011). Promoting student engagement by integrating new technology into tertiary education: The role of the iPad. *Asian Social Science, 7*(11), 61–65.

Norman, D. A., Nielsen, J., & Group, N.N. (2010). Gestural interfaces: A step backward In usability. Retrieved December 30, 2014 from http://goo.gl/ffSRd

Omar, C., Yoon, Y., LaToza, T., & Myers, B. (2012). Active code completion. In *Proceedings of ICSE '12*. IEEE Press, Piscataway, NJ, USA, 859-869.

Parker, R., Bianchi, A., & Cheah, T. (2008). Perceptions of instructional technology: Factors of influence and anticipated consequences. *Educational Technology & Society, 11*, 274–293.

Perkins, D. N., Hancock, C., Hobbs, R., Martin, F., & Simmons, R. (1986). Conditions of learning in novice programmers. *Journal of Educational Computing Research, 2*(1), 37–55.

Prince, M. (2004). Does active learning work? A review of the research. *Journal of engineering education, 93*(3), 223–231.

Race, P. (2001). *Using feedback to help students learn*. Higher Education Academy: York, UK.

Robins, A., Rountree, J., & Rountree, N. (2003). Learning and teaching programming: A review and discussion. *Computer Science Education, 13*(2), 137–172.

Schön, D. A. (1987). *Educating the reflective practitioner*. Jossey-Bass: San Francisco.

Souleles, N., Savva, S., Watters, H., Bull, B., & Annesley, A. (2014). A phenomenographic investigation on the use of iPads among undergraduate art and design students. *British Journal of Educational Technology*. Retrieved December 30, 2014 from: http://goo.gl/A6E5Ya

Swan, K., van 't Hooft, M., Kratcoski, A., & Unger, D. (2005). Uses and effects of mobile computing devices in K-8 classrooms: a preliminary study. *Journal of Research on Technology and Education, 38*(1), 99-112.

Topping, K. (1996). The effectiveness of peer tutoring in further and higher education: A typology and review of the literature. *Higher Education, 32*(3), 321–345.

Traxler, J. (2005). Defining mobile learning. In *Proceedings of the IADIS International Conference Mobile Learning 2015*, 261–266.

Wiedenbeck, S., & Ramalingam, V. (1999). Novice comprehension of small programs written in the procedural and object-oriented styles. *International Journal of Human-Computer Studies, 51*(1), 71–87.

Winslow, L. E. (1996). Programming pedagogy - a psychological overview. *ACM SIGCSE Bulletin, 28*(3), 17–22.

THE USABILITY, FUNCTIONALITY AND ACCEPTANCE OF IPADS IN HEALTHCARE PRACTICE: A STUDY OF PHYSIOTHERAPY AND OCCUPATIONAL THERAPY STUDENTS ON PLACEMENTS

ADEFILA ARINOLA[1] AND LYNN CLOUDER[2]

Abstract

As mobile devices become ubiquitous, healthcare practitioners are exploring how using technological support in the workplace could advance their practice, communication and learning. This paper discusses findings from a research study funded by the Higher Education Academy (HEA) in the UK which investigated how using iPads impacted on physiotherapy and occupational therapy students' learning, reflective practice and communication with peers and tutors during placement cycles. Similar to research carried out amongst physicians in 2009, the students found that the devices collapse 'time and space', because they permit users to access data and resources when moving between patients, wards and clinics (Prgoment, Georgious, & Westbrook, 2009). The paper also discusses how students used the iPads to interact with other professionals and patients while in hospital and community settings; as well as, the usability of the devices and associated apps for improving their learning (Clay, 2010). Apps were found to be good tools for documenting individual learning histories, engaging with learning objects and developing personalised structured education (Ifenthaler & Schweinbenz, 2013). The project adopted a participatory action research approach. Eighteen student participants used iPads during their placements in a variety of settings for a period of 5 – 10 weeks. The students were supported by visiting tutors and practice educators over an eight-month period. Interviews and focus

[1] Coventry University, United Kingdom. Email: ab0191@coventry.ac.uk
[2] Coventry University, United Kingdom. Email: d.l.clouder@coventry.ac.uk

groups were conducted with students, visiting tutors and practice educators to ascertain the utility and acceptance of the devices in practice settings. The Unified Theory of Acceptance and Use of Technology (UTAUT) model developed by Venkatesh et al. (2003) is used to analyse the acceptability of the devices in clinical settings. In particular, the research focuses on why user acceptance is challenged by established practitioners and why healthcare settings have not adapted their environs and infrastructure so mobile devices can be used more readily by practitioners.

1. Introduction

This paper explores the affordances and limitations of using an iPad as a learning and service delivery tool in clinical practice settings. The first section introduces the research in the context of affordable and accessible technology and their place if any in clinical teaching environments. The following sections outline the methodology and research sampling. The rest of the paper presents the findings and discussion.

Mobile devices are ubiquitous and multifunctional and their use in clinical settings is gradually increasing. Physicians who use mobile technology find that by collapsing 'time and space', access to data and resources when moving between patients, wards and clinics is easier than using computers or paper (Prgoment et al., 2009). Various studies show how physicians have embraced the technology in medical practice and education (Marceglia, Bonacina, Zaccaria, Pagliari & Pinciroli, 2012).

An Australian study recently reported that using it to check information just prior to seeing a patient supported clinical reasoning and decision-making (Luanrattana, Than Win, Fulcher & Iveson, 2012). Similarly, student midwives' benefited from increased confidence and immediate reassurance about their professional judgment through accessing video files on iPods (Clay, 2010). A Canadian study of nursing and medical students has highlighted the value of personal digital assistants in supporting clinical learning and preventing clinical isolation (Garnett & Jackson, 2006). Although these studies are in the minority, they suggest that supporting students on placement with mobile technology has tangible benefits for developing skills that will contribute to their employability.

The research was funded by the HEA with the aim of extending the scope of the use of mobile devices by promoting access to learning resources and interaction between users. It examines how these benefits could be extended to the development of clinical reasoning skills. In addition to bridging the gap between theory and practice and improving clinical decision-making, mobile devices offer an alternative source of information reducing reliance on busy clinical educators. The use of mobile devices as a mechanism to provide peer mentorship and support has the potential to reduce commonly experienced feelings of isolation, vulnerability and stress by opening channels of communication with university peers and academic tutors. Specialised delivery technologies such as WebApps have the advantage of not only supporting learning, but also offer an alternative means of contact and support.

There are concerns about the use of mobile technology in practice, particularly because they are synonymous with social interaction, not work or patient care. There is little evidence they make an impact on the development of students' clinical reasoning capabilities on placement, as such some view the devices with suspicion. There are also other challenges. Are there any benefits for clinical educators, visiting tutors and practice educators in relation supporting students on placement? A lot of time is devoted to supporting students on placement and much of this is travel time. Could tutors use the communication tools in mobile devices to engage with students and help them deal with the stress they experience in a timely manner? The objectives of the study were:

- to extend the evidence base on the impact of mobile learning on linking theory and practice, accessing timely knowledge and enhancing peer support to contribute to the development of students' employability through enhancing their clinical reasoning capabilities on placement;
- to identify the challenges to using mobile devices to promote learning on placement, including their acceptability with respect to professional/organisational culture;
- to identify whether students' use of mobile technology reduces reliance on clinical educators and academic tutors responsible for facilitating learning and supporting students on placement, in terms of time spent on basic teaching and pastoral support respectively; and
- to make recommendations for future health and social care professional education.

2. Literature Review

The challenges associated with the use of mobile technology in health and social care settings, such as its acceptability by clinicians, technical capability and security concerns are widely documented (Norman, 2011; Clay, 2010; Garnett & Jackson, 2006). However, mobile devices have become ubiquitous and multifunctional over the last decade; their use in clinical settings is gradually increasing. Physicians who use mobile technology find that by collapsing 'time and space' access to data and resources when moving between patients, wards and clinics is easier than using computers or paper (Prgoment et al., 2009). In medical education there are bold moves to incorporate mobile devices into the delivery of educational content, assessment and training of doctors. Researchers in Australia reported that using mobile technology to check information just prior to seeing a patient supported clinical reasoning and decision-making (Luanrattana et al., 2012). Similarly, student midwives' benefited from increased confidence and immediate reassurance about their professional judgment through accessing video files on iPods (Clay, 2010). A Canadian study of nursing and medical students has highlighted the value of personal digital assistants in supporting clinical learning and preventing clinical isolation (Garnett & Jackson, 2006). Although these studies are in the minority they suggest that supporting students on placement with mobile technology has tangible benefits for developing skills that will contribute to their employability.

3. Methodology

Physiotherapy students from one institution in the UK teamed up with Occupational Therapy students in another to investigate the use of iPads in practice settings. IPads were chosen because they provide a wide range of clinical-related resources in addition to communication and technical features. The two professions have different placement learning models and a variety of approaches to support students are adopted. Collaboration between the two HEIs means there is a broader range of practice settings for the iPads to be used as well.

The project adopted a participatory action research approach with the rationale that students will work as co-researchers throughout the phases. The mobile devices have been used by a total of 19 students. Four (4) physiotherapy students used them for a total of four months over three different placements. The second group of physiotherapy students consisted of five individuals. They also used them likewise in different practice settings. Three (3) sets of occupational therapy students used the iPads. The first group consisted of three (3) students, the second also had three (unfortunately one student withdrew) and the last group included four students. They passed the iPad to the next group after a 10-week placement in one practice setting. The placements took place throughout an academic year. In total, 14 National Health Service (NHS) trusts were involved. Each student had a practice educator on site and a visiting tutor based at the University. The visiting tutors visit their student at least once during the placement, and are responsible along with the practice educator for allocating marks for the placement. The physiotherapy students have to undertake a clinical reasoning assessment at the end of each of their five-week placements. An independent evaluator was responsible for overseeing the project.

4. Selection Criteria

Student participants and clinical educators were identified through the clinical education co-ordinator/ lead tutor. The lead tutors provided useful resources, particularly apps that were profession-specific for preloading onto the iPads.

Two physiotherapy students used their own iPads while participating in the study. Local approvals and information technology requirements were discussed with the placement educators and their Trusts. Two sites provided the students with Wi-Fi access, an additional two sites had Wi-Fi hotspots for use and the students had to rely on a free local mobile network services for access to the Internet.

The students had access to assessment forms, anatomy and physiology apps, videos of specific techniques etc. as identified mainly by physiotherapy lecturers and educators as well as the Learning Technologists. The students had independent training from the Learning Technologists and were provided with a list of guidelines for using the iPad. They were given free rein to use the devices as they chose. Discussion forums using computer-conferencing software (Skype and Facetime) were set up to enable interaction between students and their tutors/educators as well as their peers.

Students completed reflective logs and attended a focus group at the end of their placements to discuss the experiences they had while using the iPads. The logs depicted how and when the device was used, which resources were accessed and how they were used. The clinical educators log also showed how the devices were used and how they impacted on the students learning or progress. Both clinical educators and visiting tutors were interviewed at the end of each placement.

5. Findings

Students who struggled to use the iPad in clinical settings complained that they were too bulky, could not be secured, connect to the Internet or had poor battery life. Other students discussed the complexities of placements. However, the majority of student participants were keen to utilise the iPad and found that the device did indeed facilitate their placement learning. The portability of reference material, direct access to resources (especially those used by tutors in their classroom teaching and those relating to clinical guidelines and reference material), the ability to look up information on previously downloaded apps, and ease of note taking were considered very useful in the learning and practice environments.

Students reported using the iPads for a number of activities. These can be categorised into three based on interactions with the patient

1. Direct patient care, record-keeping and patient education:
 - Looking up information before attending to a patient with a condition
 - Finding information for a patient or signposting them to other agencies
 - Checking for accuracy in times of clinical uncertainty
 - Showing patient information
 - Supporting patients to manage their own health using personalised ehealth apps
 - Viewing patient tests, x-rays, etc.
 - Writing notes
 - Taking pictures of conditions, exercises, resources
2. Indirect patient care, collaboration, organising workload
 - Contacting other agencies/ colleagues
 - Storage cabinet – filing system with all their papers/books/ journal/resources in an orderly fashion
3. Learning/ improving reflective practice
 - Researching for exams/learning
 - Evidencing for exams or practice educator
 - Collaboration with peers or colleagues at work

Patient education: Participants reported that using the iPad with patients was very productive.

"I could show the students exercises and how they were doing. It is much better using the videos and pictures on the iPad than the clumsy aids in the hospital." (Physiotherapy student)

The students noted that because the iPad had a relatively large screen they could use it with patients more readily. Patients were happy to view their x-rays and other images as well as view resources, apps or information the students shared with them. In addition, the students also used the iPad to research conditions before their appointments with patients and to check "information" relating to the patient.

"The iPad is so quick and handy. I used it every time to research conditions. In the past I would have had to write things down and look it up later. But you can just do research right there. It was great, my educator and other staff also asked me to look up information." (Occupational Therapy student)

As computers were in short supply on hospital wards, the students found the iPads useful for writing notes. They did not have to wait for the computer to be free to do all the administrative work. Students also wondered if the iPad could be provided instead of PCs in the hospitals.

"The computers are so slow and outdated. They could provide trolleys with docks for the iPad so everyone could use it when and where they needed, instead of waiting for the computer to be free. It will save so much time." (Physiotherapy student)

Improving collaboration/ reflective practice: The iPads were used primarily for research, according to the feedback from the students. They used it to look for information on the Internet, refer to notes, books, journals and medical guidelines.

"I used it all the time. It was great to have it with you all the time, you could look up everything, even if you were not sure; it kind of gave you reassurance, didn't it?" (Physiotherapy student)

"I used it on the bus, at home, everywhere. You could just read anywhere you were and so useful for storing things and writing your notes and stuff". (Occupational Therapy student)

Students also suggested it was useful for showing their educators and tutors they had researched a topic and showed they were using evidence based practice.

"It is so much easier to show the educator why you are choosing the treatment option you are using and by showing the research you are also showing you are utilising evidence in your practice. I think this should influence my marks". (Physiotherapy student)

Students used the software the iPad affords for communicating with each other using social media, Skype and FaceTime (Voice over Internet protocol software). A few students used these tools to communicate with other professionals. The students also used the calendar features as well as organisation apps to manage their workload, schedules and appointments.

Learning: The iPad "redefined" the learning space for the students who participated in the research (Traxler, 2010). The students discuss using the iPad for learning *in situ* on the hospital ward, in patient homes, on the bus, while discussing conditions with their educators or with their peers using social media. The iPad did indeed for some students enable them to "do learning on the go". The affordances of mobility and portability made a real difference to the students. They were able to use these tools to facilitate their learning.

Conole at al. (2008) discuss the key functionality of technology in relation to shaping learning experiences, surmising that it can be used for information-seeking and handling (research and organisation), communication, assignment preparation and integrated learning. The findings show that the technology was indeed primarily used in the four ways mentioned. However, the students and lecturers involved in the study discuss other ways the devices could be used if the motivation and environment permitted.

1. Facilitating collaboration and communication
2. Enhance productivity
3. Capturing and integration of data
4. Promoting flexibility

Lecturers suggested iPads could enhance productivity, particularly if the students could use the device to directly communicate with their tutors. Students discuss using the devices to do more research and the flexibility to use with patients if they could ensure the protection of personal data and confidential material.

6. Challenges and Limitations

There were a number of challenges encountered by the students using the iPads. Educators seemed to have the most negative views about the use of iPads in clinical settings. Some of the challenges and limitations of using the iPads are listed below.

The students who found the device most beneficial were strong students who were able to use the device as a tool to organise their learning and develop ways to improve their practice. Such students did not rely on the preloaded apps made available for the study but downloaded the apps, software and tools they needed to aid their learning and skill acquisition. Kinash et al. (2011) argue that mobile devices do not "guarantee or preclude student learning" by themselves. The advantages of using an iPad have to be carefully channelled through a pedagogical link that could be initiated by the student or facilitated by a lecturer or educator.

Challenges encountered	Students views	Clinical educators views	Lecturers/visiting tutors views
Functionality	Inability to carry the "big" iPad around the ward and work at the same time	iPad could distract students from work. They need to attend to patients	Students not using the iPad to communicate with lecturers
Infrastructure/Environment	Limited or no connection to hospital Wi-Fi systems	Should not be carried around ward – not a tool of the trade	It may not be suitable in wards where you need to be "hands on".
Interface	Inability to integrate devices with hospital systems and records	Patients may think they are not working – using the device for social purposes	Mobility does not guarantee learning
Storage/Theft	Storage issues – cannot be used as a notebook because it could be stolen	We need to ensure it is kept safe	

Adaptability	I was not sure how to use it	There are no apps for Occupational Therapists to use in practice	iPad needs to be loaded with the relevant kind of material
Acceptance by clinicians	The qualified staff did not use it	It is not a tool of the trade	

Table 1. Challenges encountered

The students who were successfully able to deal with the challenges were encouraged and motivated by tutors who encouraged them to use the devices and supported and enabled them to use the apps or resources relevant to a particular task. Other students took the initiative to "try" resources that they used in other settings on the iPad.

"I downloaded an app that helps with revision using a Japanese resource. I had used it on a PC and was very pleased to find it available in the app store."

There were also structural, process and environmental challenges encountered by the students. The devices could not be synced with hospital systems due to restrictions. The National Health Service Hospitals/Services do not allow personal devices to link with Trust systems. The infrastructure is not designed to accommodate private devices and the students understood the management had a duty of care towards patients, protecting their personal and medical data. This challenge was discussed extensively and reported to some hospital management teams. Though some hospitals will allow the use of personal devices, there will need to be a major overhaul of the system to make it robust enough to protect the information stored on hospital systems and records.

Another challenge related to the design of the device. Participants complained it was too heavy and too big for professionals working on busy wards. The size may be ideal for viewing documents and medical records, in particular x-rays but it was not small enough to fit into a hospital tunic. In addition because it is a relatively expensive device, students worried it could be stolen if not attended to properly. In fact some students were so intimidated by the fear of theft; they stored it in cupboards and found they could not use it "on the go" as they planned, because they had to "walk to the staff room to get it every time they thought of something to use it for". This was in the end not practical.

A small number of educators were concerned that technology was disrupting their practice. They complained the iPad did not have a place on the wards because students could use more traditional tools for their learning and clinical practice. The majority of educators thought the device was timely and could improve practice; however, they did discuss appropriateness in relation to location and when engaging with patients.

"Some doctors already use the iPad on the wards and it feels like they hide behind the device, they do not communicate with the patients. We should not encourage students to use it in that way" (physiotherapy educator)

Educators in the community felt the device could be used innovatively in a variety of practice settings, especially in community medicine. Instead of carrying around many files, books and resources, the iPad is a much better device for recording, interacting with patients and communication. In hospitals the question of efficiency and hands-on care could be made but the iPad could simply replace notepads files.

The infrastructure for accessing the Internet in hospitals was found to be quite poor. The participants argued that for the device to be effective, Internet connectivity is vital.

7. Black Bag of New Tools for Clinicians

It was generally accepted that the iPad or mobile technology would become more common in Higher Education training for clinicians. Students could use the device as a learning tool more efficiently if resources were specifically designed for mobile learning. The availability of structured learning resources, which can be used on iPads or similar devices, will be advantageous to students who were not able to adapt the device for personalised learning independently. This is becoming more realistic with the increased use of various technological resources in the delivery of teaching. Interactive teaching aids are becoming a lot more ubiquitous and referencing and educational resources are being developed for sale in app stores across a range of devices. The core functionality of the device seems to be the ability to do instant research anywhere, share ideas with others and store information.

In the last twelve months the iPad and other tablets have improved their software and design to make some of the challenges listed earlier less of a concern. New models are faster, lighter and much more robust. Similarly, apps have been developed at an exponential rate since the advent of mobile technology. There are millions of educational apps and more and more are targeted at learning at HE level.

The students could creatively use the iPads in a variety of ways, in so much as the resource can be said to be a "black bag of new tools" (student). The device could become an organiser, a tool for reflection, an encyclopaedia, record keeping device, note taking pad, communication device for FaceTime, email or instant messaging, etc. All these functionalities can be used for improving student learning, their mastery of practice skills and competence as well as the confidence they develop to function as skilled practitioners. The most problematic barriers faced by the students with respect to using this device were infrastructural and acceptance of the device. The latter is an issue encountered in a number of professions.

8. Acceptance of the Devices

iPads are commonly used in business and commerce, but acceptance of the device by professionals can be tenuous. In clinical practice, doctors have embraced the devices more readily than other professions, though this is gradually changing. The first cohort of students found more resistance than the second and third. However, students still experienced a generational divide with younger practitioners more likely to embrace the devices than older, more experienced educators. Students also found acceptance was also dependent upon performance. As many acute units do not have sufficient computers, the iPads were the most efficient way of taking notes in some cases. They were particularly useful in community settings and outpatient settings where records needed to be accessed remotely and a lot of multidisciplinary working is necessary.

Using the technology acceptance model developed by Venkatesh et al. 2003, we were able to map a number of elements, which made the device acceptable. The most influential seemed to be infrastructure and ethos of the practice settings.

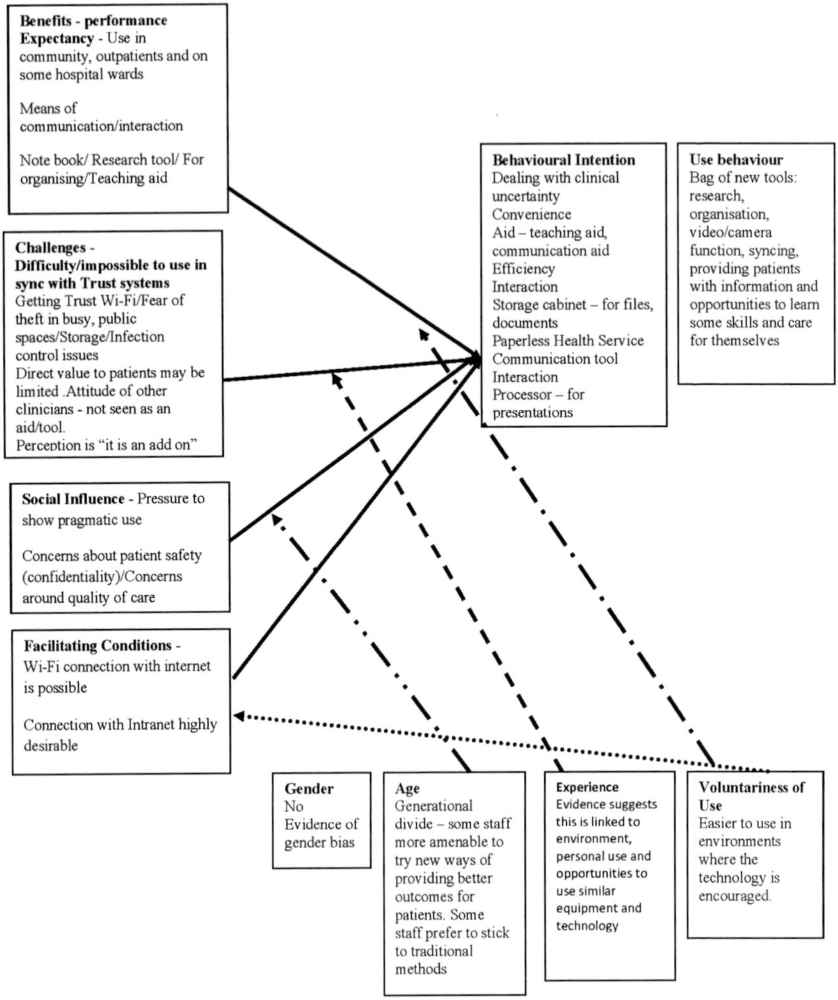

Table 2. Factors that influence user behaviour of in-clinical settings

By using the model, it is possible to outline the conditions under which the device is accepted during placement as a valuable learning tool. These are labelled in the model as Behavioural Intention and are a function of the benefits of using the device, methods used to overcome challenges, social influence from patients/policymakers and facilitators.

- Dealing with clinical uncertainty – using it for research and reflective practice
- Convenience – handy to use
- Aid – teaching aid, communication aid – resource
- Efficiency – saves time
- Interaction – tool for collaboration
- Storage cabinet – for files, documents - organiser
- Paperless NHS - when health systems no longer use paper for notes/patients (policy expected 2016)
- Communication tool
- Interaction
- Processor – for presentations

We found no gender bias during the study; instead the students and staff who were more amenable to the technology were those who were comfortable using it in other walks of life and happy to trial the device as a resources for learning.

9. Personalised Structured Education

The iPad saves students' time; they can learn a lot of information in a short time because they have access to a lot of resources. These iPad resources are usually interactive and include a variety of alternative methods of engagement (videos, games, quizzes, etc) which the students say supports their learning.

Students will benefit from apps developed to improve their learning rather than relying on mhealth applications which are often designed for practitioners or for patients who want to manage their own health. It is feasible that these kinds of educational apps will continue to evolve and be instrumental as the device becomes more ubiquitous. A lot of teaching and learning already takes place online. Many universities use Virtual Learning Environments and the concept of using tablet-friendly resources for teaching and learning is no longer farfetched.

10. Evaluation and Assessment of Application Features

Apps offer an intuitive interface between patients and clinicians (Marceglia et al. 2012). Students said the apps were very useful for interacting with patients. All the students downloaded extra apps a few paid for apps worth £2.99 - £15. The consensus among the students was they will pay equivalent of what they normally pay for a textbook to own an app.

The physiotherapy students used a lot of the apps on the device and were able to download more relevant apps. They have also been able to suggest a number of apps that will be relevant to their peers. The occupational therapists identified some apps that were had marginal relevancy to their work or education. For example while working in mental health settings they used and sought information from mental health related apps or resources. However they expressed disappointment because there were no profession-specific apps in their field of practice.

11. Conclusion

This study show that iPads can be used to support student' learning in clinical environments. The functionality of the iPad is such that it can be utilised for dual purposes. Chiefly, the iPad can be used to support students in much the same way it is used in the classroom to reinforce learning. Its portability enhances a capacity to store and retrieve a vast amount of learning resources and objects, providing a unique affordance for situated learning to take place. Students encounter a problem or a task and can access the knowledge, support or resources they need to think through the problem, discover new meaning or reinforce an idea and potentially solve the problem. Situated learning enables students to develop their own autonomous ways of learning and organising their knowledge. In effect it facilitates the development of constructivist practices (Melhuish & Falloon, 2010). The iPad also allows students to scaffold their learning, chiefly by using the organisational tools provided by the iPad as well as by using it for collaboration, connection and convergence. Secondly, the iIPad can be used as a tool for promoting patient care and service delivery.

The data focused on correlations relating to how the device improved student competence, confidence and clinical practice. Most clinical educators' felt the devices were very helpful for supporting learning. Clinicians also suggested that once hospitals and clinical settings updated their Wi-Fi infrastructure, iPads will definitely aid clinical work.

In essence the iPads enable students to retrieve relevant information seamlessly on demand, provide the capacity to organise and structure workflow more easily and dynamically, and can aid communication and collaboration between practitioner and service user. They also have the potential to support change in practice, personalised learning and drive innovation.

Though there was no obvious link to grades/marks during the placements, clinical educators and tutors acknowledged that the device could be used in a variety of ways to improve the learning experience for students during placements.

12. References

Black Book Rankings (2013, May 30). 'The Year of the big EHR switch' confirms physicians favor iPad and mobile applications. Accessed January 9, 2015 from: http://goo.gl/j3gyKR

Clay, C. (2010). Exploring the use of mobile technologies for the acquisition of clinical skills. *Nurse Education Today, 31*(6), 582-586.

Garrett, B. M., & Jackson, C. (2006). A mobile clinical e-portfolio for nursing and medical students, using wireless personal digital assistants (PDAs). *Nurse Education Today*, *26*(8), 647-654.

Ifenthaler, D., & Schweinbenz, V. (2013). The acceptance of tablet-PCs in classroom instruction: The teachers' perspectives. *Computers in Human Behavior, 29*(3), 525–534.

Kinash, S., Brand, J., Mathew, T., & Kordyban, R. (2011). Uncoupling mobility and learning: When one does not guarantee the other. In Kwan, R., McNaught, C., Tsang, P., Wang, F. L., & Li, K.C. (Eds.) *Enhancing learning through technology – education unplugged: Mobile technologies and Web 2. Communications in computer and information science* (pp. 342–350). Springer: Berlin.

Luanrattana, R., Than Win, K., Fulcher, J., & Iveson, D. (2012). Mobile technology use in medical education. *Journal of Medical Systems, 31*(1), 113-122.

Marceglia, S., Bonacina, S., Zaccaria, V., Pagliari, C., & Pinciroli, F. (2012). How might the iPad change healthcare? *Journal of the Royal Society of Medicine*, *105*(6), 233-241.

Murphy, G. D. (2011). Post-PC devices: A summary of early iPad technology adoption in tertiary environments. *E-Journal of Business Education & Scholarship of Teaching*, *5*(1), 18-32.

Norman, N. (2011). *Mobile Learning for the NHS: Research Report*. NHS South Central.

Park, Y. (2011). A pedagogical framework for mobile learning: Categorizing educational applications of mobile technologies into four types. *International Review of Research in Open and Distance Learning, 12*(2), 78-102.

Peng, H., Su, Y., Chou, C., & Tsai, C. (2009). Ubiquitous knowledge construction: Mobile learning re-defined and a conceptual framework. *Innovations in Education and Teaching International, 46*(2), 171-183.

Prgoment, M., Georgious, A., & Westbrook, J. I. (2009). The impact of mobile handheld technology on hospital physicians' work practices and patient care: A systematic review. *Journal of American Medical Informatics Association, 16*(6), 792-801.

Van Oostveen, R., Muirhead, W., & Goodman, W. (2011). Tablet PCs and reconceptualising learning with technology: A case study in higher education. *Interactive Technology and Smart Education*, *8*(2), 78-93.

Venkatesh, V., Morris, M.G., Davis, F.D., & Davis, G.B. (2003). User acceptance of information technology: Toward a unified view. *MIS Quarterly*, *27*, 425-478.

Wang, Y. Wu, M., & Wang, H. (2009). Investigating the determinants of age and gender differences in the acceptance of mobile learning. *British Journal of Educational Technology, 40*(1), 92-118.

INDEX

J

K

L

M

N

O

P

Q

S